Contents

Introduction

■ What is psychology?

The word 'psychology' comes from the combination of two Greek words, 'psyche' and 'logos'. It literally means 'the study of the mind'. However, it isn't just the mind that modern psychologists attempt to study.

When you say to people that you are studying psychology, they will often say: 'it's all just common sense, isn't it?' But there is a lot more to it than that. Psychology is a science and we can use it to understand people's behaviour and to predict how they are likely to behave in different situations. Common sense alone is not enough and it can often contradict itself. For example, you may have heard the expression 'absence makes the heart grow fonder'. This sounds like common sense. But what about the expression 'out of sight, out of mind'? This is another bit of common sense that means exactly the opposite. You can probably think of many other examples of contradictory common sense. The job of the psychologist is to take these ideas and to test them scientifically. You are also going to discover that people will sometimes do the opposite of what common sense would predict. As you follow this course you will be amazed at what you discover about people and their behaviour.

The AQA GCSE Psychology specification expects you to know and understand the work of psychologists in a variety of topic areas. We firmly believe that the best way to learn psychology is by 'hands-on' experience. You could not learn to become an expert tennis player simply by reading a textbook about tennis. You need to get onto the tennis court and try it out; hitting the ball and playing against opponents is the best way to improve your game. Equally the best way to improve your psychology is to try it out; practise doing psychology! This book will give you that opportunity. Every chapter is full of activities based on the work of famous psychologists. You will be able to conduct your own research and see how your results compare to those of the psychologists. This research then becomes part of your own personal experience, which should make it easier to remember. In other words, you will be using applied psychology to help you to learn psychology.

■ The specification

Content

AQA GCSE Psychology is examined through two question papers. The first paper is called 'Cognition and behaviour'. It covers the following four topics:

- ■ Memory
- ■ Development
- ■ Perception
- ■ Research methods

AQA Psychology

Second Edition

GCSE

Mike Stanley
Karen Boswell
Sarah Harris
Nicky Hayes
Frances Knight
Tracy Mendis

OXFORD
UNIVERSITY PRESS

OXFORD
UNIVERSITY PRESS

Great Clarendon Street, Oxford, OX2 6DP, United Kingdom

Oxford University Press is a department of the University of Oxford. It furthers the University's objective of excellence in research, scholarship, and education by publishing worldwide. Oxford is a registered trade mark of Oxford University Press in the UK and in certain other countries

British Library Cataloguing in Publication Data
Data available

978-0-19-841363-9

10 9 8 7 6 5 4 3 2 1

MIX
Paper from responsible sources
FSC® C007785

Paper used in the production of this book is a natural, recyclable product made from wood grown in sustainable forests. The manufacturing process conforms to the environmental regulations of the country of origin.

Printed in Great Britain by Bell and Bain Ltd., Glasgow.

Links to third party websites are provided by Oxford in good faith and for information only. Oxford disclaims any responsibility for the materials contained in any third party website referenced in this work.

Acknowledgements

We, the authors, would like to thank Mike Stanley, friend, colleague and mentor, for providing us with the opportunity to be involved with the writing of this book. It was his personal drive and determination that paved the way for those early meetings at OUP where we tentatively discussed the writing of a new Psychology GCSE textbook. In the following weeks it was his desire that the book should be 'just what the students need' that kept us all going.

We hope we have done you proud, Mike.

And of course, we know Mike would join us in thanking the team at OUP who kept us going throughout the whole process.

The publisher would like to thank the following reviewers and contributors for their generous help: Deb Gajic, Morag Hunter, David Latham, Howard Padley and Joseph Sparks. The publisher would also like to thank Dominic Helliwell for his help in creating the original edition of this book.

The first four chapters in this book are dedicated to these topics. They will help you to find answers to questions that have intrigued non-psychologists for years. For example:

- Why do I forget things?
- How do visual illusions trick our brains?
- What are the changes that happen to the way a child thinks as it gets older?
- How do I know if I can trust the results of a study or experiment?

The second paper is called 'Social context and behaviour'. It covers the following four topics:

- Social influence
- Language, thought and communication
- The brain and neuropsychology
- Psychological problems

The last four chapters in this book are dedicated to these topics. They will help you to find answers to other fascinating questions. For example:

- How can I read body language?
- How can I tell if somebody likes me?
- How can I give up a bad habit?
- Why are bystanders reluctant to help in emergencies?

Throughout the book, you will learn about the research methods used by psychologists to discover answers to these questions and many more.

Assessment

AQA GCSE Psychology is assessed through two written exams: Paper 1 and Paper 2. Each paper is 1 hour 45 minutes long and worth 100 marks. Each paper is split into four sections, which correspond to the four topics that you will have studied for that paper. For every topic there will be 25 marks, and a mixture of multiple-choice, short-answer and extended-writing questions.

However, although 'research methods' is examined on Paper 1 as a separate topic worth 25 marks, there will be further questions throughout Paper 1 and Paper 2 that will require you to use your knowledge of research methods and maths skills. This reflects the fact that Psychology is a scientific subject and the information we have gained about human behaviour comes from research.

When answering the exam paper, it is a good idea to try to write at the rate of approximately one mark per minute. In other words, try to divide your time up evenly and spend about 25 minutes on each topic in a paper (which is worth 25 marks). This will leave you a little time at the end to read and check your answers.

We hope that you enjoy your GCSE Psychology course and that this book helps you to prepare for your examination. We would also like to think that it will play some part in encouraging you to start thinking about how understanding human behaviour is fundamental to understanding some of the reasons for what we see going on in the world around us.

Karen Boswell, Sarah Harris, Nicky Hayes, Fran Knight, Tracy Mendis

---

Paper 1

What's assessed
- Memory
- Perception
- Development
- Research methods

Paper 2

What's assessed
- Social influence
- Language, thought and communication
- Brain and neuropsychology
- Psychological problems

How to use this book

This book contains many features that will help you to learn and revise more effectively.

Objectives

At the start of each new section you will find a list of learning objectives that are based on the requirements of the specification. These will tell you what you need to learn for this part of your course.

Getting started

These boxes contain starter activities that will introduce you to a new topic, or help you to recap what you learned in the previous section.

Key terms

This feature provides definitions of the most important terms that you need to know. Remember, all of the words or phrases that you could be required to define in an exam will be given in the key terms boxes, but there are some additional key terms that have also been defined to help your understanding.

All of the key term definitions are listed in the glossary at the back of this book.

Building skills

These activities help to test and further your knowledge and understanding. You will notice that each activity has been given a letter to help you identify what type of activity it is: 'K' stands for 'knowledge' (testing your knowledge of a topic); 'A' stands for 'application' (requiring you to apply your knowledge and understanding to a new situation or task); and 'E' stands for 'evaluation' (requiring you to evaluate information).

K A E

Going further

Many of these activities encourage you to carry out further research on the topic, either in the classroom or at home. They will help you to gain a wider or deeper understanding of the topic.

Did you know

This feature provides interesting facts and snippets of extra information about a topic.

?

Exam tip

These tips will help you with your study and exam preparation.

!

Synoptic link

This feature tells you if there is relevant information in a different part of the book, and encourages you to apply your knowledge of one topic to help deepen your understanding of another.

Practice exam questions

These questions help to test your knowledge and understanding. They are similar to the type of questions you will have to answer in your written exam.

The questions in each box are ordered according to their difficulty; this is indicated by the shading in the box, which gets progressively darker as the questions get harder.

Answers to all of the practice exam questions in this book are available online at www.oxfordsecondary.co.uk/gcsepsych.

Maths skills

 Some activities or sections in the book refer to the mathematical skills that you need to know for your Psychology course. These are indicated with a calculator icon and a number, such as '6.2.1' or '6.2.8'. The number tells you which skill is being used, as mentioned in 'Appendix A – mathematical requirements' in the specification; these skills are also listed in the 'Maths appendix' at the back of this book.

Research methods

 As mentioned on page 5, even though 'research methods' is examined as a separate topic on Paper 1, there will be questions throughout both exam papers that require you to use your knowledge of research methods. Likewise, 'research methods' has its own dedicated chapter in this book (Chapter 4), but there are also links to research methods throughout the rest of the book. The clipboard icon indicates where these links are.

Key research studies

The key research studies are investigations that are named in the specification, and are the only pieces of research that can be directly asked about on an exam paper. Each key research study has been described and evaluated in this book on a dedicated two-page spread, to ensure there is enough detail for you to answer a question on it that is worth up to 9 marks.

■ Preparing for the exam

At the end of each chapter there is a checklist of everything you should have learned for this topic, which you can use to help revise for the exam. There is also a set of practice exam questions at the end of each chapter, which you can use to test your knowledge and understanding of a topic. Answers to these practice exam questions are available online at www.oxfordsecondary.co.uk/gcsepsych.

At the end of this book there is a chapter called 'Improve your exam skills'. This includes a variety of practice questions and student sample answers. These are accompanied by commentaries that give an indication of the mark these answers would receive in an exam, and an explanation why. Use this chapter to help learn what the examiners are looking for, and how to answer questions to achieve the best mark possible.

■ Practical activities

Remember, whenever you are given the opportunity to carry out a practical activity in GCSE Psychology, you must consider the ethical issues covered in pages 92–93 in this book. Your teacher should always supervise any investigation that you are going to conduct, and needs to see your plan and detail of the procedures you intend to use before you carry out the research.

Are you ready for exams?

Memory

1.1 What are the processes of memory?

How good is your memory? Take a minute to complete this quiz. On a separate piece of paper, write down each answer that is correct for you. Be honest!

How often do you forget each of these? Choose from Never, Sometimes, Often, and Always.

a) Birthdays

b) People's names

c) Returning things you borrowed

d) Where you put something

e) What you went into a room for

f) Telephone numbers

g) Information for tests

h) Doing homework

Use this scoring system: Never = 0, Sometimes = 1, Often = 2, Always = 3. What is your total score? It should be between 0 and 24. The higher your score, the worse you think your memory is.

■ The processes of memory

Encoding (input), storage and retrieval (output)

Our memory is a bit like a computer. There are three basic processes involved with using computers: we put information into the computer (**encoding**), we keep it there until we need it (**storage**), and we get it back when we want it (**retrieval**). Our memory works in a similar way:

- we encode information into our memory

- we store it there until we need it

- we then retrieve it when we want it.

You will be able to:

- understand the processes of memory: encoding (input), storage, and retrieval (output)

- understand how memories are encoded and stored

- understand the different types of memory: episodic, semantic, and procedural memory.

Encoding: taking information into memory and changing it into a form that can be stored

Participant: someone who takes part in a study and, by taking part, provides data for the researcher to analyse

Recall: to bring a memory back into one's mind (similar to 'retrieval')

Retrieval: recovering information from storage

Storage: holding information in the memory system

A *Memory is like a computer*

Encoding

↓

Storage

↓

Retrieval

B *The flow of information in memory*

Building skills 1

Here is a list of the planets, starting nearest the Sun and working outwards through the Solar System:

Mercury Venus Earth Mars Jupiter Saturn Uranus Neptune Pluto

a) Copy out the list. Then find someone who does not know the correct order and give them 30 seconds to learn the list.

Wait for another 60 seconds and ask them to recall the list. How did they do?

b) Now find someone else who doesn't know the correct order. Copy out the list again but this time copy the phrase below it as well. Show them the information for 30 seconds.

Mercury	Venus	Earth	Mars		Jupiter	Saturn	Uranus	Neptune	Pluto
My	Very	Easy	Method	Just	Speeds	Up		Naming	Planets

Wait 60 seconds and ask them to recall the list of planets in the correct order. How did they do?

c) This activity is about encoding, storage, and retrieval. Can you identify the encoding method? How long was the information stored for? Who had the best retrieval? Why?

Building skills 2

Choose some information that you have to learn for an exam. Devise a mnemonic (a memory aid such as the one used in Building skills 1) to help encode the information. Give yourself a few minutes to learn your mnemonic. Test yourself later on today and then tomorrow. See if you can recall the information in a few days and next week.

Going further

If you recall information at set points after you have learned it, then there is a much better chance of making the memory permanent. To remember a new piece of information, you should recall it at these times after you first learn it: five minutes, thirty minutes, one hour, one day, one week, one month, and one year. Choose some information you have to learn for an exam and try this out.

■ How are memories encoded and stored?

Information enters our memory through one or more of our senses. This information has to be changed into a language or code that the brain will understand. Some information is automatically encoded without us being aware of it. Most people can probably **recall** what they had for breakfast yesterday, even though they haven't tried to remember it. Other information will only become encoded if you pay attention to it. You are unlikely to be able to remember everything you learn in your psychology lessons unless you make an effort to encode the information.

There are different ways of encoding written information. You can focus on it:

- visually – what the words look like
- acoustically – what the words sound like
- semantically – what the words mean.

How would you encode an address you have looked up? If you picture it you will be encoding it visually. If you repeat it to yourself you will be encoding it acoustically.

Task b) in Building skills 1 uses a mnemonic (a memory aid) to encode the information on the planets. You should have found your second **participant** recalled more of the planets in the correct order than your first participant. This is because the sentence was easier to encode as it has meaning to it. Encoding information semantically (by its meaning) leads to better storage and retrieval.

Did you know ?

Psychologists believe that our memories consolidate while we sleep. Consolidation means that the memories become permanent. This suggests that you should review what you have learned during the day before you go to bed.

Exam tip !

Make sure that you can explain the difference between encoding, storage and retrieval. An exam question could ask you to demonstrate understanding of the different processes.

■ Different types of memory

Getting started

Answer the following questions.

a) Where did you go on your last holiday?

b) What is the capital of England?

c) What colour is grass?

d) Can you describe your first day at secondary school?

e) Can you name an animal that has wings?

f) What did you have for breakfast this morning?

With a partner, discuss what you notice about these questions. Can you place the questions into groups?

Key terms

Episodic memory: unique memories which are concerned with personal experiences or events

Procedural memory: our memory for carrying out complex skills

Semantic memory: memories which are concerned with general knowledge rather than personal experience

Exam tip !

If you are asked to describe episodic, semantic, or procedural memory, give an example to support your description.

Episodic memory, semantic memory, and procedural memory

Psychologists believe that there are three different types of long-term memory. These are called **episodic memory**, **semantic memory**, and **procedural memory**. Episodic memory refers to the memory of personal events and experiences in your life. These memories are personal to you, such as places you have visited and events that have happened. Remembering your first day at school and where you went on holiday last summer are examples of episodic memory.

Semantic memory is the memory for facts and general knowledge. This includes knowledge about the meaning of words. Knowing that Paris is the capital of France, that elephants have trunks, and that a school is where students go to learn, are all examples of semantic memory.

Building skills 3

Look back to the Getting started activity above. Which of the questions refer to semantic memory and which of the questions refer to episodic memory? **K**

Building skills 4

Work in small groups. You will need someone with trainers or lace-up shoes in each group. **A**

The person with laces should sit with their laces undone. Ask someone else in the group to give them instructions on how to tie their laces. The person giving the instructions should not use their hands at all. The person with the laces should follow the instructions they are given exactly. Let each person in the group have a go at giving the instructions.

How successful was each person at explaining how to tie the laces? Why was this task difficult?

C *Episodic memory: last summer's holiday*

D *Semantic memory: elephants have long trunks*

E *Procedural memory: how to ride a bike*

Procedural memory is the memory for complex skills. Examples of procedural memory include how to tie shoelaces, how to swim, and how to ride a bike. They are action-based memories. In Building skills 4, you probably found it difficult to explain to someone how to tie shoelaces. This is because procedural memories are difficult to put into words. Procedural memories are stored using a motor code instead of a verbal code. This is why when children are taught to tie their laces, ride a bike or swim, they have to be shown what to do instead of just being told what to do.

Going further

Another type of memory is called flashbulb memory. Research what is meant by flashbulb memory. How is it different to episodic memory?

Building skills 5

Semantic memory and episodic memory are described as 'knowing that'. Procedural memory is described as 'knowing how'.

Why do you think they are described like this? Discuss this with a partner and share your ideas with your class.

Semantic memories and episodic memories can be described to another person because they are easy to put into words. Procedural memories are not easy to describe to another person because they are hard to verbalise. It is very difficult to explain to someone how to swim without showing the actions.

Did you know ?

When people are asked to think about an episodic or a semantic memory, different parts of the brain are active. Semantic memories involve areas towards the back of the cortex. The cortex is the outer layer of the brain where higher cognitive funtions take place, e.g. speech. Episodic memories cause more activity in the frontal cortex.

1. Which one of these is a description of storage? *(1 mark)*
   A Retrieving information from memory
   B Holding information in memory
   C Changing information so that it can be stored

2. Identify the three processes of memory. *(3 marks)*

3. Explain what is meant by the term episodic memory. Give an example of an episodic memory. *(2 marks)*

4. Explain one difference between semantic memory and procedural memory. *(2 marks)*

Practice exam questions

What are the structures of memory?

◼ The multi-store model of memory

Sensory store, short-term store, and long-term store

Psychologists believe that information passes through a series of memory stores. Information that arrives at our senses is briefly held in the **sensory store**. It only stays here for a very short period. It will quickly fade away unless we pay attention to it.

The second memory store is the **short-term store** (STS). Experiments have shown that it has a small **capacity**. It can hold approximately seven items of information. New information pushes old information out. That is why your partner probably had trouble recalling more than seven digits in the Getting started activity above. If the information in the STS is not rehearsed (repeated), it is likely to be forgotten very quickly.

The final store is the **long-term store** (LTS). Information enters this store through rehearsal. Experiments have shown that this store has a very large capacity and information can stay there indefinitely.

Building skills 1

a) Find someone who does not study psychology and show them the following list for 30 seconds.

1 0 8 6 1 7 8 9 1 9 1 4 1 9 6

Then ask them to recall as many numbers as they can in the correct order.

b) Find someone else and show them the following list for 30 seconds. Then ask them to recall as much as they can in the correct order.

108   617   891   914   196

What do you notice?

You should find that the second person was able to recall more numbers in the correct order, even though both people were presented with exactly the same numbers in the same order. This is because the first list contains too many items for the STS to hold, as the numbers were all separate bits of information. The second list is in chunks, and as each chunk counts as an item, the capacity of the STS is increased.

Key terms

Capacity: how much information can be stored

Coding: the way that information is represented to be stored

Duration: how long information can be stored for

Long-term store: memory store that holds a vast amount of information for a very long period of time

Multi-store model of memory: the theory of memory that suggests information passes through a series of memory stores

Sensory store: memory store that holds information received from the senses for a very short period of time

Short-term store: memory store that holds approximately seven bits of information for a limited amount of time

Features of each store: coding, capacity, and duration

Studies have shown that **coding** in the sensory store occurs in the same way as the information is received. For example, visual information will be coded visually. Experiments have also shown that the STS codes information acoustically (based on its sound). If a person is given a list to remember, they will try to hold it in STS by repeating it to themselves. The LTS mainly codes information semantically (based on its meaning).

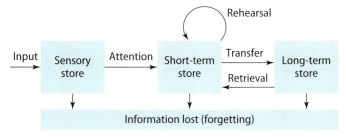

A *The flow of information through the multi-store model of memory*

Research has shown that the capacity of the sensory store is very limited. The STS can hold approximately seven bits of information. This can be increased by putting a few items together to make one chunk (see Building skills 1). The LTS can hold an unlimited amount of information.

The **duration** of sensory memory is less than one second. The duration of the STS is eighteen to thirty seconds. The duration of the LTS is unlimited.

Memory store	Coding	Capacity	Duration
Sensory	The same way in which it is received from the senses	Very limited	Less than one second
Short-term	Mainly acoustic	Approximately seven bits of information	Up to thirty seconds
Long-term	Mainly semantic	Unlimited	Unlimited

B *Coding, capacity, and duration of each memory store*

Evaluation of the multi-store model

According to the multi-store model of memory, all information has to be rehearsed to enter the LTS. We know this isn't true because you can remember lots of things that you have probably never rehearsed. For example, you are likely to be able to recall what you did last weekend, but you are unlikely to have rehearsed it. However, you probably cannot always remember things that you have rehearsed, such as information for a Maths test.

Saying things over and over again does not necessarily make them easier to recall. It is more important to understand the meaning of information so that you can say it in your own words. Other studies have shown that rehearsal which involves an elaboration of the information (such as turning it into a story) is more effective than simple repetition.

However, the studies to support the theory help us to understand why we can't always recall information from the STS and LTS.

Building skills 2

What do you think of the multi-store model of memory that has been described? Working with a partner, try to think of at least two criticisms.

Going further

With a partner, design your own study to investigate the short-term store or the long-term store of the multi-store model of memory.

You could make up your own version of Building skills 1. You could use letters, or vary the number of digits in the chunks.

 See Chapter 4 for advice on how to create an effective study.

Exam tip

Make sure you can describe how information passes from the sensory store to the STS, and from the STS to the LTS.

■ Information recall

Key terms

Primacy effect: more of the first information received is recalled than subsequent later information

Recency effect: more of the information received later is recalled than earlier information

Serial position curve: the name given to the graph that displays the results of a serial position experiment

Serial position effect: the chances of recalling any item depends on its position in the list

Primacy and recency effects in recall

The study you conducted for Building skills 3 is used to support the existence of separate short-term and long-term stores in the multi-store model of memory. It was originally conducted by a psychologist called Murdock (see the Key research study, pages 16–17).

If the last activity went according to plan, the prediction is that your participants are likely to have recalled the most words from both the start of your list and the end of your list. They are less likely to have recalled the words from the middle of the list. The words recalled from the start of the list are due to the **primacy effect**. The words recalled from the end of the list are due to the **recency effect**.

The effects of serial position

When we hear the words from the start of the list, we start to rehearse them in our head so that we can recall them later on. This transfers the words to our long-term store. However, as we are rehearsing the first few words, we miss the words from the middle of the list. We are able to recall words from the end of the list as they are still in our short-term store and so are available to be recalled, if we recall them straight away. The **effects of serial position** means that the chances of recalling any item depends on its position in the list. Therefore, items (words) at the start of a word list and at the end of a word list have the highest chances of being recalled in a free recall test.

Read Murdock's Key research study on pages 16–17 before completing the activities and questions on the next page.

C *The chances of recalling any item depends on its position in the list*

Building skills 4

Using the results you collected in Building skills 3, produce a **serial position curve** like the one in Figure A on page 16. Label the x-axis 'position of word in the list', and number it from one to twenty. Label the y-axis 'number of people who recalled the word'. **A**

Count up the number of people that recalled each word. Plot this against the position of the word.

How does your serial position curve compare to Murdock's?

Going further

Working with a partner, try to replicate Murdock's study using different variations. For example, you could use word lists of different lengths, such as 15, 30, or 40 words.

- How strong is the evidence of the primacy and recency effects for each of these lists?
- What happens if you vary the presentation times for the words in these lists?
- In the Murdock study described in this chapter, words were presented at one second per word. Try two or three seconds per word. Does this make a difference?

1a. Which one of these is a description of duration? *(1 mark)*
  A The way information is represented to be stored
  B How much information can be stored
  C How long information can be stored for

1b. Which one of these best describes the capacity of the short-term store? *(1 mark)*
  A About 3 items
  B About 12 items
  C About 7 items

2. Explain the difference in duration between the short-term store and the long-term store. *(2 marks)*

3. Describe the results of Murdock's serial position curve study. *(2 marks)*

4. Evaluate the multi-store model of memory. *(3 marks)*

Murdock's serial position curve study (1962)

Aim: To provide evidence for the existence of separate short-term and long-term stores of the multi-store model of memory.

Study design: A laboratory study in which there was control of possible extraneous variables. All procedures were standardised to ensure the study could be replicated easily. The participants were male and female psychology students. It was part of their course requirement to take part in psychological research.

Method: 16 participants were presented with a list of 20 words at the rate of 1 word per second. Once they had heard all 20 words, they were asked to recall as many words from the list as they could remember, in any order. This is called free-recall. They were given 90 seconds to recall the words. The test was repeated with the same participants 80 times over a few days. A different list of 20 words was used each time.

Results: The words at the end of the list were recalled first (known as the recency effect). Words from the beginning of the list were also recalled quite well (known as the primacy effect), but the words in the middle of the list were not recalled very well at all. Murdock displayed his results in a graph called a serial position curve (see below).

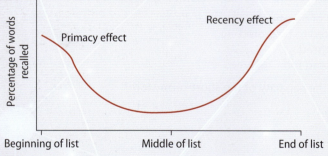

A *Murdock's serial position curve*

Conclusion: Murdock concluded that this provides evidence for separate short-term and long-term stores in the multi-store model of memory.

- The last few words were recalled well as they were still in the short-term store, and so they were readily available to be recalled. This is evidence for the existence of the short-term store.

- The first few words were recalled well as there was time for them to be rehearsed. This means they had passed into the long-term store, and so they were available to be recalled. This is evidence for the existence of the long-term store.

- The words in the middle of the list were not recalled very well because they were not in the long-term store or the short-term store.

Source: Murdock, B.B. (1962) 'The serial position effect in free recall', Journal of Experimental Psychology, 64, 482–488.

■ Support for Murdock's findings

In further studies, Murdock varied both the number of words he gave to his participants as well as the presentation time. Murdock found that the primacy and recency effects occurred in all the variations, therefore providing more support for the existence of separate short-term and long-term stores.

In another study, instead of allowing the participants to recall the words as soon as they had heard them, the psychologists gave the participants a distractor task to do (count backwards in threes). When the participants were allowed to recall the words, they found that the words from the start of the list were recalled well (the primacy effect) but participants were not able to recall the words from the end of the list. The distractor task took up the capacity of the STS so the last few words were no longer available. Therefore, this study also confirms Murdock's conclusions on the existence of the STS and LTS as described in the multi-store model of memory.

Building skills 1

Working with a partner, think of at least two criticisms of Murdock's study.   **E**

■ Evaluation

Why the study is important

■ Murdock's study provided evidence for the existence of separate short-term and long-term stores in the multi-store model of memory.

Limitations of the study

■ The participants in Murdock's study were given lists of words to learn. Remembering word lists is not the type of memory task that people usually have to do in their everyday lives. In the real world, people use their memories for remembering the things they have to do, for revising for exams, for work, and for general day-to-day life. Therefore, it can be argued that the study lacks ecological validity (see page 73).

■ Murdock's participants were all a similar age and were all students studying an introductory psychology course. Would the results have been different if the participants were of different ages, from different courses, or from different professions? Psychology students may try to work out the aim of a study, or impress the experimenter. Therefore, they may produce different results to non-psychology students.

■ Some psychologists now disagree with the idea of separate short-term and long-term stores. Some see short-term memory as an active part of long-term memory.

■ Other psychologists believe that it is very simplistic to view memory as having one long-term store, and suggest there is more than one type of long-term store (for example: episodic, semantic, and procedural memories).

Going further

Create a poster to summarise the key points of the multi-store model of memory and Murdock's serial position curve study. The poster could be in the form of a table, spider diagram, or other imaginative way of summarising the key points.

Exam tip   !

When describing the results of Murdock's study, make sure you are clear that words at beginning and the end of the list were recalled more than the words in the middle.

1.2 Key research study: Murdock

Getting started

What can you remember about the primacy and recency effects in recall?

a) Jot down a definition of the primacy effect. Now write down a definition of the recency effect.

b) Draw a brief sketch of a serial position curve. Mark the primacy and recency effect in the correct positions on the curve.

■ The theory of reconstructive memory

What is reconstructive memory?

Bartlett thought that memory was not just a stored copy of facts. He said that we change our memories to fit in with what we already know, even though we think we are remembering exactly what happened. This is known as **reconstructive memory**.

When you play 'Chinese whispers' (see Building skills 1), the other people in your group probably think they are passing on your message accurately. Without realising, they actually change it so that it makes more sense to them. Bartlett believed that this happens because if you are trying to recall information and you cannot remember the small details, your mind will fill in the gaps with details that make sense and fit in with the rest of the information.

Bartlett investigated his theory of reconstructive memory in an experiment called 'War of the Ghosts' (see pages 20–21). He used a method called serial reproduction. Serial reproduction is meant to duplicate the process by which stories are passed down through generations, and how gossip and rumours are spread.

The 'War of the Ghosts' story is very confusing to most people. It is about two men who go to a river to hunt. They hear some war noises and hide. Then five men in a canoe come along and ask the two men to go with them to make war on some people. One goes with them and the other doesn't. They travel up the river to a town and a big fight breaks out. You can read the full text of the story below. Would you be able to recall the story in detail to another person? Would you recall the events that took place in the correct order?

War of the Ghosts

One night two young men from Egulac went down to the river to hunt seals and while they were there it became foggy and calm. Then they heard war-cries, and they thought: 'Maybe this is a war-party'. They escaped to the shore, and hid behind a log. Now canoes came up, and they heard the noise of paddles, and saw one canoe coming up to them. There were five men in the canoe, and they said: 'What do you

Objectives

You will be able to:

- understand the theory of reconstructive memory

- understand the concept of 'effort after meaning'

- understand Bartlett's 'War of the Ghosts' study

- recognise factors that affect the accuracy of memory: interference, context, and false memories.

Key terms

Effort after meaning: making sense of something unfamiliar after it has happened

Reconstructive memory: altering our recollection of things so that they make more sense to us

Building skills 1

Have you ever played 'Chinese whispers'? Write a short and simple message, about 10 to 15 words long. Get a few of your class to stand in a line about one metre apart. Now whisper your message into the ear of the first person in the line. They should then whisper the message to the next person, and so on down the line until the message reaches the last person. Ask that person to say the message out loud.

How does it compare with your original message? The chances are that it will be quite different. Why?

think? We wish to take you along. We are going up the river to make war on the people.'

One of the young men said, 'I have no arrows.' 'Arrows are in the canoe,' they said. 'I will not go along. I might be killed. My relatives do not know where I have gone. But you,' he said, turning to the other, 'may go with them.' So one of the young men went, but the other returned home.

And the warriors went on up the river to a town on the other side of Kalama. The people came down to the water and they began to fight, and many were killed. But presently the young man heard one of the warriors say, 'Quick, let us go home: that Indian has been hit.' Now he thought: 'Oh, they are ghosts.' He did not feel sick, but they said he had been shot.

So the canoes went back to Egulac and the young man went ashore to his house and made a fire. And he told everybody and said: 'Behold I accompanied the ghosts, and we went to fight. Many of our fellows were killed, and many of those who attacked us were killed. They said I was hit, and I did not feel sick.'

He told it all, and then he became quiet. When the sun rose he fell down. Something black came out of his mouth. His face became contorted. The people jumped up and cried. He was dead.

Effort after meaning

In the 'War of the Ghosts' study, Bartlett showed that memory is not an accurate recording of what has happened. He said that memory is an active process that involves **effort after meaning**. This means that we make sense of something unfamiliar after it has happened. We try to fit what we remember with what we already know and understand about the world.

As a result, we often change our memories so that they become more sensible to us. This process involves making assumptions, or guesses, about what could or should have happened. For example, if you try to remember what your dentist's waiting room looks like, you will probably find that your memory is influenced by what a typical waiting room should look like. You are more likely to recall this, rather than what it actually looks like. Therefore, we may mistakenly remember things that aren't really there, because they make sense within the situation.

Evaluation of the theory of reconstructive memory

The theory of reconstructive memory is important because it emphasises the influence of people's previous knowledge and background on the way they remember things. The theory has many benefits for everyday life. It teaches us that we must be very careful when giving, or listening to, eyewitness accounts of events such as accidents or crimes. Witnesses might think that they are being accurate but, in trying to make sense of what they saw, they may unconsciously alter the facts.

It also helps us to understand why two people who are recalling the same event might have completely different versions of the story. It does not necessarily mean that one of them is lying. They each might genuinely believe that their version of the story is accurate.

Despite the theory being developed during the early 1900s, the idea that memory is reconstructive is still very popular today.

Building skills 2

Read the story 'War of the Ghosts'.

a) Jot down your thoughts as you read it. Does it make sense to you? Why/why not?

b) What do you think Bartlett's participants thought when they heard it for the first time?

Exam tip

If you are being asked to define 'effort after meaning', try to give an example to support your definition.

A *Do you remember what your dentist's waiting room looks like?*

Bartlett's 'War of the Ghosts' study (1932)

Aim: To see if people, when given an unfamiliar story to remember, would alter the information so that it makes more sense to them.

Study design: Laboratory study in which there was some control of possible extraneous variables. All procedures were standardised to ensure the study could be replicated easily. The participants were undergraduate students studying English at Cambridge University.

Method: Each participant was asked to read a story called 'War of the Ghosts', which is a Native American folk tale (see pages 18–19 for the full text of the story). They were told to read the passage twice through to themselves, at their normal reading pace. About 15 minutes later, they were asked to retell the story to another person. That person then had to retell the story to another person, and so on, like a game of 'Chinese whispers'. A record was made of the story that each person reported, allowing Bartlett to know what the changes were from one person to the next.

Results: After the story was passed on ten times:

- the passages became much shorter
- there were lots of omissions
- there were changes to the detail
- the order of events was changed.

The story had gone from 330 words to 150 words. All mention of ghosts disappeared despite the title being emphasised by Bartlett to the first participant. Unfamiliar names were changed into familiar ones, canoes were changed to boats, and paddling was changed to rowing. Despite the complex nature of the story, the final version of it was a clear story of a fight and death.

A Bartlett's participants read a story called 'War of the Ghosts'

Conclusion: Bartlett concluded that our memory is not an exact copy of what we hear. It is distorted by what we already know about the world. Therefore, our memory is influenced by our own beliefs and stereotypes.

Source: Bartlett, F.C. (1932) Remembering, Cambridge University Press.

■ Support for Bartlett's findings

Other psychologists have since replicated Bartlett's study using the 'War of the Ghosts' story, and found similar results.

In another study, white participants were shown a picture of a black man and a white man having an argument. Once they had seen the photo, they were then asked to describe it to another person, who then had to describe it to someone else, and so on. Just like Bartlett's study, the detail changed at each retelling. The major change was that participants said the weapon was held by the black man, when in fact the white man had been holding it. This supports Bartlett's findings and shows that memory is an active process and can be changed to 'fit in' with what we expect to happen based on beliefs and stereotypes.

■ Evaluation

Why the study is important

- Bartlett wanted to test memory in a meaningful way. Before his research, memory had mainly been tested using meaningless material such as nonsense word lists.

- His study is more relevant to the way we use our memories in everyday life than studies that involve learning word lists. In the real world, we often tell people about what others have said to us, and this will often be passed on.

Limitations of the study

- Many people disagree that Bartlett's study tested memory in a meaningful way. They say that the 'War of the Ghosts' story is deliberately confusing and not similar to our everyday experiences. Bartlett recorded the stories at each 'retelling' to see how they had changed. However, written data is very difficult to score.

- Some psychologists criticised the type of participants used in the study. Bartlett used students who were studying English at Cambridge University. It was argued they were likely to be much better at reading and verbalising a story than people who were older, or younger, or who were not studying English.

B *Participants recalled the black man as holding the weapon*

Building skills 1

Working with a partner, think of at least two evaluations of Bartlett's study.

Going further

Working with a partner, try to replicate Bartlett's study using a few participants.

Design a study to see how the telling of a story changes from person to person.

You will have to think carefully about how you can measure the amount of information recalled at each telling of the story. You will need to devise a clever scoring technique.

 See Chapter 4 for advice on how to design an effective study.

Exam tip

If you are asked to evaluate a study, remember that you can include why it is important as well as any limitations it might have.

1.3 Key research study: Bartlett

Factors affecting the accuracy of memory

Getting started

What affects your memory?

Try to think of an occasion when you just could not recall something that you thought you knew.

What do you think might have caused that to happen?

Interference

Research has shown that things that take place between learning and recall can affect the accuracy of our memory. This is known as **interference**. Interference can occur in two ways:

- Things that we already know can cause problems when we try to take in new information. For example, you know your old postcode, but cannot remember your new one.

- New things that we learn can cause problems when we try to recall information that we learned before. For example, you can remember your new postcode, but not your old one.

Interference is often tested by giving one group of participants a list of words to learn, followed by another list of words to learn. A second group of participants is only given the first list to learn. All participants are then asked to recall the first list of words. The recall of the first group is usually much lower than the recall of the second group. This is because the second list of words acts as interference.

Context

Have you ever gone to another room for something and then, when you got there, forgotten why you were there? This happens to a lot of people. Why do you think this happens?

Building skills 3

A

Working with a partner, choose twenty words, and write them as a list on a sheet of paper. Make ten copies of the list.

Find ten participants and give them two minutes to try to learn the list. After that, collect the word lists and divide the group into two smaller groups. Take one of these groups to another room or out into the corridor. Give them two minutes to write down, in silence, all the words they can recall. At the same time, your partner should ask the remaining group, who are still in the room, to do the same thing.

Did one group recall more words than the other group?

The prediction is that the group that stays in the room will have recalled more words on average. Why do you think this happens?

Studies on **context** have shown that recall of information is higher if learning and recall take place in the same context. Therefore, in Building skills 3, the participants who stayed in the room should have had a higher recall than those who recalled in a different context.

B *Why do people forget what they were looking for when they enter a new room?*

One study on context used deep-sea divers as participants. They were asked to learn a list of words. Some learned and recalled in the same contexts (on shore or underwater), while others learned and recalled in different contexts (learned underwater and were tested on shore). The recall of words was higher when both learning and recall took place in the same context.

False memories

How well can you trust your memory? How certain can you be that a memory you have from a childhood event is accurate? Remembering something that has not actually happened is known as a **false memory**. Research on false memories has shown that it is very easy for a false memory to be planted in someone's mind.

In one study, participants were questioned about their childhood. The researcher used information from their parents to describe some true events, as well as a false event about getting lost in a shopping centre. About 25 per cent of participants believed that they had actually been lost and could also give some detail about what had happened while they were 'lost'.

Building skills 4

Try to think of at least two problems with the research into factors that affect the accuracy of memory.

E

In Building skills 4 you might have said that research on interference and context involves giving participants lists of words to learn. This is not really how we use our memory in everyday life, so these studies lack ecological validity.

You may have said that learning underwater is also quite an unusual context, and unlikely to be one that most people experience. However, the results do show clearly that a change in context between learning and recall does affect recall.

A lot of studies into false memories can be criticised for the lack of a **standardised procedure**. The 'lost in the shopping centre' study involved each participant being described events from their own childhood, before being introduced to the false event. As the events in their childhood were different for each participant, the information they were given (the false memory) was also different. This means that the study was not fully standardised. See page 70 for more detail on standardised procedures.

C *Research has shown that it is easy to plant a false memory in someone's mind, such as getting lost in a shopping centre as a child*

Going further

A famous case of a false memory is Hillary Clinton's description of her arrival in Bosnia in 1996. Her report of events was very different to what actually occurred on the day.

Research other famous cases of false memories.

Practice exam questions

1. What is meant by a false memory? *(1 mark)*

2. Identify one factor, other than context, that has been shown to affect the accuracy of memory. *(1 mark)*

3. Describe the results of Bartlett's 'War of the Ghosts' study. *(2 marks)*

4. Briefly evaluate research into the theory of reconstructive memory. *(4 marks)*

1 Revision checklist

Processes of memory

☐ explain how memories are encoded and stored

☐ explain the processes of encoding, storage and retrieval

☐ explain the differences between these three types of memory: episodic memory, semantic memory and procedural memory

See pages 8–11

Structures of memory

☐ describe and evaluate the multi-store model of memory (referring to sensory, short-term and long-term stores)

☐ explain the features of each store (coding, capacity and duration)

☐ know what is meant by primacy effects and recency effects (in relation to memory recall)

☐ explain the effects of serial position

☐ **key research study:** describe and evaluate Murdock's serial position curve study

See pages 12–17

Memory as an active process

☐ describe and evaluate the theory of reconstructive memory, including the concept of 'effort after meaning'

☐ explain how different factors affect the accuracy of memory, including interference, context and false memories

☐ **key research study:** describe and evaluate Bartlett's 'War of the Ghosts' study

See pages 18–23

Practice exam questions

1. What is meant by the term 'encoding'? *(2 marks)*

2. Charlie and Alfie are brothers. Charlie was talking about a birthday party he had when he was younger.

   Charlie: 'My favourite party was when I had a clown and he made balloon animals.'

   Alfie: 'That wasn't your party, that was mine.'

   Mother: 'Alfie is right, that happened at his party, not yours Charlie.'

   a) Use your knowledge of one factor that affects memory to explain what has happened to Charlie's memory in the situation above. *(2 marks)*

   b) Identify and briefly outline one other factor that might affect the accuracy of memory. *(2 marks)*

3. Testing the duration and capacity of short-term memory often involves using laboratory experiments. Outline one advantage and one disadvantage of using laboratory experiments in memory research. *(4 marks)*

4. Two students were talking about a psychology test they had to revise for.

   Mike: 'I've been trying to revise for the psychology test this week by saying the information over and over again. I still don't remember it though.'

   Caroline: 'You need to do something with the information, turn it into a story or understand what it really means.'

   Describe and evaluate the multi-store model of memory. Refer to the conversation above in your answer. *(9 marks)*

5. Describe one study in which the primacy effect and the recency effect in recall have been investigated. Include in your answer the method used, the results obtained and the conclusion drawn. *(5 marks)*

6. Which one of these is a description of the capacity of memory? *(1 mark)*

   A It is how long information can be stored for

   B It is how much information can be stored

   C It is the way in which information is stored

When a question like this is worth two marks, it means there are two separate ideas that need to be covered in the answer. For the term 'encoding', the two ideas are about information being *changed* and *stored*.

This question is worth 4 marks and has two different parts. This means that the part of your answer about 'one advantage' will be worth up to 2 marks, and the part about 'one disadvantage' will also be worth up to 2 marks. It is therefore important to write about both an advantage *and* a disadvantage, rather than focusing a lot of time and effort on only one of these things.

When a question asks for a reference to a conversation, it is important to use a reference that is relevant to the question being asked.

When you are describing a method, make sure you describe all of the conditions of the independent variable and the dependent variable.

2.1 What are sensation and perception?

Getting started

Sensation is the information that we receive through our senses. Our senses are active all the time, receiving different kinds of sensory information. Take a minute to note down some information you are receiving right now. Think about each of these senses:

- vision (what can you see?)
- hearing (what can you hear?)
- smell (can you smell anything?)
- touch (are parts of your body in contact with anything?)
- taste (can you taste anything?)
- proprioception (what positions are parts of your body in?)
- kinesthesia (are you moving at all?).

■ Sensation

The information we receive through our senses is known as **sensation**. We have special sensory organs which detect information from the outside world, or from inside our bodies, and convert that information into tiny electrical signals. That process is called transduction.

The problem is that we would receive a lot more information than we could cope with, if we really paid attention to everything. We hear lots of sounds which do not really matter and we see things which are not important to what we are doing at that time. The same goes for the other senses. So we need to interpret or make sense of the information that we receive, and that process is known as **perception**.

Building skills 1

Perception is about making sense of what our senses tell us. Different senses require different types of perception. Link the different kinds of perception listed below with the relevant sense.

Senses: vision, hearing, smell, taste, touch

Type of perception	Sense
Auditory perception	
Olfactory perception	
Tactile perception	
Visual perception	
Gustatory perception	

Objectives

You will be able to:

- identify key features of the process of sensation
- distinguish between sensation and perception
- explain what is meant by perception.

Key terms

Perception: how we interpret or make sense of the sensory information that we receive

Sensation: the information that we receive through our senses

Synoptic link

The electrical signals are carried to the brain by special cells called neurons, which take the information to the part of the brain that will de-code it, so we can make sense of it. See Topic 7.3, pages 151–153.

Did you know

People who are missing one sense often find that their other senses become stronger to compensate. For example, blind people often have very acute hearing, and deaf people can be very sensitive to subtle touches or slight movements.

Building skills 2

Sometimes, our senses can fool us. Try making up two parcels, each weighing 1 kilogram. One parcel should be quite small, and the other quite large. Ask other people to lift up each parcel and tell you if they think one is heavier than the other.

Usually, people will think that the large parcel weighs less than the small parcel. This is because we expect a large parcel to weigh quite a lot, so when we pick it up we are surprised that it is not heavier. As a result, we think that the large parcel is light, while the small one seems heavy.

A

A *Which is heavier?*

■ Perception

We need to make sense of the information we receive from our senses. This is what perception is all about. If we did not organise the information somehow, we would get overwhelmed and not know what anything meant. When we use our eyes, for example, our sensory organs receive information about lightness, darkness, and colour, which is picked up as tiny dots; each sense receptor picks up just the information from one little part of the whole visual field that you can see.

But we do not see a mass of tiny dots, even though that is what our visual receptors receive. Instead, we see patterns, shapes, people, and things. We may see them clearly or faintly. Sometimes we do not even see a proper shape, just a suggestion of a shape, but our experience allows us to make it out so that we can see what is there. This is because of the processes of perception.

Visual perception – that is, how we perceive the information received by our eyes – is the most important sense for human beings, although not for all animals. For this reason psychologists have studied perception in detail, and we know quite a lot about how it works.

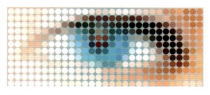

B *What do the dots show?*

Going further

You can see how much our senses influence each other by exploring the relationship between vision and taste.

1. Choose four clear but differently flavoured drinks, for example fruit-flavoured clear water drinks.

2. Use food colouring to change the colours to colours people would not expect, for example colour a strawberry flavoured water with orange, or turn a lime-flavoured water red.

3. Ask your friends to taste them, and see how many of them can judge the flavours correctly.

Exam tip **!**

When distinguishing between two terms, remember that examples can be helpful and could earn extra marks.

Practice exam questions

1. Decide whether each of the following statements is true or false.
   a) The information that our sensory organs detect from the world around us is converted into tiny electrical signals. *(1 mark)*
   b) The information that our sensory organs detect from the world around us is already organised and easily understandable. *(1 mark)*

2. Using an example, explain the difference between 'perception' and 'sensation'. *(4 marks)*

2.2 How do we perceive?

■ Visual cues

Judging distance

The image that our eyes receive is two-dimensional, like a picture spread out in front of us. But we live in a three-dimensional world, and if we are to avoid bumping into things or getting run over by traffic, we need to know how far away things are. Judging distance is something that we do without thinking. However, it is a complicated thing to do.

We do it by using key bits of information, known as **depth cues**. These cues tell us about the third dimension of the real world – depth, or distance – and they allow us to work out how near something is to us, or how far away it is. It is an important survival tool.

We can see some depth cues in pictures, even though pictures are only two-dimensional – that is, they have height and width, but not the third dimension, which is depth. Pictures use a set of cues which are called **monocular depth cues**, because we can use them even if we are looking with just one eye. They help us to tell how far away things are, but not perfectly. Other depth cues need two eyes, and involve comparing the slight differences in the images that each eye receives. These are called **binocular depth cues**, and they make our depth perception much more accurate.

Monocular depth cues

The best way to identify monocular depth cues is to work out how you would indicate distance if you were drawing a picture of a scene and trying to make it as much like a photograph as possible. One cue you might use is the way that things further away often appear to be higher up.

This is a cue known as **height in plane** (Figure A). Another possible cue is the way that things that are closer to you seem to be larger. This depth cue is known as **relative size** (Figure B).

Occlusion is another depth cue. You can see in Figure C how an object which is covering up another object appears to be closer to us. The fourth depth cue that you might use in a picture is known as **linear perspective**. This is the way that straight lines seem to be pointing towards to a single point on the horizon (Figure D). This point is known as the vanishing point because the lines disappear when they reach it. The vanishing point is a useful cue if we want to show distance in a landscape.

Did you know ?

Having two good eyes is essential for people whose activities depend on precise judgements, such as gymnasts or goalkeepers. Even everyday activities, like driving or crossing the road, are more difficult if we only have one eye to see with.

A *Height in plane*

B *Relative size*

E *Firefighting is one of the professions in the UK that requires good eyesight before you can join*

Exam tip !

If you are asked to explain a monocular depth cue, a drawing (such as those in Figures A–D) could be helpful. However, it is also important to take into consideration the amount of time you might need to do this.

C *Occlusion*

D *Linear perspective*

Binocular depth cues

Binocular depth cues are ways of identifying how far away things are, which we can use because we have two eyes at the front of our heads. This means that we see two images which are nearly (but not quite) the same. By comparing these two images, our brains work out how far away things are. Using binocular cues allows us to be much more accurate in our judgements of depth.

There are two main ways that binocular cues work:

■ One way is by detecting the difference in our eye muscles. We focus our eyes differently to see things that are closer, to how we focus to see things that are further away. The brain detects these differences in how the muscles are working, and uses it as a cue to distance. This cue is called **convergence**.

■ The other way is by comparing the images received by the two eyes. If something is close to us, there is quite a difference in what the two eyes see. But if it is further away, there will be less of a difference between the images: after about 10 metres, the difference is hardly noticeable. This cue also depends on having two eyes and is called **retinal disparity**.

> **Key terms**
>
> **Convergence:** a form of depth perception which uses how eye muscles focus on images
>
> **Retinal disparity:** a form of depth perception which compares the images from two eyes, side by side

Building skills 2

A

You can see how much your eyes converge on near objects by working with a friend, each of you watching the other.

Hold out your hand at arm's length, and focus on the tip of your finger. While your friend watches your eyes, slowly bring your finger closer to your face, until it nearly touches your nose, keeping your eyes focused on the tip. The angle of your eyes will change as the finger gets closer. Then ask your friend to do the same, while you watch.

Building skills 3

A

You can see how different the images are that your two eyes receive quite easily.

Take a pencil or pen, hold it out at arm's length, and close one eye. With that eye closed, line up the pencil vertically with something on the far horizon or on something as far away as you can see. Without moving the pencil, close that eye and open the other one. The pencil will seem to have moved in relation to the object in the distance.

Now try the same thing, but this time lining the pencil up with something close to you. How much does that image move?

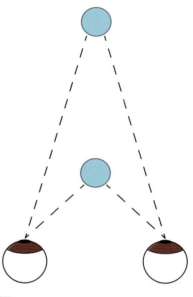

F *Convergence*

1. What are binocular depth cues? *(2 marks)*

2. Identify and explain one monocular depth cue. *(3 marks)*

3. Explain how 'convergence' helps us to perceive how far away objects are. *(2 marks)*

Practice exam questions

Getting started

Take a moment to look at what you can see around you. Narrow your eyes to cut out the details, and try to see it as just shapes and colours, or try looking through a sheet of very old transparent plastic.

Notice how what you can see is grouped almost automatically into lighter and darker blocks. Look again, and notice areas of different colours.

Now, imagine that you only have five blocks of shading to describe what you see: very light, light grey, mid-grey, dark grey, and black. Which bits of what you can see would be darkest – that is, black? Which bits are lightest, so would be white? How would you allocate the other three shades?

Would you still have an idea of what you are looking at?

Objectives

You will be able to:

- outline Gibson's direct theory of perception

- define key terms related to direct perception

- explain the importance of movement in direct perception.

Key term

Motion parallax: the way that the visual field changes with movement, with close objects seeming to move more than objects that are further away

■ Gibson's direct theory of perception – the influence of nature

Direct perception is the idea that we perceive simply by using the information we receive through our senses. This gives us enough information to make sense of the world. James J. Gibson, who developed the direct theory of perception, believed that the key to understanding perception is to remember what it is used for. People (and animals) do not just receive passive images of the world. We are active in it, and that activity is part of our perception because it changes the visual images we receive. For example, if we are moving along a road, the visual image we receive changes. Things close to us appear to move fast as we go past them, while things further away do not seem to move as much. This is known as **motion parallax**. It only happens if we move, and it combines with the other depth cues to help us judge distances accurately.

We can use other cues as well. We do not just see blocks of colours when we look around, because colours have different textures – patterns of shade, mixtures of tones, or smoothness – which tell us what they are like. For example, if you look at a lawn or a wide area of paving, the bits which are closest to you will look more detailed, showing individual blades of grass or individual bits of stone or concrete. Further away, it will seem smoother, and the furthest parts will look even smoother (see Figure A). This happens as the depth cues of relative size and height in plane combine to change the apparent texture of what we are looking at. It produces a texture gradient, in which things that are further away look smoother. The same thing happens with colour to produce a colour gradient: colours are brighter close up, and paler when they are further away (Figure B).

A *Gradient of texture*

B *Gradient of colour*

Gibson saw texture gradients and colour gradients as even more examples of how the real world gives us plenty of information for perception. The real world, he argued, is three-dimensional, and where we stand and how we move about in it is as much a part of real-world perception as shape and colour.

An ecological theory

Direct perception is all about what perception is for. It is sometimes called the ecological theory of perception, because Gibson believed that perception evolved in order to help an animal deal best with its environment. So humans, birds, and primates have developed colour vision because that helps them to pick out ripe fruits and berries in trees, and they have developed good depth perception because this is essential for jumping across branches or running away from distant threats in grasslands.

Dealing with our environment includes our own actions, as well as the information we receive. A tree stump offers us different possibilities for action: we could stand on it to see further, we could sit on it for a rest, we could use it as a table, we could hit it with a stick to make a sound that carries a long way, and so on. Gibson argued that our perception of objects includes the possibilities for action which they afford (their affordances). So affordances are also part of direct perception. We are not just looking at the environment as if it were a movie, totally separate from us. We perceive what is around us in terms of ourselves, and what it allows us to do. Gibson's theory of direct perception tells us that we live in a perceptual world, which is not just three-dimensional but includes our own behaviour as well. So according to Gibson, we do not need to make **inferences** or guesses about what we are seeing. We have enough information from our senses to be able to understand the world around us.

Evaluation of Gibson's direct theory of perception

■ The theory does indicate that some perceptual abilities – like perceiving depth – might be due to **nature**, and that we do not always need to use past experience to perceive the world around us. There is evidence from infant research that depth perception might be innate or inborn.

■ The theory focuses on movement and how perception depends on the way visual cues change as we move. This is sensible as we never perceive anything from a static point of view, and even when we try to keep still our eyes are in constant motion.

■ The theory suggests that sensation and perception are the same process, but we know from illusions such as Figure C that they are separate processes. Here we sense the black shapes on a white background, but we perceive a horse and rider.

■ It is also the case that we know our past knowledge and information about the world affects some of our perception. We often interpret something depending on what we expect it to be rather than what actually is (Figure D).

C *What does this image show?*

D *Can you spot the mistake in this sign?*

Can you believe what you see?

■ Visual illusions

Visual illusions happen when our visual perception is 'tricked' into seeing something inaccurately. Some of them happen because the brain uses inappropriate strategies for interpreting the sensory information it is receiving. This can happen for several reasons, including:

- ■ **misinterpreted depth cues** – wrongly applying the 'rules' of depth perception

- ■ **ambiguity** – when an image could equally well be one thing or another

- ■ **fiction** – creating something that isn't really there, to complete an image

- ■ **size constancy** – keeping our original perception of the size of an object, even when the information received by the eyes changes.

Objectives

You will be able to:

- ● describe some common visual illusions

- ● outline four cognitive strategies which can create visual illusions

- ● explain how the Ames room illusion works.

Key terms

Ambiguity: having more than one possible meaning or interpretation

Fiction: the perception of an object or movement that is not present in the stimulus

Misinterpreted depth cues: when a depth cue is used inappropriately

Size constancy: the way we keep our original perception of the size of an object, even when the information received by the eyes changes

Visual illusion: a visual perception which is wrong or misinterprets what is actually there in reality

Building skills 1

Psychologists have studied many different visual illusions, and some of them are illustrated below and on pages 34–35. Before you read any further, look at Figures B to H and see if you can find an example of each of the types of cognitive strategy listed above.

A

Cognitive strategy	Illusion
Misinterpreted depth cues	
Ambiguity	
Fiction	
Size constancy	

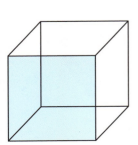

A The Necker cube

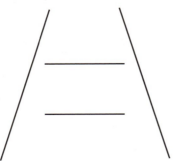

B The Ponzo illusion

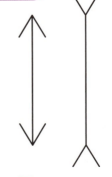
C The Müller-Lyer illusion

■ Explaining visual illusions

Depth cues (see Topic 2.2) help us to identify distance, but in a line drawing they can be misleading. The Ponzo illusion (Figure B) uses the depth cue of linear perspective. The two outer lines of the drawing create an illusion of perspective, as if they were railway lines stretching out before us. Unconsciously, we see the top inner line as being further away than the bottom line, so we perceive it as longer. But if we measure the lines, we find that they are exactly the same.

A similar process happens with the Müller-Lyer illusion (Figure C). With the left line in Figure C on page 33, the outward-pointing arrowheads seem to be 'pushing' the line towards us, whereas the inward-pointing arrowheads on the right line suggest that it is further away. Because we perceive the left line as being closer, we see it as shorter than the other one.

Ambiguity is another source of visual illusions. Sometimes there are two equally possible explanations. The shape in the Rubin's vase illusion (Figure D) might be a vase, or it might be two faces seen from the side. We can see either the vase or the faces, but not both at the same time. If we look at the vase, the faces disappear; if we look at the faces, the vase disappears. In this case, the brain copes with the ambiguity by focusing on one explanation or the other.

Sometimes, though, an image is so ambiguous that the brain cannot decide. The Getting started activity showed how the Necker cube (Figure A) seems to flip backwards and forwards. The drawing is perfectly balanced – that is, it can be seen either way – so your brain cannot decide which is the 'right' way round. Both hypotheses are equally possible, and therefore it flips the perceived image from one to the other.

A third type of illusion, fiction, is created by our own minds. The Kanizsa triangle (Figure E) is a good example. The triangle is not really there – it is a fiction that our perception has created, suggested by the shapes around it – but it appears so clearly that it even seems to stand out from the paper. The perceptual system generates an image which fills in the gap to create something plausible. We can see fictional movement too: if we see two lights next to one another, flashing alternately, our perceptual system joins them up so it looks as if there is one light moving from side to side. This is known as the phi phenomenon, and it is common in 'moving' advertising signs or Christmas decorations.

Visual constancies

Perceptual constancy is how we perceive objects as being the same (constant), even if the visual image we are receiving is quite different. A teacup seen from two different angles makes very different shapes on the retina of our eyes, but we still see it as the same shape because we apply constancy scaling, making allowances for those changes. That is called shape constancy (Figure F).

A similar thing happens when we see people in the distance: we do not see them as growing larger when they walk towards us, even though that is happening in the visual image. Instead, we apply size constancy,

D *Rubin's vase*

E *The Kanizsa triangle*

F *Shape constancy: a teacup*

seeing them as the same size in reality. The Ames room (Figure H) uses size constancy to produce a visual illusion. If we look at it from a special viewpoint, we see one person as being much larger than the other. It works because, although the room looks square, it is not really. The person who looks smaller really is further away, but the lines of the room are carefully drawn so the viewer does not see it that way (Figure G).

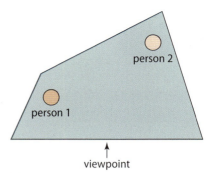

G *How the Ames room works*

H *The Ames room*

Did you know ?

The ambiguous images and paradoxical illusions used by the artist M. C. Escher (see for example Figure I) were developed when he worked closely with psychologists exploring how visual illusions worked. Escher's impossible figures show how we automatically try to turn every image we perceive into a three-dimensional object, even when it cannot be three dimensional and is only two dimensional.

Going further

Collect other examples of visual illusions that you have come across, and work out which perceptual process creates their effect. Remember that they may use more than one at the same time.

Exam tip !

It would be helpful to know which of the explanations for visual illusions can be used to explain the Ponzo illusion, the Müller-Lyer illusion, Rubin's vase, the Ames Room, the Kanizsa triangle and the Necker cube.

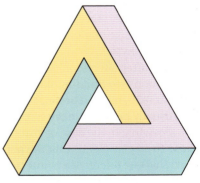

I *A paradoxical illusion*

Practice exam questions

1. One explanation for visual illusions is size constancy. Explain what is meant by 'size constancy' in this context. *(1 mark)*

2. Identify and explain one visual illusion. *(3 marks)*

Getting started

When you are looking for a friend in a crowd of people, what is it that you look for? Have you ever misidentified someone, thinking that it was your friend and then finding out that it wasn't?

Choose one particular friend and write down the clues you would use to identify him or her in a crowd, such as in a shopping centre. What sort of thing would you look for? How would you be sure it was him or her and nobody else?

Objectives

You will be able to:

- outline Gregory's constructivist theory of perception

- explain the role of inference in constructive perception

- define key terms related to constructive perception.

Key terms

Constructivist theory: the idea that our perception is built up from our prior knowledge and experience

Nurture: the idea that our characteristics and behaviour are influenced by our environment

■ Gregory's constructivist theory of perception – the influence of nurture

The **constructivist theory** of perception argues that our past knowledge and experience is essentially the most important thing in making sense of what is around us. Richard Gregory developed this theory, saying that our perception works by making reasonable guesses about what we see, on the basis of what it is most likely to be. These are known as perceptual hypotheses – the 'most probable' explanations for the visual information that we are receiving. Generally, Gregory argued, these hypotheses are accurate because the real world offers so much information, and we do not need to look for any other explanations.

The importance of visual illusions

For Gregory, certain types of visual illusions provide important evidence for the constructive approach to perception. Some illusions tell us something about the physiological mechanisms of the visual system – for example, negative after-effects happen as our visual cells recover from continuous stimulation (see Building skills 1). Other kinds of illusions, such as those on pages 33–35, happen because the perceptual system is misusing strategies that usually help it to make sense of the information it is receiving. In the case of visual illusions, using those strategies means that the perceptual system makes wrong inferences or guesses about the data. Gregory believed that perception involves cognitive processes: we do not just perceive the information that we receive, we also use our stored knowledge and experience in perception.

■ Evaluation of Gregory's theory of perception

- There is a lot of evidence to support the idea that the interpretations we make of the sensations we receive are affected by our past experiences. Both of the key research studies in this chapter (see pages 42–45) suggest that the

A *How do nature and nurture combine to help us make sense of what we see?*

perceptions of the participants were affected by their expectations or how they were feeling at the time of the study. This supports the idea that nurture can have an effect on perception.

■ Not everyone agrees with the explanations given for the effects of some illusions. Some have suggested that the Müller-Lyer illusion works because the arrowheads on the lines make them look like the near edge of a building, or the far corner of a room, so we think one line might be nearer to us than the other. However, the illusion still works when there are circles instead of arrowheads on the lines, and this does not seem to fit with our past experience of buildings affecting our perception (see Figure B).

■ All we can really say is that both nature and **nurture** have an effect on the way the sensations we receive become our perception of the world around us.

B *How does the Müller-Lyer illusion work?*

■ Top-down and bottom-up theories

Gregory's theory is a top-down theory, which means that it takes higher mental processes and shows how they shape the way we interpret the information the eyes receive. It suggests that perception is influenced by nurture: all the learning and past experiences we have gained. On the other hand, Gibson's theory, in Topic 2.3, is a bottom-up theory. This is because it takes the basic information which our eyes receive and shows how that basic information can produce the higher mental process of perception. This theory suggests that perception is influenced by nature: inborn biological factors rather than learning. Oddly, both of these theories can be right: Gregory's model works for some kinds of visual information – particularly when the information we are receiving is uncertain or ambiguous – while Gibson's model works in more everyday situations, where we have extra information from movement and textures.

1. Evaluate Gregory's constructivist theory of perception. *(4 marks)*

2. Explain how perception uses inferences from visual cues and past experience to construct a model of reality. *(9 marks)*

Practice exam questions

Getting started

Make up a set of about 30 cards, all the same size, which have words written on them in four different colours. 15 of these words should be ordinary, everyday words like 'apple' or 'paper'. The other 15 should be words which are not swear words, but could be slightly embarrassing, such as 'crotch' or 'penis'. Make sure your two lists contain words of the same length, and share the colours randomly between all the cards you have made.

Next, shuffle one of the two sets of cards and, using a timer on your phone or a second hand of a watch, ask someone to sort the cards into different colour piles as quickly as they can. Time how long it takes them. Then shuffle the other set of cards, and ask them to do the same. Compare the two times to see if one took longer than the other. What conclusions can you draw?

Objectives

You will be able to:

- explain what is meant by perceptual set
- identify factors which can generate perceptual set
- describe some examples of perceptual set.

Key terms

Culture: a group of people who share similar customs, beliefs, and behaviour

Expectation: the beliefs we have about what we are going to experience

Innate: inborn or inherited – that is, not learned

Perceptual set: a state of readiness to perceive certain kinds of stimuli rather than others

■ Perceptual set and expectation

At any one moment, we are receiving far more information than we can possibly take in. So we need to select what we are going to notice, choosing what is important and leaving out what is not. One way that we achieve this is by 'focusing' our perception, so that we are more ready to perceive certain things than others. We do this by developing a state of readiness, which psychologists refer to as **perceptual set**. This does not have the same meaning as when a jelly is set: it is used in the same way as at the start of a race, where athletes are told to 'Get ready, get set, GO!'. To be 'set' means to be fully ready and prepared, anticipating what is coming so that we can act on it effectively.

All our cognitive processes – memory, decision-making, learning, and perception – can be affected by set. We remember different things when we are in different moods; for example, a bad mood makes us more ready to remember annoying or unpleasant things, while a good mood makes us more likely to remember good things. We make different decisions depending on what we are expecting, or even on what we have just seen. We are more prepared to learn some things than others – for example, babies learn rhymes more easily than ordinary sentences because they are set to learn through repetition. And we are more likely to perceive things if our perception is set to notice that kind of thing.

Expectations are an important way that our perceptions become set. Bruner and Minturn's study (see pages 44–45) shows how expectations can influence how we interpret what we see. To take another example: people who have been shown pictures of birds' heads are set to see birds' heads. When they are then shown Figure A, they often say it is a duck's head, because they expect to see more birds' heads. However, if they had previously been shown pictures of rabbits' heads, then they probably would have given a different answer.

Synoptic link

Bartlett's 'War of the Ghosts' study (see Topic 1.3) showed us how set can affect memory too. The people trying to recall the story were ready to remember certain kinds of details but not others, and so they adjusted their accounts to fit what they thought was likely to have happened.

A Can you see the two different animals in this image?

B Is this like a modern phone?

■ Culture and perception

Expectations are not the only factors that can influence how we make sense of what we are seeing. The way we are brought up and the **cultures** we are brought up in can influence our perception too. For example, in modern Western society we grow up with lots of line drawings and cartoons. They are not particularly realistic, but we are used to them because we see them so often in children's books (see Figure B). One of the conventions in that type of drawing is the use of perspective. So if a Western child is asked to draw an animal, they usually draw it from the side – in fact, they may be told it is wrong if they do anything else (see Figure C).

C Is this like an elephant?

This does not apply, though, to children who have grown up in traditional tribal societies, where they do not have picture books or cartoons. If they are asked to draw an animal, they often draw it as if it were spread out flat (see Figure D). The reason for this is that they are drawing what they perceive, and what they perceive is the whole animal – they know that it has a head, tail and four legs, not just two, so that is what they draw. The perception of the Western children has been shaped by their exposure to line drawings and perspective, so they draw what looks like only half of the animal to someone who is not used to Western culture. But children from traditional environments do realise that these half-pictures are meant to be an animal, even if they think it is not correct.

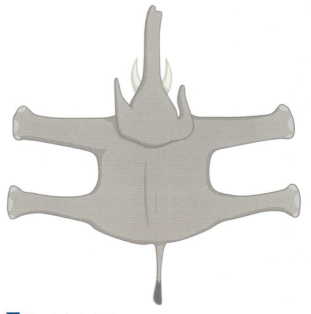

D The whole elephant

39

Building skills 1

Find some very early learning books for children, such as alphabet books or very simple first readers. Look at the pictures in them, and compare them with images of the real thing that they are representing, which the children would have come across in their everyday lives. How much do the pictures reflect the child's reality? What do you think these images are actually teaching those children?

K **E**

Key terms

Emotion: the moods or feelings that a person experiences

Motivation: the drives and needs that cause a person to act in a particular way

■ Emotions and motivation

We all experience a range of **emotions** and moods. Sometimes we are happy, sometimes we are annoyed, sometimes we are sad, and so on. These emotions can influence what we perceive as well. They contribute to our perceptual set, by making us more likely to perceive things in a way that is in line with how we feel. For example, children who are getting excited about Christmas tend to draw pictures of Santa Claus which are bigger and include more presents, than they do after Christmas when it is all over and they are not excited any more. In a similar way, someone who is upset about something is more likely to notice upsetting actions or events, and may just not notice positive things that are happening. They may also interpret what they see in an ambiguous picture in a very negative way (Figure E).

E *Is the person on the left about to help or hurt the older man?*

Motivation is what makes us do things. We have lots of different types of motives, ranging from physical motives, like being hungry or thirsty, which encourage us to eat or drink, to social, like wanting to keep in with our friends, or looking for respect from other people. The range of emoticons available on most modern keyboards shows us just how varied our emotions and motivations can be (Figure F). Our motivation can influence

F *Emoticons*

our perception as well – 2.6 Key research study: Gilchrist and Nesburg (page 42) looks at a study of how perception can be affected by hunger.

Our perception can also be affected by social motives, such as worrying what other people think of us or whether somebody likes us. In those cases, we often notice any little detail of other people's actions that fit with our motivation, and ignore information which does not fit.

G *What we think of other people can affect how we perceive them*

Building skills 2

Try composing a **A** **E** message to someone else consisting entirely of emoticons, then see how many people can interpret what it says. Are there ambiguities in your message that you had not realised were there? What does this suggest?

Did you know **?**

Our emotions and motivations can influence how we see ourselves, as well as how we interpret other experiences. Many people with anorexia, for example, see themselves as being fat when they look in the mirror, even though other people would say that they were very thin.

Going further

Try investigating whether hunger affects your friend's responses to words. Use two lists of ten words each, such as the ones that have been started for you below. Read out each word and ask your friend to give an example of it, then go on to the next word until the list is finished. Time how long it takes them to complete each list. Repeat this activity just before lunch, changing the order of the words in each list. See if they are faster at answering list A than list B.

List A   Fruit, meal, drink, food, snack

List B   Building, plant, country, car, street

Can you think of any other reason why the words in List B might take more time to respond to than those in List A, regardless of whether someone is hungry or not? What is the problem, and how would you address this problem?

Exam tip **!**

Be prepared to write answers to questions that ask you about several different topics in one question. The synoptic links in each chapter guide you to where this might occur.

Practice exam questions

1. Identify a factor that affects perception. *(1 mark)*

2. Outline the method used by Gilchrist and Nesberg in their study of motivation (see pages 42–43). *(3 marks)*

3. Describe and evaluate the Bruner and Minturn study of perceptual set (see pages 44–45). *(9 marks)*

Gilchrist and Nesberg's need and perceptual change study (1952)

Aim: To investigate how motivation affects perception.

Study design: Laboratory experiment

Method: 26 university students volunteered to go for 20 hours without any food, and to only drink water. They were **randomly allocated** to be in one of two groups: one which actually went without food, and the other, a control group, which had their normal meals during the 20 hours.

In the experiment, the participants were told that they would see a set of pictures on a screen for 15 seconds. Then the screen would be turned off. After 15 seconds, they were told they would see the pictures again, but they would not look the same. Their job was to adjust each picture so that it looked the same as the one they had seen before.

The pictures were a set of four colour images taken from magazines, showing typical meals: T-bone steaks, fried chicken, hamburgers, and spaghetti. In the second showing, the researchers had changed the brightness of the pictures, and the participants were asked to adjust the brightness of the pictures by turning a knob. They were tested at the beginning of the study (just after their lunchtime meal), after 6 hours, and after 20 hours.

Results: The control group showed little difference in their memory of the brightness of the pictures as time went on. But as the experimental group became hungrier, they judged the pictures to be brighter. Chart A shows the differences between the two groups on the different occasions.

Conclusion: Hunger can affect the way that we perceive images of food, which suggests that motivation affects perception.

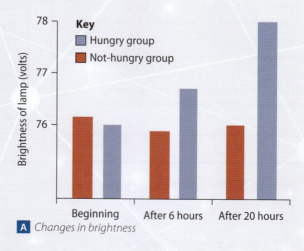

A *Changes in brightness*

Source: Gilchrist, J. C. and Nesberg, L. S. (1952) 'Need and perceptual change in need-related objects', Journal of Experimental Psychology, *44, 369–376*

■ Evaluation

Why the study is important

- The study showed that motivation can affect our perception.

- The study had ecological validity because the participants really were hungry.

- The study was carefully controlled, with matched timing and exactly the same conditions for both groups, apart from hunger. This means it would be easy for other researchers to replicate the study.

Limitations of the study

- There were not very many participants and they were all students of a similar age, so it is difficult to apply these results to other types of people.

- The participants were volunteers so their behaviour might not have been representative, as they were keen to take part in the study. They might also have guessed what the study was about, which could have also affected their behaviour.

Building skills 1

Gilchrist and Nesberg added another condition to their study, which involved 48 participants going without food or drink for 8 hours. They were tested in the same way but using pictures of drinks. On the last occasion, they were tested, then allowed a drink of water or orange juice, and then tested again. The average measures of the brightness of their adjusted images were:

- Thirsty group: at start 79; after 6 hours 82; after 8 hours 83; after a drink 79.

- Non-thirsty group: at start 81; after 6 hours 81; after 8 hours 81.5; after a drink 81.5.

  Convert these findings into a bar chart.

Key term

Random allocation: sorting participants into groups in a way that depends on pure chance

Synoptic link

In Chapter 4 you will learn about experimental design. This is a typical laboratory experiment. Can you identify the independent variable, the dependent variable, and some of the controls used in this study?

Did you know

Hunger can also affect your level of arousal (see Chapter 7), making you more tense. That is why having something to eat or a milky drink before you go to bed can help you to sleep.

Going further

Hunger and thirst are important sources of motivation. Human beings have other motives too, such as the need for achievement, or competitiveness. Design a study which would explore whether this type of motive can affect perception.

2.6 Key research study: Gilchrist and Nesberg

Bruner and Minturn's perceptual set study (1955)

Aim: To investigate how expectations can direct perception.

Study design: Laboratory experiment

Method: 24 student participants were asked to take part in an experiment on recognising numbers and letters. Letters or numbers were flashed up very quickly, at first faster than the eye could see, at 30 milliseconds, and then increasing by 20 milliseconds each time. The participants were asked to draw the letter or number as soon as they could recognise it.

The test **stimulus** was a broken 'B', which had a small gap between the curved part of the letter and the straight line. This meant that it could be seen as either the letter B or as the number 13 (see Figure A).

Half the participants were shown a series of four stimulus letters (L, M, Y, and A) as training for what to do. Then they were shown the test stimulus. After that, they were shown a series of test numbers (16, 17, 10, and 12) followed by the test stimulus. Then they were shown a series of mixed letters and numbers, again followed by the test stimulus. So each participant saw the test stimulus three times: once when they were expecting a letter, once when they were expecting a number, and once when they expecting either to come up.

The other half of the participants had the same procedure, except that they were **counterbalanced**. They were shown the stimulus numbers first, followed by the test stimulus, then the letters followed by the test stimulus, and then a mixture of letters and numbers followed by the test stimulus.

A *The stimulus figure*

Results: Most of the participants drew an open figure, like a '13', when they were expecting a number to come up, and a closed figure, like the letter 'B', when they were expecting a letter. When they were expecting either a letter or a number they produced mixed results: some people drew a '13' and some drew a 'B'.

Conclusion: The researchers concluded that the participants' expectations had directly affected how they interpreted the stimulus figure.

Source: Bruner, J. S. and Minturn, A. L. (1955), 'Perceptual identification and perceptual organization', Journal of General Psychology *(53), 21–8*

■ Evaluation

Why the study is important

- The study was carefully controlled and counterbalanced, so it could be replicated, increasing the reliability of these findings.

- The study showed the importance of human experience and context in perception, challenging the idea that perceptual rules always work the same way (as stated by Gibson).

- The study confirmed how recognition can be influenced by expectation. It provides support for Gregory's explanation of how we interpret information.

Limitations of the study

- There were not very many participants.

- The participants were all volunteers so their behaviour might not have been representative, as they were keen and enthusiastic participants. They might also have guessed the purpose of the study, which could have affected the results that were produced.

- The task was not very similar to perception in real life, where we are rarely faced with invented ambiguous figures, so it lacked ecological validity.

Building skills 1

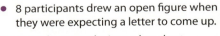

In one part of the study, the researchers found the following results:

- 22 participants drew an open figure when they were expecting a number to come up.
- 16 participants drew an open figure when they were expecting either a number or a letter to come up.
  - 8 participants drew an open figure when they were expecting a letter to come up.

Convert these results into a bar chart.

Key terms

Counterbalancing: an arrangement in which half of the participants in an experiment are given the conditions in one order (A followed by B) while the other half are given them in the opposite order (B followed by A)

Stimulus: something that is detected by the sense receptors, which the nervous system will react to

Synoptic link

This experiment used counterbalancing as an experimental control. You will learn about experimental control in Chapter 4. Why is counterbalancing important, and what does it control?

Did you know **?**

Early subliminal advertising showed people information so quickly that they did not notice it, although it still affected them. But it could backfire: when a cinema owner flashed 'ice-cream' subliminally on the screen, some people bought ice-cream, but others complained that the cinema was too cold. It is illegal to use subliminal advertising now.

Going further

Bruner and Minturn based their study on the principle of closure identified by the Gestalt psychologists. What is the principle of closure, and how is it relevant to their study?

2.6 Key research study: Bruner and Minturn

2 Revision checklist

Sensation and perception

☐ explain the difference between sensation and perception

See pages 26–27

Visual cues and constancies

☐ understand the differences between monocular and binocular depth cues

☐ describe how four monocular depth cues work: height in plane, relative size, occlusion and linear perspective

☐ describe how two binocular depth cues work: retinal disparity and convergence

See pages 28–30

Visual illusions

☐ understand how the following can create visual illusions: ambiguity, misinterpreted depth cues, fiction and size constancy

☐ explain how the following visual illusions work: the Ponzo illusion, the Müller-Lyer illusion, Rubin's vase, the Ames Room, the Kanizsa triangle and the Necker cube

See pages 33–35

Gibson's direct theory of perception – the influence of nature

☐ describe and evaluate Gibson's direct theory of perception

☐ explain the role of motion parallax in perception

See pages 31–32

Gregory's constructivist theory of perception – the influence of nurture

☐ describe and evaluate Gregory's constructivist theory of perception

☐ explain how inferences are used to construct a model of reality

See pages 36–37

Factors affecting perception

☐ explain what is meant be perceptual set

☐ explain how culture, motivation, emotion, and expectation can influence perception

☐ **key research study:** describe and evaluate Gilchrist and Nesberg's need and perceptual change study

☐ **key research study:** describe and evaluate Bruner and Minturn's perceptual set study

See pages 38–45

Practice exam questions

1. **a)** What is meant by the term 'sensation'? *(2 marks)*

   b) Sadiq suspected that a glass of milk might not be safe to drink. He tested it by using his nose. Which sense is Sadiq most likely to be using? *(1 mark)*

   A   Sight

   B   Smell

   C   Touch

   c) When Sara drank the coffee that Sadiq had made for her, she suspected that the milk might not be safe to drink. Which sense is Sara most likely to be using? *(1 mark)*

   A   Hearing

   B   Taste

   C   Touch

2. **a)** Describe Gibson's direct theory of perception. *(5 marks)*

   > When describing theories and concepts, examples may be helpful in showing understanding.

   b) Use your knowledge of psychology to evaluate Gibson's direct theory of perception. *(5 marks)*

   > When asked to evaluate a theory or piece of research, using generic comments that are not developed will earn very few marks. Remember to be specific and to develop your points.

3. **a)** One explanation for visual illusions is ambiguity. Explain what is meant by 'ambiguity' in this context. *(1 mark)*

   b) Which of the following visual illusions can be explained by ambiguity? *(1 mark)*

A The Ponzo illusion   B The Müller-Lyer illusion   C Rubin's vase

4. **a)** Imagine that you have been asked to conduct a study to investigate how motivation affects perception. Use your knowledge of psychology to describe:

   - what task you would do to carry out your study
   - what you would measure
   - the results you would expect to find in your study. *(5 marks)*

   > When the question asks for the task that would be used in your study, your answer needs to give the control condition as well as the experimental condition for the suggested task.

   b) Identify two ethical issues that you would need to consider in the study you have described in 4 a). *(2 marks)*

   c) Outline how you could deal with the ethical issues that you identified in your answer to 4 b). *(2 marks)*

3 Development

3.1 How does the brain develop?

Getting started

Look at the human brain in Photo A. What do you know about the brain? Can you name any structures in the brain? Can you describe their functions?

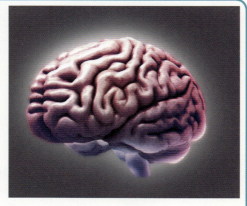

A *The human brain*

Objectives

You will be able to:

- understand how the brain develops from simple neural structures in the womb

- identify and describe structures of the brain: the brain stem, thalamus, cerebellum, and cortex

- understand the development of autonomic functions, sensory processing, movement, and cognition

- understand the roles of nature and nurture in brain development.

■ Early brain development

Simple neural structures in the womb

Brain development begins during the third week of pregnancy. The multiplying cells form a structure called the neural plate. This folds over onto itself to form a tube-shaped structure, called the neural tube.

During the fourth week (see Photo B) the neural tube begins to divide into a spinal cord (green), forebrain (blue), midbrain (grey) and hindbrain (orange).

During the sixth week the forebrain divides into two areas (pink and yellow). Part of the pink area goes on to form the **cortex**. Part of the yellow area develops into the **thalamus**. **Neurons** and **synapses** begin to develop in the spinal cord, which allows the foetus to move around and react to its environment.

By the fifteenth week, the **cerebellum** (upper orange area) has formed from the hindbrain. By the sixth month of pregnancy, the brain is fully formed, although it does not reach its full size for a while yet. During the last three months of pregnancy, folds begin to form on the cortex. This gives the brain its wrinkled appearance. At birth, the brain is 25 per cent of its adult size.

Synoptic link

Neurons and synapses develop in the very early stages of human growth. Think about how these continue to be of importance as we learn how to do or remember things. See Topic 7.3 to learn more about neurons and synapses.

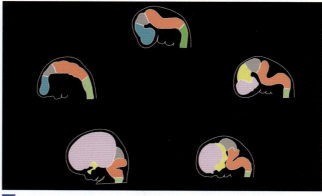

B *Neural structures in the womb at week 4 (upper left), week 5 (top), week 6 (upper right), week 8 (lower right), week 15 (lower left)*

■ The brain stem, thalamus, and cerebellum

The **brain stem** is shaped like a widening stalk. It connects the spinal cord to the brain. It controls basic **autonomic functions** such as breathing, heart rate, blood pressure, and sleeping. By week six of pregnancy, the baby's heart beats regularly and blood pumps through the main vessels.

The thalamus, known as the 'deep chamber', is found in the centre of the brain. It can be viewed as a **sensory processing** station. It receives messages from the senses and turns them into appropriate behavioural or motor responses. All sensory information passes through the thalamus on its way to the cortex (where **cognition** takes place).

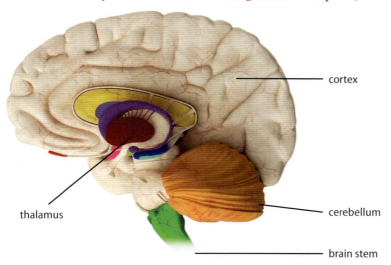

C *Cross section of the human brain*

Building skills 1

Working with a partner, take it in turns to try the following activity. **A**

Stand up straight with your feet together and your hands by your side. Now close your eyes. Try and stay in this position for one minute. Your partner will time you and tell you when a minute has passed.

The test you have just tried is called the Romberg test. It can be used to see if a person has a problem with their balance, which they may show through unsteadiness. The test is used to help diagnose whether someone has a problem with their spinal cord, which leads to a loss of motor coordination. However, the test cannot be used on its own to diagnose this problem, as there may be other reasons why someone shows unsteadiness during the test.

The cerebellum, known as the 'little brain', is located at the back of the brain behind the brain stem. It coordinates movement and balance. It receives information from the cortex and other areas of the brain, and fine-tunes it into a motor activity such as walking.

If a person suffers damage to the cerebellum, they are likely to have difficulty with muscle coordination, keeping their balance, and with fine motor skills. For example, they would have trouble typing or riding a bicycle.

Key terms

Autonomic functions: involuntary bodily functions such as breathing and heart rate

Brain stem: the part of the brain that controls basic functions such as breathing and heart rate

Cerebellum: a small, wrinkled structure at the back of the brain which coordinates motor movement, dexterity, and balance, among other things

Cognition: the mental processes involved in gaining knowledge; these include thinking, planning and problem solving

Cortex: the outer layer of the brain where higher cognitive functions take place, e.g. speech

Neuron: a specialised nerve cell which generates and transmits an electrical impulse

Sensory processing: the brain receives messages from the senses and turns them into appropriate motor and behavioural responses

Synapse: the small gap between the dendrite of one neuron and the receptor site of the next one, which allows signals to pass between them

Thalamus: the part of the brain that passes information from the sense organs to the cortex

Did you know

Research suggests that the human brain is not fully developed until you are in your mid-20s or possibly even your 30s.

Exam tip !

Make sure you can identify and briefly describe the brain stem, thalamus, cerebellum, and cortex.

The cortex

The cortex, also known as the cerebral cortex, is the outer layer of the brain. It starts to function around the time a baby is born. It is associated with higher cognitive processes and is divided into four lobes (sections). Each lobe is associated with different functions:

- occipital lobe – processes visual information

- temporal lobe – involved with hearing

- parietal lobe – processes information related to touch on the skin like heat, cold, and pain

- frontal lobe – associated with cognitive activities such as thinking, planning and problem solving.

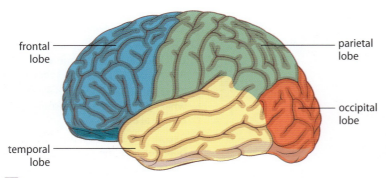

E *The cortex is divided into four lobes*

The roles of nature and nurture

The roles of **nature** and **nurture** in brain development are widely debated in psychology.

Psychologists on the nature side of the debate believe that your characteristics and behaviour are inherited from your parents. Those on the nurture side of the debate believe that your characteristics and behaviour are influenced by your environment, and develop after birth depending on the experiences you have.

Psychologists use different methods to study the roles of nature and nurture in brain development, including looking at twins, newborn babies, and animals.

Twin studies

Identical twins share exactly the same genes whereas non-identical twins do not. If both identical twins have the same characteristic, it is evidence that the characteristic is due to nature. A number of studies have shown that the IQs of identical twins are very similar, implying that nature has a major role in intelligence.

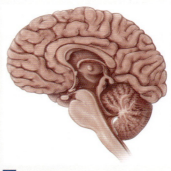

Another study looked at a pair of identical twins who were raised apart from the age of four weeks. They were very similar when they met for the first time aged 39. They both had the same car, went on holiday to the same place, and both bit their nails. It was concluded that nature plays more of a role in personality than nurture.

Newborn babies

It is useful to study newborn babies because there will be very little impact of nurture on a baby before birth. Psychologists have found that besides being able to cry, babies can also recognise faces. This implies that nature is responsible for these abilities. As babies are not able to talk until much later on, it is believed that nurture is responsible for language development.

Animals

In one study, baby rats were kept in cages on their own with no toys. Another group of baby rats were kept in a cage together with lots of stimulating toys. The rats that lived in the group in the stimulating environment developed bigger brains and demonstrated better problem-solving skills than the rats that lived on their own. This supports the idea that nurture is very important for early brain development.

> ### Building skills 3
>
> What problems can you think of in using twins, newborns or animals to investigate the roles of nature and nurture in brain development? **E**

Twin studies are useful but you have to be careful when analysing the results. Identical twins may have more characteristics in common than non-identical twins, but this may not be due entirely to nature. Identical twins tend to be treated in very similar ways by parents, therefore nurture could still play a role.

You also have to be careful when drawing conclusions about human development and behaviour from studies using animals. What applies to animals may not necessarily apply to humans because humans are more complex. However, animal studies are useful when it is not possible to conduct experiments on humans.

> ### Did you know ?
> By the age of 2, the brain is about 80 per cent of its adult size.

> ### Exam tip !
> When defining a term be careful not to use the term in your definition. For example, you would not achieve any marks for saying that 'nature means that our characteristics are from nature'.

> ### Going further
> Investigate which human characteristics are believed to be the result of nature, and which are believed to be influenced by nurture. Discuss your findings with a partner. Do you agree? Why/why not? Try to give examples to explain your thoughts.

> ### Synoptic link
> Topic 6.2 on pages 126–127 considers the similarities and differences between animal and human communication. You could use your learning in this topic to expand your analysis there: consider how nature and nurture could influence communication development.

> **Practice exam questions**
>
> 1. Which one of the following best describes the brain stem? *(1 mark)*
>   A The part of the brain that controls basic functions such as breathing
>   B The part of the brain involved in coordinating movement and balance
>   C The outer layer of the brain where higher-level processing takes place
>
> 2. Describe the role of the thalamus. *(2 marks)*
>
> 3. Outline how the role of nurture in brain development can be investigated. *(4 marks)*

What is Piaget's theory of cognitive development?

■ Piaget's theory of cognitive development

Piaget (1896–1980) studied children's **cognitive development**. He believed that **schemas** were the key to cognitive development and he described how they developed as a child grew up. Schemas are blocks of knowledge that develop in response to our experiences of the world. He believed that babies are born with simple schemas for sucking and grasping. As the baby grows, new schemas develop.

Schemas develop through **assimilation** or **accommodation**. Assimilation occurs when new information is added to an existing schema. For example, babies will use the sucking schema with fingers and other things that they put in their mouth. However, in order to suck through a straw, the basic sucking schema needs to be changed. This is called accommodation.

Building skills 1

Josh holds a pen in the same way that he holds a pencil. This is assimilation. However, he has to change his grip when he is given a paintbrush for the first time. This is accommodation.

A

Working with a partner, think of at least one more example of assimilation and accommodation. Share your ideas with your class.

A Piaget teaching children in a classroom

Key terms

Accommodation: changing a schema, or developing a new schema to cope with a new situation

Assimilation: adding new information to an existing schema

Cognitive development: the changes that take place over time in a person's thinking and intellect

Concrete operational: the ability to apply logic to physical (concrete) objects to solve problems

Conservation: knowing that the amount of something stays the same, even though its appearance may change

Egocentric: not being able to see things from another person's point of view

Pre-operational: before logic – being unable to apply reason to solve problems

Schema: a cognitive model of people, objects, or situations; based on previous information and experiences which helps us to perceive, organise, and understand new information

■ The four stages of development

Piaget believed that there are four stages to children's intellectual development. He said that all children pass through the stages in the same order, and roughly at the same ages.

Sensorimotor stage: 0–2 years

In this stage, children learn about the world through their senses (sensori-) and by doing things (motor). The main feature of the **sensorimotor** stage is that the child develops object permanence (knowing that objects still exist even when they are out of sight).

To investigate object permanence, Piaget gave a child a toy to play with. Then, while the child was watching, Piaget took the toy and hid it underneath a blanket. He watched to see whether or not the child would search for the toy. He found that children under the age of eight months did not search for the toy, whereas children aged eight months and older did. Therefore, he concluded that they had developed object permanence.

Pre-operational stage: 2–7 years

The main feature of the **pre-operational** stage is that children are **egocentric**. To investigate this, Piaget showed children a model of three mountains. He then placed a doll somewhere beside the model (see Figure C). The child was then shown photos that had been taken from each side of the model. The child had to choose the photo showing the view that the doll could see.

He found that children under the age of seven chose a photo that showed their own view. However, children aged seven and older were able to choose the photo that showed the doll's view. He concluded that children are no longer egocentric from the age of seven.

Concrete operational stage: 7–11 years

Piaget believed that by the time children reached the age of seven, they had developed the ability to conserve and were acting in the **concrete operational** stage.

To investigate **conservation** of number, Piaget showed children two identical rows of counters. He then asked the child if there were the same amount of counters in each row. When the child agreed there were, he spread out one of the rows of counters while the child watched. He then asked the child again if there were the same amount in each row. Children under seven said there were not, whereas children aged seven and over said there were.

> **Exam tip** !
>
> Make sure you can name and briefly describe all four stages of Piaget's theory. A question asking you to describe a stage will require an answer that is clear and concise.

> **Key term**
>
> **Sensorimotor:** learning through the senses and by physical (motor) activities

B *A child showing object permanence*

C *The three mountains experiment*

Before the change

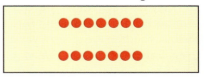

After the change

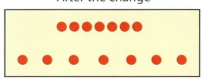

D *Conservation of number experiment*

Getting started

Without looking back, can you name the three stages of Piaget's theory you have looked at so far?

Describe, or draw, the experiments Piaget used to test children's understanding in each stage.

Key term

Formal operational: the ability to apply logic in an abstract (non-physical) way to solve problems, for example mental calculation

Formal operational stage: 11+ years

Piaget believed that a main feature of the **formal operational** stage is that children can solve problems in a systematic way. Children were given different lengths of string and a number of weights that could be attached to the string. The child's task was to investigate what factor affected how fast the pendulum would swing. The child had to vary the length of the string, and the number of weights attached.

Piaget found that children under the age of 11 would attempt to change both the weight and the length of string at the same time. However, after the age of 11, children would solve the problem systematically. For example, they would keep the length of string the same, while they changed the weights in turn, from the lightest to the heaviest. Therefore, Piaget concluded that a main feature of this stage was that children could solve problems systematically.

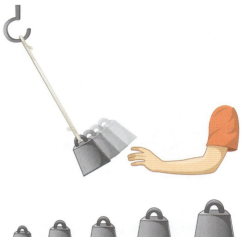

E *The pendulum task*

■ The role of Piaget's theory in education

Piaget believed that a child's intelligence develops from discovering things for themselves. He said that children needed to explore objects and situations to learn about them. Piaget also said that children had to be ready to learn, and that they would only gain new concepts if they were at the right stage of development for what they were learning.

Building skills 3

Create a poster to summarise Piaget's four stages of development. The poster should include the names, the ages, and the main features of each stage. The poster could use a table or spider diagram or some other imaginative way of summarising the four stages.

K

Building skills 2

How do you think Piaget's ideas are used in nurseries and schools? Try to think of at least three different ways and explain the purpose of each.

A

You may have suggested that nurseries and early years at primary school have a heavy focus on discovery learning. That is, children are given a variety of objects and allowed to explore them in their own way. For example, they may have a water table and work out for themselves which objects sink and which float.

You may also have suggested that giving children science problems to solve either on their own, or in groups, allows them to learn from their experiences.

F *Piaget's theory in education*

Applying Piaget's theory to education

- Teachers should take a readiness approach. They need to present opportunities for the child to learn new concepts only when they are at the right stage of intellectual development and ready to learn.

- Children should be taught in a child-centred way. The teacher should provide the materials and allow the child to discover the answers to problems for themselves.

- Teaching materials for science and maths should consist of actual objects that a child can manipulate. For example, string and weights to investigate the pendulum task.

■ Evaluation of Piaget's theory of cognitive development

Other psychologists have since shown that the ages Piaget said children could do certain tasks at are incorrect. Recent studies have demonstrated that babies develop object permanence before eight months. It has also been shown that children lose their egocentric thinking, and can conserve, before the age of seven; see McGarrigle and Donaldson's 'Naughty Teddy' study (page 58) and Hughes' 'Policeman Doll' study (page 56). It has also been suggested that people enter the formal operational stage much later than age 11, and some people will never reach it.

Psychologists also criticise Piaget's theory because of the way he conducted his experiments. For example, in the conservation tasks, he asked children the same question more than once (before and after the movement of counters). This may have led children to believe that their first answer must have been wrong so they should change it.

Piaget's theory has also been criticised because of the way he collected his data. He used small samples that were unrepresentative of most children. He did a lot of research on his own children. The questions he put to children were not always standardised as each child was treated differently.

However, despite these criticisms, Piaget's work has led many other psychologists to study children's cognitive development. His methods of testing children's intellectual development were new and fun, and they used simple resources which others could easily replicate. His research has had a major impact on early years education, where his ideas are still being used today.

Going further

Search the Internet for clips of children completing conservation of number, volume and mass experiments. Describe how conservation of volume and mass experiments are carried out. If you have young children in your family, you could ask their parents for permission to try out these experiments on them.

If several of you do this, compare the results of your experiments. How do they differ? How are they similar? Think about why this might be.

Building skills 4

What do you think of Piaget's theory? Working with a partner, try to think of at least two evaluation points. **E**

Synoptic link

Read more about standardised procedures on pages 70–71.

Exam tip

Make sure you answer the question set. Do not describe everything you know about Piaget's theory if the question only asks about one of his stages.

1. Which one of the following is a description of assimilation? *(1 mark)*
   A Dylan holds a big spoon in the same way that he holds a baby spoon
   B Dylan has to change his spoon grip to hold a fork

2. Identify and briefly describe the second stage of Piaget's theory of cognitive development. *(3 marks)*

3. Describe one way in which Piaget's theory of cognitive development could be applied to education. *(2 marks)*

Practice exam questions

Hughes' 'Policeman Doll' study (1978)

Aim: To see if children can see things from another person's point of view, at an earlier age than Piaget's theory suggested.

Study design: A laboratory study in which there was some control of possible extraneous variables. All procedures were standardised to ensure the study could be replicated easily. Thirty children between the ages of three-and-a-half years and five years took part in the study.

Method: The children were shown a model with two intersecting walls that formed a cross. A policeman doll was placed on the model. The child was asked to hide a boy doll so the policeman doll could not see him.

The policeman was then placed in different positions on the model, and the child was asked to hide the boy each time. This was to ensure the child understood the task. If the child made mistakes, they were told and were allowed to try again. This was rarely necessary because the children seemed to understand the task straight away.

Then the actual experiment began. Another policeman doll was placed on the model and the child was asked to hide the boy doll so that neither policeman doll could see him. This was repeated three times so that a different section of the grid was left as the only hiding place each time.

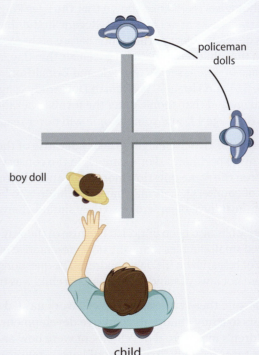

A 'Hide and seek' – the child had to hide the doll from the policemen

Results: 90 per cent of the children aged between three-and-a-half and five years were able to hide the boy doll from the two policemen dolls.

Conclusion: Children aged between three-and-a-half years and five years can see things from someone else's point of view if the situation is familiar to them, and the task makes sense.

This was very different to Piaget's findings that children were egocentric until seven years of age.

Source: Hughes (1978) cited in Donaldson, M. (1978) Children's Minds, *London: Fontana.*

Building skills 1

What do you think of Hughes' 'Policeman Doll' study? How might the children have viewed the activities they were asked to do?

Working with a partner, try to list at least two reasons why children were able to see things from someone else's point of view at an earlier age than Piaget found in his 'three mountains' experiment.

Building skills 2 A

Working with a partner, design an ethical experiment that could be used to test whether children are egocentric or not.

See Chapter 4 for advice on how to design an effective experiment.

You could make up an experiment similar to the three mountains task, or the policeman task, or you could design your own.

Try your experiment out on other members of your group.

In Building skills 1, you might have said that the policeman task makes more sense to children as it resembles a game of hide and seek, which most children understand and have played. You may also have suggested that the policeman task is easier than the three mountains task. Hughes believed the three mountains task was too difficult because it required children to do two things. They had to choose the doll's view, then they had to match it to a photograph. The policeman task was easier because they only had to do one thing: hide the doll from the two policemen.

■ Support for Hughes' findings

Another psychologist designed a version of the three mountains task that used children's television characters. They found that three- and four-year-olds could give the correct answers when the television characters were used. Hughes also gave children a simpler version of the three mountains task. He found many three- and four-year-olds could then give the correct answers.

This provides more support for the view that Piaget underestimated the age at which children could see things from someone else's point of view.

Going further

Search the Internet for clips of children completing egocentrism experiments. If you have children in your family, you could ask their parents for permission to try out the experiments.

Consider your results against those of Hughes. Are they similar? Consider why or why not.

However, Hughes' first experiment can also be criticised. The children were tested in an unusual environment and by someone unfamiliar to them. Perhaps if the children were in their own environment, and the experimenter was familiar to them, more would demonstrate that they are no longer egocentric at an even younger age.

■ Evaluation

Why the study is important

■ It showed that contrary to Piaget's conclusions, children younger than seven are not always egocentric.

Limitations of the study

■ The task involved hiding from a policeman, which is not a situation that young children are likely to have experienced. If it involved hiding from a parent, or another child, more children might have got the correct answers.

McGarrigle and Donaldson's 'Naughty Teddy' study (1974)

Aim: To see if children developed conservation skills at an earlier age than Piaget found, if the change to the materials was accidental.

Study design: A laboratory study in which there was some control of possible extraneous variables. All procedures were standardised to ensure the study could be replicated easily. Eighty children between the ages of four and six took part in the study.

Method: The children were shown two rows of counters and asked if there was the same amount in each row. Then a glove puppet called 'Naughty Teddy' made an appearance. Naughty Teddy accidentally messed up one row of counters in front of the child. The messed-up row was spread out to look longer than the other row. The experimenter pretended to be really cross with Naughty Teddy and told it off. The child was then asked if there were the same amount of counters in each row.

A *Naughty Teddy accidentally messed up one row of counters*

Results: 62 per cent of the four- to six-year-olds stated that there was still the same amount of counters in each row, therefore they could conserve. Only 16 per cent of four- to six-year-olds answered the question correctly in Piaget's conservation of number study, when the adult made the change to the counters.

Conclusion: Children younger than the age of seven can conserve if the change to the materials is seen to be accidental. When Naughty Teddy messes up the row of counters and spreads them out, younger children know that the amount of counters has not changed.

Source: McGarrigle, J. and Donaldson, M. (1974) 'Conservation Accidents'. Cognition, 3, 341–350.

Building skills 1 **E**

What do you think of McGarrigle and Donaldson's 'Naughty Teddy' study?

Try to give two reasons why children were able to conserve in their experiment at an earlier age than in Piaget's experiment.

Building skills 2 **A**

Working with a partner, design your own conservation experiment.

 See Chapter 4 for advice on how to design an effective experiment.

You could design one on conservation of number (the counters experiment), or one on conservation of volume or mass (you will need to investigate those experiments first).

Try out your experiment on other members of your group.

In Building skills 1, you might have said that because Naughty Teddy made the change, it was seen by the children as being an accident. Therefore, they knew that the number of counters could not have changed. Also, as an adult makes the change to the counters in Piaget' experiment, the child may think that the adult must have changed something, so they should give a different answer to their first answer.

■ Support for McGarrigle and Donaldson's findings

Other psychologists have also found that children develop conservation skills before seven years of age. In one study, psychologists replicated the conservation of number experiment, but they only asked the question once. They showed children the two rows of counters in silence. Then, once the psychologist had spread out one of the rows of counters, they asked the question 'Is there the same amount in each row?'. They found that more six-year-olds got the answer correct than Piaget found, therefore offering more support to McGarrigle and Donaldson's conclusion that children can conserve before the age of seven.

However, McGarrigle and Donaldson's experiment can be criticised. The children used in the study were tested by an adult stranger in an unusual environment. Perhaps if the adult making the change was familiar to them, and they were in their usual environment, more children between the ages of four and six would be able to conserve.

Exam tip **!**

If you are asked to describe an experiment on conservation, make sure you describe the method clearly. This could include things like whether the child was asked the same question before, and after, the counters were spread out.

■ Evaluation

Why the study is important

- It showed that contrary to Piaget's conclusions, children younger than seven can conserve.

Limitations of the study

- Over 30 per cent of children still failed to conserve when 'Naughty Teddy' made the change.

- The study was replicated by another psychologist who found that although more children could conserve when 'Naughty Teddy' was used, the results were not as high as McGarrigle and Donaldson had found.

What are the effects of learning on development?

Getting started

Read the following statements. Decide whether you agree or disagree with each one.

a) People are born with a set level of intelligence and cannot really do much to change it.

b) It does not matter how much intelligence someone is born with, they can always increase it.

Which statement did you agree with? Why?

Objectives

You will be able to:

- understand Dweck's Mindset Theory of Learning
- know the difference between a fixed mindset and a growth mindset
- understand the role of praise in learning
- understand the role of self-efficacy beliefs in learning
- understand what is meant by a learning style
- recognise different learning styles including verbalisers and visualisers
- understand Willingham's Learning Theory and his criticism of learning styles.

■ Dweck's Mindset Theory of Learning

Dweck developed a theory called the **Mindset Theory of Learning**. The theory explains how students can achieve success in their learning. Dweck specifically talks about maths and science, although the theory applies to all subjects and sporting activities. Dweck believes that there are two types of mindsets:

- **Fixed mindset** – students believe that their intelligence is unchanging. They believe it is genetic and there is nothing they can do to change it.

- **Growth mindset** – students believe that their intelligence comes from hard work. They believe that it can be increased by putting time and effort into learning.

When a student is faced with a challenge, the type of mindset they have will affect how they deal with it. Dweck believed that a fixed mindset student will give up very quickly. However, a growth mindset student will keep on trying, which will increase their chances of succeeding.

Building skills 1

Look back at the Getting started activity above. Which statement do you think refers to a fixed mindset? Which statement do you think refers to a growth mindset? Why?

B *A student with a growth mindset keeps trying*

In the Getting started activity above, statement a) refers to a fixed mindset. Statement b) refers to a growth mindset. A person's mindset can be measured by asking them to agree or disagree to a number of statements similar to those in Getting started above.

A *A student with a fixed mindset gives up quickly*

Changing mindsets

Psychologists have shown that mindsets can be changed through training. In one study, students were taught about what happens in their brain each time they learn something new and difficult. The students who were taught this lesson showed a major improvement in their exam results, compared to a control group who did not receive the lesson.

The role of praise in learning

Dweck believes that the type of **praise** or positive feedback a student receives from their teacher affects their mindset. She suggests there are two types of praise:

- Person praise – the student is praised for their intelligence. For example, they are told they are clever, or they are told they are a great scientist.

- Process praise – the student is praised for their effort and the processes they use in completing a task. For example, they are praised for the strategies they use, or the progress they have made.

Students who receive person praise believe their successes and failures are something beyond their control. Students who receive process praise believe their successes and failures are due to the amount of effort they put in.

In one study, students were given an online maths game to play that gave them feedback on their effort, strategy, and progress. This was different to the usual maths games that provide a score as feedback. It was found that with the new game, students made more effort, used more strategies, and persevered for longer than they usually did. It was concluded that the type of praise a student receives has a big impact on their learning.

■ Evaluation of Dweck's Mindset Theory of Learning

- The theory helps us understand how students can increase their exam grades.

- It informs teachers that mindsets can be changed, and explains how they can change them.

- There are studies to support Dweck's theory, which suggests her findings are accurate.

■ The role of self-efficacy beliefs in learning

Self-efficacy is the belief in your own ability to succeed at a task. A student with a strong sense of self-efficacy puts in effort to achieve their goals. They will challenge themselves with difficult tasks, and are likely to be successful. A student with a low sense of self-efficacy believes they will not be successful, so they are unlikely to try. They will avoid challenging tasks, and are less likely to achieve their goals.

Students can increase their sense of self-efficacy by:

- being successful at something
- observing other people succeed at something due to their effort
- being persuaded they can achieve by a role model such as a teacher
- being guided through a task.

Key terms

Mindset Theory of Learning: a theory that describes how students can achieve success in their learning

Fixed mindset: the belief that ability is genetic and unchanging

Growth mindset: the belief that ability comes from hard work and can be increased

Praise: an expression of approval

Self-efficacy: the belief in your own ability to succeed at a task

Building skills 2

Working with a partner, try to list at least two evaluations of Dweck's theory.

E

Exam tip

Make sure that you can explain the difference between a fixed mindset and a growth mindset: using examples can help you.

Going further

Test your mindset at http://mindsetonline.com/testyourmindset.

Learning styles

Key terms

Learning styles: the different ways that a person can process information

Verbaliser: someone who processes information by speaking and listening (auditory processing)

Visualiser: someone who processes information by looking at it (visual processing)

Visual, Auditory, and Kinaesthetic (VAK)

In Getting started above, you chose your preferred learning style according to the VAK theory.

The VAK theory states that there are three **learning styles**: visual, auditory, and kinaesthetic.

- Visual learners learn best by reading or seeing pictures. They like to see what they are learning. They remember things by what they look like.

- Auditory learners learn best by listening. They like to hear something, or speak it to learn it. They remember what they have heard.

- Kinaesthetic learners learn best by doing something. They like to move or make what they are learning. They remember best when some type of physical activity is involved.

Verbalisers and Visualisers

Another theory of learning styles calls learners **verbalisers** or **visualisers**. In Building skills 4, if you chose statement a), you are a verbaliser. If you chose statement b), you are a visualiser.

- Verbalisers process information verbally. They prefer to learn from written information, and they like to write things down. They think using words.

- Visualisers process information visually. They prefer to learn from pictures and diagrams. They think using pictures.

Building skills 3

K

Which statement did you choose in the Getting started activity above?

According to the VAK theory of learning styles, are you a visual, auditory, or kinaesthetic learner? How does the statement suggest this?

Building skills 4

K

Choose one statement that best describes how you prefer to learn.

a) I like to write about things. I think things through in my mind like I'm talking to myself.

b) I like to visualise things in my mind. I do mental maths by imagining I can see the numbers on paper.

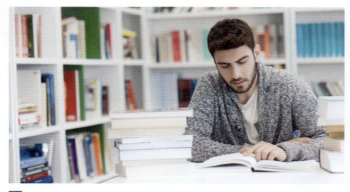

C *Verbalisers learn from written information*

D *Visualisers think using pictures*

■ Willingham's Learning Theory and his criticism of learning styles

Many people believe that if you teach a student in the way they learn best (their preferred learning style), then they should learn better. For example, if you have a kinaesthetic learner, the teacher should make sure the lesson involves them doing something active instead of sitting still and listening. If you have a visual learner, you should make sure the lesson involves pictures and diagrams to illustrate concepts.

However, Willingham disagrees with this. He believes that learning styles do not exist in the ways suggested above. In his learning theory he points out that there is no experimental evidence to support their existence. Studies also show that teaching students in their preferred learning style has no effect on their exam results.

Willingham agrees that students may have a better visual or auditory memory, but he says it does not help in the classroom. This is because teachers usually want students to remember what things mean, not what they sound or look like. He says that whether the information is presented visually or audibly, the student needs to extract the information and store its meaning. This may explain why teaching students in their preferred learning style has no effect on their exam results: a student's ability to store information is more important than how they learned the information.

Willingham believes that students should be taught using the best method for the content being taught. For example, in a lesson on structures of the brain, all the students need to see a diagram of the brain, not just those with a visual learning style. In a language lesson, all students need to hear how words are pronounced, not just those with an auditory learning style. In addition, if a student has difficulty taking in a particular type of information, they need to be given the opportunity to practise dealing with that type of information.

Exam tip

Examiners will expect you to use specialist vocabulary accurately. Make sure you know the difference between similar words such as verbaliser and visualiser.

Going further

Do you want to know what type of learner you are according to the VAK learning style theory? Complete the online test to find out: www.rdi.co.uk/what-type-of-learner-are-you

Practice exam questions

1. Which one of these is a description of a fixed mindset? *(1 mark)*
   A The belief that ability comes from hard work and can be increased
   B The belief that ability is genetic and unchanging
   C The belief in your own ability to succeed at a task

2. Explain the difference between a verbaliser and a visualiser. *(2 marks)*

3. Describe the role of praise in learning. *(4 marks)*

4. Explain Willingham's criticism of learning styles. *(4 marks)*

3 Revision checklist

Early brain development

- [ ] explain how the brain develops from simple neural structures in the womb
- [ ] identity and describe the roles of the brain stem, thalamus, cerebellum and cortex
- [ ] explain how these parts of the brain control autonomic functions, sensory processing, movement and cognition
- [ ] explain the roles of nature and nurture in brain development

See pages 48–51

The effects of learning on development

- [ ] describe and evaluate Dweck's Mindset Theory of Learning
- [ ] understand the difference between fixed mindset and growth mindset
- [ ] explain the role of praise in learning
- [ ] explain the role of self-efficacy beliefs in learning
- [ ] describe different learning styles, including verbalisers and visualisers
- [ ] outline Willingham's Learning Theory and his criticism of learning styles

See pages 60–63

Piaget's theory of cognitive development

- [ ] explain and evaluate Piaget's theory of cognitive development (including the four stages of development: sensorimotor stage, pre-operational stage, concrete operational stage and formal operational stage)
- [ ] explain the concepts of assimilation and accommodation
- [ ] Apply Piaget's theory to education
- [ ] understand how children's egocentricity and conservation skills change as they get older
- [ ] **key research study:** describe and evaluate Hughes' 'Policeman Doll' study
- [ ] **key research study:** describe and evaluate McGarrigle and Donaldson's 'Naughty Teddy' study

See pages 52–59

Practice exam questions

1. Briefly describe what the cortex is and identify one role of the cortex.

   (3 marks)

2. Look at the table below. It shows the scores from an IQ (intelligence) test that was given by a psychologist to pairs of identical twins.

Pair	A	B	C	D	E	F	G
Twin one	102	99	122	88	108	76	84
Twin two	108	93	116	92	106	77	87
Difference	6	6	6	4	2	1	3

   The psychologist wanted to know the average differences in intelligence between the twins.

   a) Look at the difference column in the table. Calculate the median difference. *(1 mark)*

   b) Look at the difference column in the table. Calculate the mode score for the differences. *(1 mark)*

   c) Look at the table below that shows the median differences between identical and non-identical twins.

Identical twins	4
Non-identical twins	9

   What do these results suggest about the role of nature in IQ (intelligence)? *(3 marks)*

3. What is meant by the term 'egocentricity'? *(2 marks)*

4. Discuss how the findings of research studies can be used to evaluate Piaget's theory of cognitive development. *(4 marks)*

   > Be careful with this question to avoid just evaluating research studies or just evaluating Piaget's theory. Your answer should refer to both the findings of research studies *and* Piaget's theory.

5. Read the following conversation between two teachers at a school:

   Teacher one: 'I don't think that learning styles are important and I never find out what my students' learning styles are.'

   Teacher two: 'I've spent hours working out each student's learning style and trying to teach them in a way that matches how they learn. I don't understand why this hasn't improved their exam results.'

   Explain Willingham's criticism of learning styles. Refer to the conversation above in your answer. *(4 marks)*

   > Even if you don't know the answer to a question like this, you should still make a reference to the conversation because if you give a relevant reference, you can still get some marks.

6. Explain the difference between a fixed mindset and a growth mindset. *(2 marks)*

7. Discuss the role of praise in learning. *(3 marks)*

4 Research methods

4.1 What is the experimental method?

Getting started

Find out from your class how many people listen to music when they are doing their exam revision or homework.

Find out how many people think that listening to music makes them work better.

Put the answers up on the board.

Objectives

You will be able to:
- understand variables
- formulate testable hypotheses
- understand the different kinds of experiments in psychology.

■ The null hypothesis and the alternative hypothesis

Psychologists believe that studies of human behaviour should be carried out in scientific settings whenever possible. This means that the researcher will follow the procedures that have been used by all scientists, such as controlling the setting of the research and making accurate measurements so that other researchers can replicate or redo the study to check the results. The most common method used in science is to conduct **experiments**. The following sections show how psychologists do this.

A **hypothesis** is a testable statement that makes it very clear what the researcher is investigating. A **null hypothesis** is a general statement that no 'things' affect each other or 'nothing is happening', for example 'What you watch before bed has no effect on how well you sleep'. Scientists produce alternative hypotheses about events that they think are happening and then test these ideas. This often involves a prediction about how one **variable** will affect another variable, for example 'Watching scary films before bed affects how quickly you fall asleep'.

■ Formulating hypotheses

Most research in psychology starts with an idea about how human behaviour is affected by factors like personality, time or noise. Psychologists want to test these ideas in a scientific way. Sometimes an idea can be quite vague, such as:

Does listening to music affect how well students learn?

The researcher will then try to rewrite the vague idea into a more precise hypothesis. For the question about students who listen to music while learning, we need to identify the two variables that we are interested in studying. As the researcher is going to conduct an experiment, the two variables have special names. These are called the **independent variable (IV)** and the **dependent variable (DV)**.

Key terms

Alternative hypothesis: the hypothesis the researcher tests by conducting a study and collecting data, which attempts to show the null hypothesis is not supported

Condition: an experiment is usually organised so there are two trials, after which the performances of the participants are compared; these are the conditions of the experiment

Dependent variable (DV): the factor which will be measured in an experiment to see if changing the IV has had an effect

Experiment: a research method in which the researcher tries to control all variables other than the independent variable (IV) and dependent variable (DV); this allows the researcher to identify a cause-and-effect relationship between the IV and DV

Hypothesis: a testable statement about the relationship between two variables: the independent variable (IV) and the dependent variable (DV)

Independent variable (IV): the factor which will be varied or changed in an experiment to look for an effect on the other variable

Null hypothesis: a hypothesis that exists and states that no variables affect any other variables

Variable: a factor or thing that varies: it can change

The two variables are:

- something to do with whether or not there is music playing while the studying is happening (IV)

- something to do with how well the students learn (DV).

You have probably realised that the IV, DV, hypothesis, and experiment are all related to each other. When you design an experiment you need to identify the IV and DV so that you can then write these in the hypothesis. You can do this by asking yourself to complete the following:

This experiment is looking at the effect of _____ (the IV) on _____ (the DV).

The first gap in the sentence is filled in with the IV, or two **conditions** of the experiment that are being altered or manipulated by the researcher. The second gap will be filled in with the DV, or the performance of the participants that the researcher plans to measure.

In the 'Music study' experiment, the answer would be:

This experiment is looking at the effect of the presence or absence of music on the score in a learning test. The IV has to have conditions that can be compared; music is present compared with music is absent. The DV has to be a behaviour that is measured, so a test of some sort with a score.

For this experiment, the IV is the presence or absence of music and the DV is the score on a learning test.

Once you have identified the IV and DV it is easy to write the hypothesis. A suitable hypothesis for this experiment would be:

The presence or absence of music has an effect on the score in a learning test.

The hypothesis produced for the experiment above about the effect of music on learning is called an **alternative hypothesis**. This is because it is what the psychologist is interested in investigating. The null version of this hypothesis would be:

*The presence or absence of music has **no** effect on the score in a learning test.* (The idea that 'nothing is happening'.)

■ Different kinds of experimental method: laboratory, field, and natural

All researchers try to carry out experiments in controlled settings so that they can be sure that the only variable that affects the DV is the IV. However, it is not always easy to control every other thing that could affect the DV.

A laboratory experiment is an experiment carried out in highly controlled environments like a laboratory. In this case the setting is often artificial, or not where people would usually produce this behaviour.

A field experiment is a setting in which the behaviour would normally occur. If the research is looking at how someone is dressed affects whether they are helped or not, then the researcher might have confederates (people working for them) who follow a scripted behaviour of falling down when smartly or scruffily dressed.

A *Studying with music*

Synoptic link

You should look back through your notes and any Key research studies you have met so far and try to identify the IV and DV in any experiments you have studied.

Building skills 1

With a partner discuss this idea: Does exercise make you more alert in class? You need to conduct a study using the experimental method, so you will have to:

- identify the IV and DV, then
- write the hypothesis.

B *Studying without music*

The pedestrians who are around when this happens are just shopping. Their responses to the 'fall' will be their normal behaviour. The IV of whether the person needing help is dressed smartly or not, is still controlled by the researcher (see 5.3 Key research study: Piliavin, page 114).

A natural experiment is one in which the IV is not under the control of the researcher. This occurs when the conditions of the experiment are already fixed, such as studies looking at gender or age differences. When the behaviour of males and females, or younger and older people, is compared, the researcher does not determine which participants are in the different age or gender groups. This is determined by the age or sex of the person.

■ How experimental design varies

Getting started

Imagine that you were asked to carry out the 'Music study' experiment from pages 66–67 to see if learning is affected.

Would you use the same people to learn something while listening to music and then without music? What might be the advantages of doing this?

Can you think of any problems if you did have the same people doing the two different tasks?

Discuss this in your class.

■ How participants are used in an experiment

There are lots of different ways of using people in an experiment. The researcher has to decide which **experimental design** would be most suitable for the alternative hypothesis that is being tested. Sometimes the design chosen is determined by the hypothesis being tested. For example, if the researcher is comparing the self-esteem of males and females, then in one group there would be all males and in the other group all females. In other investigations the researcher could decide either to have the same people in both conditions or to use different people.

The three types of experimental design are called **independent groups**, **repeated measures**, and **matched pairs**, and they are described below.

Independent groups

In this design, the people who are available to take part in the experiment are usually divided into two groups. One group takes part in one of the conditions of the experiment and the other group takes part in the remaining condition of the experiment. In the 'Music study' experiment, one group of people would learn with music present and the other group of different people would learn without music present.

Repeated measures

In this design, there is one group of participants. These participants take part in both conditions of the experiment. For the 'Music study' experiment, all the participants would learn some material with music present and they would also learn some material without music present.

Matched pairs

In this design, the people who are available for the experiment are tested before they take part. The test is used to match people into pairs. The pairs are made of two people who each have very similar qualities that are important in the study. They could be identified as Pair Aa, Pair Bb, and so on. One member of the pair takes part in one condition of the study (that group comprises A, B, C, and so on). The other member takes part in the other condition (that group comprises a, b, c, and so on).

Even though the people in the two groups are different people, the researcher treats the data collected as if each pair of scores came from one person. Identical twins are often considered to be perfect matched pairs in psychology research.

Building skills 2

In groups, look at Table D and discuss the different types of experimental design. Think of an experiment which might suit each different type and explain your choice. To get you thinking about experimental designs, you could use the experiment above about how listening to music or working in silence might affect scores on a learning test.

A   **E**

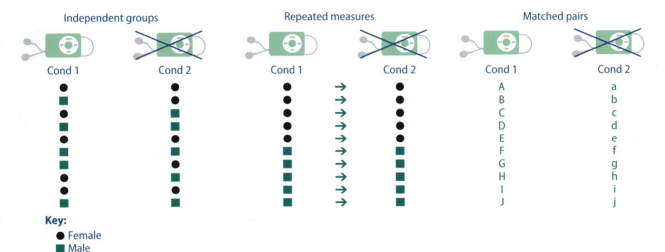

Key:
- ● Female
- ■ Male

C *Three possible experimental designs*

■ Strengths and weaknesses of each design

	Strengths	Weaknesses
Independent groups	• There are no **order effects** because people only take part in one condition. • Often, the same material can be used for the task in both conditions. • Participants cannot work out the aim of the study because they only take part in one condition.	• There are different people (**participant variables**) in the two conditions so that may be why the results are different. • You need more people for the study. To get 10 in each group you need 20 people.
Repeated measures	• The people in both conditions are the same, so there are no participant variables. • You only need 10 people to get 20 results because each person produces two 'scores'.	• There are order effects as people have to do two tasks. • You may need two tasks (they cannot learn the same list twice). • Participants may work out the aim of the study because they take part in both conditions.
Matched pairs	• Participant variables are reduced. • There are no order effects. • Often the same material can be used for the task in both conditions.	• Matching is difficult, time-consuming and not always successful. • Some participant variables are still present.

D *Experimental designs: strengths and weaknesses*

■ Standardised procedures in experiments

Getting started

Imagine you are trying to find out whether the presence or absence of music does affect the learning score a student might obtain.

What other things might affect the learning score of the student? Anything that might have an effect would need to be controlled. Discuss your ideas with the rest of your class.

As you have seen, an experiment is a carefully organised procedure. With **standardised procedures**, a set sequence applies to all the participants when necessary. This makes the experiment unbiased. It means that the researcher is trying to control all the variables and events so that the results of the experiment can be related only to the IV.

■ Extraneous variables, their possible effects, and how these can be controlled

Extraneous variables (EVs) are variables other than the IV that might affect the DV if they are not controlled. If we go back to the 'music study' experiment then EVs are things other than the presence or absence of music (IV) that might affect the learning score (DV). Possible problems could be:

■ Time allowed to do the test – if participants in the 'music present condition' have more time than those in the 'music absent condition', that could affect the scores in the test. The results would be due to the fact that people in one condition had higher learning scores because they had twice as much time as people in another condition. The solution would be to allocate the same amount of time for doing the test to both conditions.

■ Difficulty of the questions in the test – if participants in the 'music present condition' have easier questions than those in the 'music absent condition', then that could affect the scores in the test. One solution would be to use the same questions in both conditions. Another would be to have two learning tests of equal difficulty.

Building skills 3

In the Getting started activity above you came up with ideas for extraneous variables that needed to be controlled. Now think of ways in which you could control these extraneous variables.

A

■ Instructions to participants

Another issue that a researcher must consider when standardising procedures, concerns the **instructions** given to participants to make sure they know what to do. This includes verbal information – what is said to participants – and written information.

Objectives

You will be able to:

- understand what is meant by a standardised procedure

- understand extraneous variables, their possible effect, and how to control for them

- understand the importance of instructions given to participants

- understand randomisation

- understand allocation to conditions

- understand counterbalancing

- understand the strengths and weaknesses of the experimental method

Key terms

Extraneous variable (EV): a variable that is not the IV but might affect the DV if it is not controlled

Instructions: the written (or verbal) information given to participants during an experiment

Randomisation: using chance to provide an order for a procedure

Standardised procedures: a set order of carrying out a study that is applied to all participants when necessary

The information that is said or written for participants might affect the way they participate in the study and therefore their scores or performances. That could be an EV. The usual practice is to write as much of this information as possible and ensure that each participant receives the same information. This is usually done in sections:

■ Briefing – this is what is said/ written to encourage a person to agree to participate. It contains ethical information about consent, anonymity, the right to withdraw, and so on.

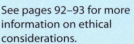

E *Participants must be fully debriefed to make sure they understand their role in the study*

■ Standardised instructions – these are clear instructions about exactly what the participant will have to do in the experiment.

■ Debriefing – this explains the study in detail so that each participant is absolutely sure of the aim of the study, that is, why they were doing what they were doing in the condition(s). Ethical issues are addressed again, especially the opportunity for the participant to withdraw their data if they feel unhappy about their performance.

Synoptic link

See pages 92–93 for more information on ethical considerations.

■ Randomisation

Randomisation means making sure that there are no biases in procedures.

This might, for example, be used when the experimenter has constructed a list of 20 words for participants to learn. These words are of equal difficulty because they are all everyday nouns with six letters. The experimenter has to decide the order in which they should be presented to the participants. Instead of the experimenter choosing the order, randomisation is used.

All 20 words are written on separate pieces of paper and put in a bag. The first word is pulled out of the bag and written down at the top of the list. This is repeated until all 20 words have been put on the list. The order of words has now been randomised. Each word had an equal chance of being selected first for the list and the experimenter left the final order of the words to chance. Then the researcher has to be sure that all participants are presented with the words in that same order.

Going further

Can you think of any other extraneous variables that would need to be controlled if you were to carry out the 'Music study'?

In pairs, work out why having the same learning task in both the music present and music absent conditions would not be appropriate in a repeated measures design. What solution(s) can you think of for this problem?

■ Allocation of participants to conditions

Random allocation

An important issue is how participants in a study are put into the conditions of the experiment. The researcher should not have any influence over which participants go into which condition of a study. If the researcher chose which participants were in which condition it would be a form of bias. The results might be due to this bias rather than the IV.

When the design is independent groups, the experimenter can use **random allocation** to achieve this. If 20 people are available for the study, the experimenter can put ten pieces of paper with 'A' on them and ten with 'B' into a bag. Each participant takes a piece of paper from the bag and that determines the condition they take part in.

In a similar way, using matched pairs design, the researcher will allocate the people in each pair randomly. This could be achieved by putting the letters for a pair in a bag (A and a) and getting one participant to select a letter. This is then repeated for every pair. All those who select the capital letters could do Condition 1 and the rest could do Condition 2.

Of course, with repeated measures design, there is no random allocation to one of the conditions because each participant has to complete both conditions. There is another procedure used to try to make this experimental design less biased.

Counterbalancing

When the experimental design is repeated measures, all the participants have to take part in both conditions. We have seen that this might cause order effects. In order to even these out, a procedure called **counterbalancing** is used. This means half of the participants complete Condition 1 then Condition 2; the other half complete Condition 2 then Condition 1. This will not get rid of order effects but it will share the effects equally between the two conditions.

F *Two possible ways of putting the participants of a study into the conditions of the experiment*

■ Strengths and weaknesses of the experimental method

It is important to remember that there are many strengths, as well as weaknesses, to the experimental method. There is no best way of finding out about human behaviour, so researchers choose the most appropriate method for their investigations.

	Laboratory experiments	Field experiments	Natural experiments
Strengths	• Lots of control of EVs means it is easier to establish cause and effect, so the researcher can be sure that the IV affected the DV. • The high levels of control and standardisation mean the experiment can be replicated and the results confirmed. • There is high objectivity because opportunities for bias are reduced in the standardised procedures.	• The setting is natural with realistic tasks, so there is high ecological validity. • There is still control of the IV and even some EVs. Replication is possible. • Participants are unaware they are in a study so their behaviour will not be affected and the results will be valid.	• When the IV is naturally occurring, such as gender or age, this is the only type of experiment that can be conducted. • The high levels of control (of all except the IV) and standardisation mean the experiment can be replicated and the results confirmed. • There is high objectivity because opportunities for bias are reduced in the standardised procedures.
Weaknesses	• The settings can be artificial, with unrealistic tasks, so there is a lack of ecological validity. • Participants are aware they are in a study so their behaviour can be affected, and the results may be misleading or lack validity.	• Reduced control of EVs means it is harder to establish cause and effect, so the researcher is less sure that the IV affected the DV.	• There is no random allocation of participants to conditions of the experiment, as the IV is not under the control of the researcher. • The settings can be artificial, with unrealistic tasks, so there is a lack of ecological validity. • Participants are aware they are in a study so their behaviour can be affected, and the results may be misleading or lack validity.

Practice exam questions

1. Describe how an experimenter could use repeated measures in a study where participants are all timed sorting cards:
   • in the presence of an audience – Condition A
   • in the absence of an audience – Condition B. (*2 marks*)

2. Identify the IV and DV in the experiment outlined in Question 1. (*2 marks*)

3. Identify a possible EV in the experiment outlined in Question 1. Explain how the EV could be controlled. (*3 marks*)

4. Write a suitable hypothesis for the experiment outlined in Question 1. (*2 marks*)

5. The researcher decided to counterbalance the conditions in the study in Question 1. Explain why this is an appropriate standardised procedure for this experiment. (*2 marks*)

6. Briefly discuss the strengths and weaknesses of using the experimental method to investigate the effects of the presence and absence of an audience on a card-sorting task. (*6 marks*)

What are sampling methods?

■ Target populations and samples

When psychologists conduct research, they are interested in finding out how people behave in certain situations. The **target population** is the group of people the researcher wants to study. What a researcher cannot do is to test every person to find this out. Instead, research is carried out using small groups of people. The people who take part in an investigation are the participants and as a group they are the **sample** for the study. The small sample of participants will be selected from the much larger group called the target population.

The important issue for the researcher is that the sample of people in a study is **representative** of the target population. If they are, then the researcher can assume that the behaviour of the sample matches the behaviour of the target population. This means that the results of the study can be generalised in that the results can be said to apply to not just the sample but to the target population as a whole.

■ Sampling methods

 Sampling methods refer to the strategies that are used by researchers to obtain people who will take part in their studies. Four different types of sampling methods are discussed below.

Random

In a **random sample** every member of the target population has an equal chance of being selected for the sample. This means that the researcher must identify all the members of the target population, number each person, and then draw out the required number of people. If the target population is small, then all the numbers can go into a hat to be drawn out. If it is large, then a computer program can be used to do this. This sampling method is fair and not biased because the researcher cannot choose the individual participants. However, the sample might not be representative because, for example, the researcher could draw out too many females just by chance, which could cause a bias in the data collected.

Opportunity

Opportunity sampling means choosing people who are members of the target population and are available and suitable to take part. Often, these people are known to the researcher so they may not represent the target population very well. This could produce a biased sample. The chosen participants may also try to 'help' the researcher by behaving in ways that support the hypothesis being tested, so their results could be unreliable. However, it is a quick, easy way to collect people for a study.

Systematic

Systematic sampling involves selecting every nth member of the target population. For example, if the researcher decides that 'n' will be 'seven', every seventh person in the target population is selected. This is unbiased because the researcher cannot choose the individuals but it is not random because the people who are first to sixth in the population do not get a chance to be selected.

Stratified

Stratified sampling is the most complex of the sampling methods. The researcher must identify the subgroups in the target population and work out what proportion of that target population each group represents. For example, in a school there are several subgroups: teachers, other staff, students in each year, and so on. If the teachers make up 10 per cent of the whole school target population then 10 per cent of the sample must be teachers. This is repeated for each subgroup. Once the researcher knows what proportion needs to be selected for the sample, a random sample of each subgroup is taken. This is very time consuming. However, it will provide an unbiased and very representative sample of people for the study.

Sampling method	Strengths	Weaknesses
Random	No researcher bias Likely to be representative	Time-consuming
Opportunity	Quick and easy	Not likely to be representative and may have researcher bias
Systematic	Simple procedure with no researcher bias	Sample may not be representative
Stratified	Very representative	Very time-consuming

A *Summary of the strengths and weaknesses of sampling methods*

Building skills 1

Imagine you have been asked to design a study to investigate whether listening to music or working in silence affects scores on a learning test.

Which sampling method would you choose to use in the study and why would you choose this method? Discuss your choice with others in your class.

Exam tip

You will only gain credit for answers about strengths and weaknesses of sampling methods if the points you make apply to the method you are discussing. Make sure you stay focused and do not just try to tell the examiner everything you know about every sampling method.

Going further

You should always pay attention to the sampling method used in psychology research. This can have implications for the results of the study.

If you have studied some topics already you might like to refer back to the Key research studies discussed and evaluate:

a) the sampling method(s) used, and

b) its possible effect on the results.

Practice exam questions

1. A researcher used an opportunity sample to collect participants for his investigation. Identify one problem with this method and explain how it could be overcome. *(3 marks)*

2. Outline what is meant by random sampling and give a practical example of how a random sample could be achieved. *(4 marks)*

Objectives

You will be able to:

- understand the survey methods of questionnaires and interviews
- understand closed and open questions, and structured and unstructured interviews
- understand the strengths and weaknesses of questionnaires and interviews, including ecological validity.

■ Survey methods

In this section we will look at methods used by researchers that are not experiments. The sampling methods we have seen already also apply to these non-experimental methods. Researchers are also still interested in trying to find possible connections between variables, but in non-experimental methods these are just referred to as variables and not the IV and DV. In a **survey** about aggressive behaviour and the media, a researcher could be looking for a possible connection between Variable 1: aggressive behaviour, and possibly Variable 2: types of video games played.

■ Questionnaires

A questionnaire is an example of a survey method that is used to collect large amounts of information from a group of people who are often spread out across the country. The researcher must design a set of questions that the people who take part in the survey will answer. The participants in surveys are often called 'respondents' because their behaviour is a response to a question. All the respondents will answer all the questions and the researcher must try to make sure that the answers given provide information that is needed for the investigation.

There are different types of questions that can be used on a questionnaire. Each type produces a different type of information.

Closed questions

Closed questions are questions where the range of possible answers is determined by the researcher. The respondents are required to tick a box or underline/circle the answer that fits their response. Examples of three closed questions are shown on the next page.

Key terms

Closed question: a question where the possible responses are fixed, often as 'yes' or 'no' options

Questionnaire: a set of standard questions about a topic that is given to all the participants in the survey

Survey: a method used for collecting information from a large number of people by asking them questions, either by using a questionnaire or in an interview

> For each of these questions, underline the answer that most closely applies to you.
> 1 Are you female?   Yes/No
> 2 Do you watch TV?   Never/Sometimes/Often
> 3 Do you play video games? Never/Sometimes/Often

Closed questions provide the researcher with data that is easy to collate or put together. The researcher can work out quite quickly the percentages of people who responded 'Yes/No' or 'Never/Sometimes/Often'. Then a bar chart can display the responses.

However, there is little detail in the answers given. Also, because the respondents do not have the opportunity to explain their answers, the researcher does not know why they chose that particular response. Another problem can be that the respondents are not exactly sure what the difference between 'Sometimes' and 'Often' might be, so they choose 'Sometimes' as a safe answer. The same thing often happens when people are given 'Don't know' as an option. They pick it because they do not want to give a definite answer of either 'Yes' or 'No'.

A *Answering a questionnaire containing closed questions*

Going further

In pairs, write an answer to the following question: 'How do you feel when you play a video game?' Explain your answer.

Check your partner's response to this question, and then the responses from the rest of the class. What do you notice?

Getting started

Compare the responses to the video game question in Going further on page 77 with the types of responses given to closed questions.

What do you notice about these two types of questions?

Open questions

Open questions are questions where the respondent can write an individual answer and they are given space to do so. The answers to these questions generally provide lots of detail. The respondents are able to explain their answers, so they feel less frustrated than when they have to choose an answer from restricted options that might not fit exactly what they want to say. These questions provide the researcher with lots of information about behaviour, often with explanations for why a person has produced a particular behaviour.

However, problems can occur when open questions are used on a questionnaire. It is very hard to collate, or group together, all the individual responses into an overall pattern because each response is different. Sometimes researchers have to produce categories of responses and fit the individual answers into these categories. However, this will mean that the detail and depth of information in the individual responses might be lost because the researcher has tried to summarise the findings.

Here are some examples of open questions:

Answer each of these questions as clearly as you can.
1 What kinds of TV programmes do you watch and why do you choose these?
2 Why do you enjoy playing video games?
3 How would you answer someone who says video games are too violent?

Writing questions for a questionnaire

It is very important for the researcher writing a questionnaire to be sure that the questions are clear and unambiguous. The words used in the questions should not be emotive because this might upset the person filling in the questionnaire and affect the honesty of their answers. Also, the meaning of each question must be obvious to the reader. When questions are unambiguous their meaning is absolutely clear. This means that the respondents are sure of exactly what a question is asking and exactly how to give an answer to it. Researchers must make sure that 'closed' questions do not have more than one question in them. It would not be easy for the respondent to work out

B *How would you design a questionnaire to find out if video games are too violent?*

whether they should answer both questions or just focus on one. Taking all this into consideration is likely to increase the ecological validity of the questionnaire. The researcher can be more confident that the answers given are a true account of the behaviour of the respondents.

Building skills 1

Look at the following questions. What might be the problems with the way they have been written?

K

a. How many hours a week do you spend playing video games?

Up to 1 hour   2–3 hours   More than 5 hours

b. Playing video games is a waste of time and makes people aggressive.

Agree   Disagree

■ Strengths and weaknesses of questionnaires

The main strength of using questionnaires to find out about behaviour and attitudes is that a great deal of data can be collected quickly. That is why large organisations often use questionnaires to get feedback quickly from their customers. Closed and open questions both have strengths and weaknesses, so it is often useful to have both types in a questionnaire. Closed questions are easy to score and open questions provide detailed information. Open questions also allow people to explain their answers so the researcher knows why the particular answer has been given. Questionnaires are ethical because people are fully aware that they are filling in the questionnaire and they know what the questions are asking.

However, there are some weaknesses. Questionnaires provide the answers respondents want to give and there is no way of checking that the answers are actually true. This means that the results of the questionnaire could be misleading for the researcher. When closed questions are used, the researcher does not know why a particular answer was chosen.

Did you know **?**

Lots of questionnaires are posted out and the return rate can vary between 5 and 54 per cent. The results of such a questionnaire might reflect the answers of a very small group of people who do not represent the population, and therefore the results cannot be generalised.

C *'How do I feel when ...'*

■ Interviews

Interviews involve the researcher in direct contact with the respondent, who in this case is called the interviewee. This is often face-to-face contact but could be over the telephone or over the Internet using a video link. The vast majority of interviews involve a questionnaire and the researcher can record the answers at the time of the interview. Alternatively, they can record the interview itself and then play back the content later to analyse the responses. Interviews are not a just a 'chat', even though they usually involve two people talking to each other. They are focused on a particular topic.

There are two types of interview:

■ **Structured interview** – in this type of interview the questions are all pre-set and every interviewee will be asked exactly the same questions in the same order. The researcher cannot ask an extra question based on an interesting point made by the interviewee. It is often the case that the questions are closed but some may be open.

■ **Unstructured interview** – in this type of interview the researcher will have decided on the topic and may have a starter question, but the next question will be based on the response made by the interviewee. This means that each person interviewed will have a different set of questions and it is the interviewee who directs the discussion. There will generally be a mixture of both open and closed questions.

Strengths and weaknesses of interviews

In general, interviews produce large amounts of data, which is considered to be a strength of this method. They also provide information about people's thoughts and feelings that cannot be found by just watching behaviour. The data from structured interviews can be collated and analysed easily. The data from unstructured interviews are detailed and have ecological validity.

The weaknesses of the interview method are similar to those of the questionnaire method. The researcher cannot be sure the interviewee is telling the truth, so the data may not be accurate.

D *In an unstructured interview, the interviewee will direct the discussion*

Structured interviews lack detail and may be frustrating for:

■ the interviewer, who wants to ask another question

■ the interviewee, who cannot explain the answer they have given.

Data from unstructured interviews may be difficult to collate and analyse.

E *Interviews often involve face-to-face contact*

Building skills 2

K **A** **E**

1. Try to interview someone about the use of mobile phones by students in your school or college. If you work in small groups you need to decide whether your group will use either a structured or an unstructured interview.

   Make sure each person in the group has a copy of the questions. Those who decide to use an unstructured interview will need to keep a record of the questions that were asked. Each person in the group should interview one person and bring the results back to the group. Each group should analyse the results and present the findings to the class.

2. What did you discover:
   ● about mobile phone use
   ● about interviewing people?

Remember to be sensitive when you ask your questions. If an interviewee seems uncomfortable about answering a question, just move on.

Exam tip

When you are answering questions about the strengths or weaknesses of questionnaires and interviews, you must make it clear whether you are referring to open or closed questions in a questionnaire, or to structured or unstructured interviews with either open and/or closed questions.

Synoptic link

Which of the key research studies use interviews or questionnaires as part of their method?

Practice exam questions

1. What is a survey? *(2 marks)*

2. Distinguish between each of the following:
   a) closed questions and open questions *(3 marks)*
   b) structured interviews and unstructured interviews. *(3 marks)*

3. Outline one strength and one weakness of conducting a survey using questionnaires. *(4 marks)*

Getting started

So far, the methods you have looked at have involved studying the behaviour of groups of people. This is because researchers often want to find explanations of behaviour that can be applied to all people. However, there are times when researchers focus their attention on unique individuals whose behaviour is not usual.

In small groups of three or four, discuss what kinds of behaviours produced by individual people or a distinct group of people might be of interest to psychologists.

Objectives

You will be able to:

- understand the method of case studies

- understand the strengths and weaknesses of case studies.

Key term

Case study: an in-depth investigation of an individual, a small group, or an organisation

■ Case study method

A **case study** is an in-depth investigation of an individual or of a unique group. Case studies are carried out by professional psychologists who work in environments, such as hospitals, prisons, or therapy centres. The information in a case study can be from a number of sources. Sources include interview details about the person's life – these are biographical details. There might also be work records or school records if the person is a child. The psychologist might carry out observations of the person or test the person using some kind of scale, such as a personality test.

The case study is written up as a description of the individual or group. The psychologist will then interpret the information using psychological theory to decide how to use the information collected. If the case study is of a single person this will usually involve what treatment should be offered. Otherwise it will be used to support or challenge a theory.

Exam tip

Remember that case studies are carried out by professional psychologists, so you should not attempt to conduct a case study of your own. However, in the examination you may be asked how or why a psychologist might carry out a case study, so make sure you have investigated this.

Strengths and weaknesses of the case study method

The following list highlights some of the main strengths of the case study method:

- Case studies provide detailed information about individuals rather than collecting just a score on a test from a person.

- Case studies record behaviour over time, so changes in behaviour can be seen.

- A single case study that shows us that a theory is not correct is very useful. It will encourage researchers to change the theory and make it more accurate.

A *Conducting a case study*

There are some weaknesses too:

- The data collected can be very subjective. The method relies on the individual who is being studied remembering events, and these memories might not be accurate or reliable. Also, the interpretations made by the psychologist could be biased and therefore the content of the case study might be unreliable.

- The information from the case study cannot be applied to anyone else because it is unique.

- There are ethical issues, especially of confidentiality, right to withdraw, and protection from harm. The last might occur because very often the person being studied is someone who is suffering from psychological problems. This means they could be vulnerable.

Building skills 1

Choose a famous psychologist whose work you have enjoyed studying while you have been taking your GCSE course. Think about the theories and/or the research this person produced and why you were interested in the information. Imagine you have the opportunity to meet with that psychologist. What questions would you ask him or her? What kinds of information would you want to get from this meeting? Write down some examples of:

- the personal information you might ask about
- the questions about the work of the psychologist that you might ask
- any other information you would require, such as how their work affected their life.

Do you think you would enjoy the opportunity to do this kind of research? Discuss this with your group.

K **A**

Sometimes a case study will be carried out to add to our understanding of human behaviour in general rather than our understanding of a particular person. Gregory and Wallace famously investigated a man who had been blind from infancy, but whose sight was restored by an operation when he was an adult. Gregory and Wallace discovered that the man was not affected by visual illusions. Gregory used this information to support his theory that visual perception in humans is affected by experience of the world.

Gregory found that the man whose sight was restored did not think the horizontal lines in the Ponzo illusion (Figure B) were of different lengths, whereas most people who look at the illusion believe the horizontal line at the top is longer than the horizontal line at the bottom.

Going further

There are some famous studies of individuals in psychology. Sigmund Freud wrote accounts of many people, including 'Little Hans', the 'Rat Man', 'Dora' and the 'Wolf Man'. Other famous investigations have been carried out studying 'Genie' and 'HM'.

Use the Internet and other library resources to research at least one of these individuals and any others you might discover. You can then present your findings about these people to the rest of your class.

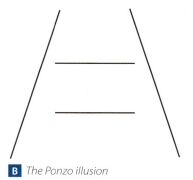

B *The Ponzo illusion*

Synoptic link

You could apply this discovery by Gregory and Wallace to your work on visual illusions and perception in Topic 2.4. Think about why it was also important to Gregory's constructivist theory of perception as outlined in Topic 2.5.

---

1. Give two reasons why a psychologist might choose to investigate behaviour using the case study method. *(2 marks)*

2. Identify one weakness that might arise when a researcher uses the case study method. *(1 mark)*

3. Explain how the weakness you identified in Question 2 could be dealt with by the researcher. *(2 marks)*

Practice exam questions

Getting started

Imagine you want to know how people behave at pedestrian crossings. In particular, you would like to find out if they obey the 'red man' or not and, possibly, whether there are any gender differences in pedestrian-crossing behaviour. You could carry out a survey and ask people what they do at pedestrian crossings.

a) What problems might there be if you did this?

b) Can you think of another way that you might be able to collect data about pedestrian-crossing behaviour?

Objectives

You will be able to:

- understand observation studies, including categories of behaviour

- understand inter-observer reliability and how to establish it

- understand the strengths and weaknesses of observation studies.

Key terms

Categories of behaviour: the separate actions that are recorded as examples of the target behaviour

Observation study: a method of collecting information about behaviour by watching and recording people's actions

◼ The observational method

Observation is a technique that is used in research. When we call a study an **observation study**, this means the data collected has been observed and recorded. An observer identifies the behaviour and then decides how to record that behaviour. With this method, the researcher usually decides to watch behaviour as people produce it. Researchers want to be certain that the behaviour they are recording is 'normal' behaviour, and seeing the behaviour occur naturally is one way of making sure that this is the case. In most natural observations, people are observed in their usual environments and the researcher does not interfere with the location at all. Sometimes, researchers do make something happen so that the natural responses of people can be recorded. One example of this is as follows.

While on duty, a nurse received a telephone call from a 'doctor' in psychiatry who instructed the nurse to give medicine to a patient on the ward. The researchers watched the nurse to see if she obeyed the illegal instruction or refused. (Nurses are not allowed to give medicine if the instruction comes from a phone call.) As far as the nurses in the study were concerned, the setting was their normal place of work, so their behaviour was natural, but the researchers had changed a very small part of the environment (they introduced the phone call), so they could be there to watch what happened.

Imagine you had decided to conduct an observation of bystander behaviour. If you wanted to find out whether people help when someone drops their shopping, there are several possibilities:

- You could stand in the street hoping someone might drop their shopping, which is not very likely to happen.

- You could bump into someone and hope that their shopping drops, which is not acceptable.

- You could ask a confederate or co-researcher to drop some shopping near to where you are in the street and you could record the actions of the pedestrians.

A *A nurse giving medicine*

There are some occasions when data is collected by conducting an observation study in a 'laboratory setting'. This is not necessarily an actual laboratory. It just means that the place where the observation is carried out has been organised by the researcher to make it easy for the observation to be conducted. Therefore, the people being observed are brought into a special room where they can be seen and recorded. This would mean the experiment has been conducted using an observational technique to collect the behaviour. This kind of observation might lack some ecological validity because the people being observed would know that the study is taking place.

Categories of behaviour

In order to make sure that an accurate record of behaviour can be made, researchers use a **categories of behaviour** system. In an observation of playground behaviour, the target behaviour is 'playground behaviour'. However, the observers would not know what they were to look for if that was the only information they had. Behaviour categories are used to make it clear exactly how to record the actions that have been seen. For the playground study, suitable categories would be as shown in Table B.

C *Hopscotch*

	Categories of behaviours			
	Running	**Hopping**	**Skipping**	**Standing**
Boys	卌 卌 卌	II	I	II
Girls	III	卌 III	卌 III	I

B *A tally chart showing categories of behaviour for observation of playground behaviours in boys and girls*

D *Skipping*

Building skills 1   K A

In pairs, design a record sheet containing behavioural categories which you could use to record the behaviour of males and females at a pedestrian crossing. You need to think of all the ways in which people could use the crossing, and then create categories for the behaviours you want to record. Remember, pedestrian crossings have red and green lights that are supposed to control the way people use them.

Compare your record sheet with those of other pairs.

E *A pedestrian crossing*

Exam tip   !

Remember, if a question asks you to explain a term, you cannot use that term in your answer. Students often write, 'Observation studies are studies in which the behaviour of people is observed.' This will not gain credit. You need to write about 'investigations in which the behaviour of people is watched and recorded'.

Synoptic link

Consider how the observational method is used to understand prosocial behaviour, for example in Topic 5.3 and in Piliavin's subway study (Topic 5.3 Key research study: Piliavin).

Strengths of the observational method

The observational method is usually very high in ecological validity. For many of the behaviours that humans produce, especially social behaviours, this method is the most sensible and reliable way of finding out about what people really do. When researchers ask people what they think they would do the answers are often misleading – either because people are not sure or because they do not want to give an honest answer in case they 'look bad'.

Observation studies record real behaviours that are full actions. Many people criticise research like memory research because the participants learn lists of words. They argue that this is a very small behaviour that hardly relates to the person at all, or how people use their memories in everyday life. Observation studies record whole behaviours that people really do produce regularly.

Weaknesses of the observational method

There are still some weaknesses because, although researchers can see and record the behaviour, they do not know *why* it occurred. This means the researcher must make a judgement about the reason for the behaviour and that judgement could be incorrect.

An observer might make a mistake when recording the behaviour, or the people who are being watched might become aware of this and change their behaviour. Either of these events would affect the accuracy of the results.

Finally, there are often ethical issues involved in studies where people are not aware that they are being watched. If a researcher wants to record natural behaviour, then they cannot inform the people involved, so there will be an invasion of privacy and a lack of consent.

Synoptic link

The ethical issues raised in Topic 4.7 can help you assess the strengths and weaknesses of the observational method.

Did you know

'Non-participant observation' is where a researcher does not participate in the behaviour of the study but watches from a distance or in a separate location. 'Participant observation' is when the researcher becomes a member of the group or institution they are observing. For example, one researcher became a teacher in a school for many months so that he could observe the relationships between pupils and teachers.

F *Observation can be carried out by watching people from a distance*

G *Is one of the group observing the non-verbal communication of the others?*

■ Inter-observer reliability

When an observation study has been conducted, the record of the behaviours that have been watched has to be an accurate record. The researcher needs to be sure that every time a behaviour that fits the behavioural categories occurs it is recorded. This can be a major problem because in many observation studies the actual behaviour will have passed, so it cannot be seen again.

A solution to this problem is to use the following procedure.

- The researcher designs a record sheet with suitable behaviour categories for the observation they wish to conduct.

- Two observers each have a copy of the same record sheet and watch the same behaviour/location at the same time for the same period of time, recording what they see on their own individual record sheet.

- At the end of the observation period the observers compare their record sheets.

If they have been recording consistently, they will have matching or very similar records of their observations. This means that they will have established **inter-observer reliability**. If the two record sheets are very different, then both will have to be discarded. This is because it would not be possible to work out which observer's record is accurate.

Building skills 3

Design a study that uses the observational method, which is appropriate for your local environment. This could involve watching people in a shopping centre where you observe whether men and women carry their shopping bags differently, or whether or not they hold the door open for people following them into and out of shops. You might look at non-verbal behaviour in cafes. You could even design a study to watch the behaviour of characters in a TV programme.

K **A**

Use what you now know about carrying out an observation study, categories of behaviour, and how to establish inter-observer reliability. Design a record sheet that is appropriate for your observation study.

Exam tip

!

Sometimes students think that having two observers means that, if one observer misses a behaviour, the other will spot it and that would be a 'good thing.' In fact, that would not make the observation reliable. In order to achieve high inter-observer reliability, both observers should consistently record the behaviours every time they occur.

Building skills 2

E

There is a possible problem with the data that a researcher has collected at the end of the observation period in a study. It may not be an accurate record. Can you think of any reasons why this might be the case? Discuss this with the rest of your group.

Researchers have to find a solution to this problem. What could they do to make sure their record of the observation period is accurate?

Going further

1. Conduct the observation study you planned in Building skills 3, using materials that you have designed. Then prepare a short report on what you did, what your findings were, and what patterns of behaviour (if any) you discovered.

2. When you have heard the reports of other pairs/groups who carried out an observation similar to yours, discuss the results together. Consider the data collected overall. Look for similar patterns of behaviour and discuss why any differences might have occurred.

3. Was there any inter-observer reliability in the record sheets in the observations of your class?

---

1. Explain one reason why observation studies can be said to have ecological validity. *(3 marks)*

2. Two psychologists conducted an observation study of males and females parking their cars in a supermarket car park. Explain why the psychologists decided that they should both record the behaviour of the drivers. *(3 marks)*

3. Briefly discuss one ethical issue that might occur in an observation study and explain how this issue might be dealt with. *(3 marks)*

4. Discuss one strength and one weakness of observation studies in psychology. Use examples of research to support your answer. *(6 marks)*

Practice exam questions

Getting started

Every member of your group should write their height and their shoe size in centimetres on a piece of paper. (You can measure everyone against a wall in the room to get their heights and each person can draw around their foot on a piece of paper and measure the length if necessary.)

Hand in the pieces of paper; there is no need for names. Write the pairs of measurements for each person on the board. Do you notice any pattern in the data you have collected? How could you display the data using a graph or diagram?

Objectives

You will be able to:

- understand what is meant by 'correlation'
- draw appropriate scatter diagrams
- understand the strengths and weaknesses of correlations.

■ Correlations in psychology

Sometimes, researchers are interested in seeing if there is a particular kind of **relationship** between two variables. In an experiment the relationship is a 'cause and effect' one. Changing one variable, such as the amount of noise (IV), has an effect on the other variable, such as the number of words someone recalls (DV). Remember, in experiments other extraneous variables are controlled so that we can say with more certainty that the IV did affect the DV (see Topic 4.1).

There are times when the researcher does not change or manipulate a variable. Instead, two variables are just measured and the researcher looks at how they are related to each other. These variables could be behaviours that people produce, such as the number of cigarettes people smoked in a year and the number of colds those people had in the same year. They could also be qualities, such as how happy a person rates themselves to be and how motivated they are at work. Psychologists use **correlation** to try to establish whether or not there is a pattern in the connection between the two variables.

Correlation is *not* a research method; it is a statistical technique that is used to analyse and display the possible association or relationship between two variables. Each variable has to be measured as a score or value of some sort. These scores can then be plotted on a special graph called a **scatter diagram** (see Figure C as an example). To produce a scatter diagram the data has to be collected in pairs. Usually each person in the study provides a pair of scores, one score for each variable being measured. Sometimes, researchers correlate data that comes from two separate people. For example, in research into depression, pairs of twins each provide a score on a test, such as an anxiety scale, and the data from each twin is plotted as a pair of scores.

In the Getting started activity, each member of your group provided two measurements: their height and foot size. This data can be displayed in a scatter diagram.

Key terms

Correlation: a technique used by researchers to establish the strength of a relationship between two variables

Positive correlation: a relationship between two variables in which, as the value of one variable increases, the value of the other variable also increases

Relationship: a connection or association between two or more variables

Scatter diagram: a type of graph for representing correlations

How to plot a scatter diagram

To draw a scatter diagram, the horizontal axis (x-axis) represents the scale for one variable, such as foot size in centimetres, and the vertical axis (y-axis) represents the scale for the other variable, such as height in centimetres. For each pair of scores, you find the point on the x-axis that represents the foot size and find the point on the y-axis that represents the height. Where the lines intersect, put a dot or cross on the diagram. This means that each point or cross on the diagram represents a pair of measurements.

Building skills 1

 Plot a scatter diagram to display the data collected in the Getting started activity opposite. Remember to give your diagram a title that refers to the relationship between both of the variables.

K

A *People are different heights*

B *Shoe sizes are different*

Positive correlation

Figure C shows a **positive correlation**. In a positive correlation, as the value of one variable increases so does the value of the other variable. The scatter diagram shows that, as the number of umbrellas being carried by people increases, the number of puddles on the ground increases. These two patterns are found to occur at the same time.

Remember, the positive correlation does not tell us what causes this relationship, only that the relationship can be identified.

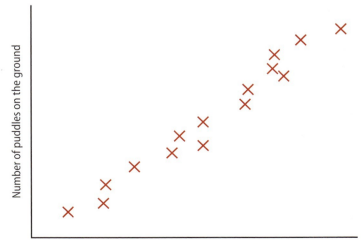

C *Scatter diagram showing positive correlation*

Negative correlation

Figure D shows a **negative correlation**. In a negative correlation, as the value of one variable increases, the value of the other variable decreases. The scatter diagram shows how, as the number of passengers on a train increases, the number of sandwiches for sale in the buffet car at the end of a journey decreases.

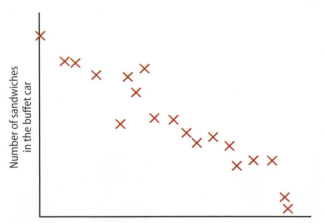

D Scatter diagram showing negative correlation

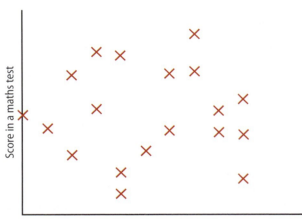

E Scatter diagram showing no correlation

No correlation

Figure E shows **no correlation** between the number of pets owned and the score in a maths test.

Building skills 2

K

Look at the scatter diagram you drew displaying your foot sizes and heights. Did you find a positive correlation? Most correlations for these two variables would usually result in a positive relationship. What does the relationship you found indicate about foot size and height in your group?

Check your title for the scatter diagram and, if necessary, rewrite it making sure it now includes reference to the type of correlation you have found.

F What is the relationship between puddles and umbrellas?

Prediction

If you look at the scatter diagram in Figure C, you can see that when there are lots of umbrellas being carried there are also lots of puddles on the ground. This allows us to make a **prediction** based on the type of correlation we have found. When we have identified a particular kind of relationship between two variables, we only need to measure one of the variables to predict, or 'guess', the likely measurement of the second variable. We can predict that on a day when there are lots of umbrellas being carried there will also be lots of puddles on the ground. What we cannot say is that carrying umbrellas causes puddles on the ground.

The only method that can establish a cause and effect relationship is an experiment. This is because the experimental method controls the extraneous variables that could also be causes. In a study where the variables are just measured, it may be something else that has caused the positive relationship, as in the case of the number of umbrellas being carried and the number of puddles. In this particular example, the cause may well be the fact that it is raining!

■ Strengths and weaknesses of correlation

Correlation is a very useful technique for research in psychology. Here are some of the strengths:

- Correlation allows a researcher to see if two variables are connected in some way. This means that once a relationship has been found, the researcher can use a different method, such as an experiment, to try to find the cause of the results.

- Correlation can be used when it would be impossible or unethical to carry out an experiment. Researchers cannot force people to smoke in order to see if they then develop lung cancer. However, plotting the rates of smoking against lung cancer does tell us that they are related. This knowledge can influence behaviour and further research.

There are also weaknesses in the use of correlation:

- Correlation does not indicate which of the two variables measured caused the relationship to occur. It is sometimes the case that other variables are the cause of the pattern seen on a scatter diagram.

- In order for a correlation to be informative, there does need to be a large amount of data for each variable so that the possible pattern can be seen. This means that the researcher needs to take lots of measurements of both variables so that the pattern in the data can be reliably identified. Correlations based on small populations are not very reliable.

Exam tip

Remember, the heading for a scatter diagram:

- must always use the phrase 'relationship between ...' or 'association between ...' rather than 'the effect of ...'
- should not seem to suggest one variable has caused the other
- should not be a question such as 'Is height related to foot size?'
- must contain the correct relationship phrase (positive correlation, negative correlation, or no correlation).

Going further

See if you can find some examples of research that has used correlation. To get you started you could look up research into attractiveness and marital choice. Another study investigated the relationship between eye movements and dreaming. Use the Internet, textbooks, and the Key research studies to help you find examples.

Present your findings to the rest of your group.

Did you know

One researcher discovered that when pets such as hamsters, snakes, and rats were kept in rooms by hospital wards, patients often said they had lower stress levels.

1. What is meant by the term 'positive correlation'? *(2 marks)*

2. Explain why correlation can be useful in psychology. *(2 marks)*

3. What is the difference between an experiment and a correlation study? *(2 marks)*

Practice exam questions

What are ethics in psychology?

Objectives

You will be able to:

- understand ethical issues as outlined by the British Psychological Society Codes

- consider ways of dealing with ethical issues.

Key terms

British Psychological Society (BPS) guidelines: the ethical guidelines produced by the British Psychological Society in its Code of Ethics and Conduct (2006) and Code of Human Research Ethics (2014), which govern the work of all practising and research psychologists

Ethical issues: points of concern about what is morally right

■ Codes of Ethics: The British Psychological Society (BPS)

The Code of Ethics and Conduct (2009) and Code of Human Research Ethics (2014) of the British Psychological Society underpin the activities of all practising psychologists. When you conduct any practical work for your GCSE course, you too are covered by this code so you must ensure that whatever research you do, it is ethical. This means you need to understand the **ethical issues** that relate to your practical work and make sure that you follow the **British Psychological Society (BPS) guidelines** in everything that you do to the best of your ability and under the supervision of your teacher.

Respect

Psychologists should respect people as individuals and avoid unfair or prejudiced practices. The data collected should be confidential and anonymised so that people cannot be identified in the research. This can be especially important in cases studies where individuals might be identified more easily because of the amount of information given about them.

Participants should give informed consent. This means that they should know fully what they are consenting to and that they must be told what the study is about before they agree to take part. Psychologists should avoid deception, which means people should not be misled about the research. However, the BPS does recognise that some research would be impossible if everything was revealed at the start. Researchers must inform participants as soon as possible about any minor deception that has taken place. It would be acceptable to ask people to take part in a 'memory study' and tell them later that it was to investigate the effect of organised and randomised word lists on the number of words recalled.

Going further

There are some studies in psychology that have caused a great deal of concern because of the way participants were treated. Research them on the Internet. Some names to get you started are Stanley Milgram and Mary Ainsworth. Find out what they did and then discuss whether you think the research was justified or not.

There are special issues when participants are under 16. They should be asked to give their own consent, if that is appropriate. It is important to note that consent from parents, guardians, or someone acting in the place of a parent, such as a teacher at school, is also required. If people are being observed in public places their privacy should be respected, so there should be no secret filming on mobile phones, for example.

Finally, participants have the right to withdraw from the research at any time and can withdraw their data too. They must be made aware of this right.

A *Guards are in a position of power*

Competence

Psychologists should only give advice if they are qualified to do so. Certainly, GCSE students must recognise that they have no qualification for giving advice.

Responsibility

Researchers must protect the participants from harm. The risk of harm from participation in psychology research should be no greater than the risk from everyday life. The psychological and physical health of participants should not be at risk.

Participants should be debriefed at the end of the investigation to ensure they understand fully the true aim of the research. Only then can they make an informed decision about withdrawing their results.

Integrity

Psychologists should behave with honesty and fairness in all their interactions, with all people. It is essential that psychologists consider whether the benefits of the research can be said to outweigh the possible costs to participants in that research.

Building skills 1

You need to start thinking about ethical issues and how these occur in all research. Look at the studies that have been mentioned in this chapter. For each study, list the possible ethical issues that you think would need to be addressed.

A

Did you know ?

University students took part in a prison experiment, in which one group of students were guards and the other group were prisoners. The experiment had to be stopped after six days because the 'guards' became sadistic and the 'prisoners' became withdrawn and depressed.

Exam tip !

In an examination question, make sure that an ethical issue you identify is appropriate for the study described. You should identify the issue, such as 'right to withdraw', then explain why it is an issue in that particular study, and how it could be dealt with.

Synoptic link 🔗

Consider the importance of ethics in the design of the child studies carried out in Topic 3.2 Key research study: Hughes and 3.2 Key research study: McGarrigle and Donaldson.

Practice exam questions

1. Identify one ethical issue that might occur in a study of perceptual set. Explain why it is an issue and how it could be dealt with. *(4 marks)*

2. Explain why researchers have to take special care when they wish to investigate the behaviour of young children. *(4 marks)*

Getting started

A researcher gave participants two memory tests: one in silent conditions and another in noisy conditions (listening to music). For each condition the participants had a score out of 20.

Another researcher asked participants to explain how they felt their memory was affected when they tried to recall information when it was quiet, and also when it was noisy because music was playing.

Think about the data collected by the two researchers. What advantages can you see for collecting data in these ways? What problems could there be with the data? Discuss your ideas with the rest of your class.

■ Quantitative and qualitative data

We have looked at the different methods used by researchers to find out about human behaviour. These include experiments, observations, and survey methods. No matter what the method is, the researcher will collect data that is either in a numerical form or in a non-numerical form.

Quantitative data is data in numerical form, such as scores on a test or times taken to do a task. This type of data is usually easy to display as percentages or averages, and in graphs, but there will not usually be an explanation for why a particular score was achieved.

Qualitative data is data in descriptive (non-numerical) form, such as verbal or written answers to questions, or records of observed behaviour. This type of data is usually rich in detail and there might be an explanation for why the behaviour occurred. However, it is often hard to collate or put together lots of individual responses, so this data can be difficult to summarise.

The methods used by researchers are never only quantitative or only qualitative. If a researcher carried out an observation study and rated the happiness of the person observed on a scale of 1 to 10, then the observation study collected quantitative data and the study could be described as a quantitative study. However, if the researcher had observed the person and written a description of their 'happy behaviours', then the study could be described as using a **qualitative method**. We cannot say experiments are quantitative and observations are qualitative. How the experiment is described will be determined by the type of data collected.

Objectives

You will be able to:

- understand the difference between a quantitative method and a qualitative method

- distinguish between quantitative and qualitative data

- distinguish between primary and secondary data

- use appropriate statistics to present and analyse data collected in a study

- interpret and display quantitative data

- understand the basic characteristics of normal distribution.

Key terms

Primary data: data collected firsthand from the source (participants), by the researcher

Qualitative data: data in descriptive (non-numerical) form, such as verbal or written answers to questions, or observed behaviour

Qualitative method: any method which provides descriptive (non-numerical) data

Quantitative data: data in numerical form, such as scores or times taken to do a task

Quantitative method: any method which provides numerical data

Secondary data: data that is already published and just used, rather than gathered, by the researcher

■ Primary data and secondary data

Primary data is data that has been collected firsthand from the source (participants) by the researcher. **Secondary data** is data that is already published and simply used by the researcher. The majority of data collected in psychological research is primary data.

■ Descriptive statistics

The data in Building skills 1 is in the form of times taken to solve a puzzle (in seconds). This is called the raw data. However, researchers usually want to identify patterns in behaviour rather than concentrate on individual performances. The various means of summarising data are outlined below.

Calculating averages

There are three types of average that can be calculated: **mean** (or arithmetic mean), **median**, and **mode**. Each of these averages will be calculated using the data from Building skills 1.

Mean

The mean is calculated by adding together all the values in a set of scores and then dividing the total by the number of values in the set.

> Condition A:
>
> mean = 23 + 19 + 24 + 47 + 23 + 20 = 156 (total number of seconds) ÷ 6 (number of values) = 26
>
> Condition B:
>
> mean = 45 + 44 + 43 + 44 + 46 + 48 = 270 (total number of seconds) ÷ 6 (number of values) = 45

Median

The median is the middle value in a set of scores. To find the median you must arrange all the values in order from lowest to highest. Then you must find the middle value. If there is no middle value because you have an even number of values, then find the midpoint of the two middle values.

> Condition A:
>
> 23, 19, 24, 47, 23, 20 arranged in order, becomes:
>
> 19, 20, 23, 23, 24, 47. The midpoint of 23 and 23 is 23 so the median is 23.
>
> Condition B:
>
> 45, 44, 43, 44, 46, 48 arranged in order, becomes:
>
> 43, 44, 44, 45, 46, 48. The midpoint of 44 and 45 is 44.5 so the median is 44.5.

Building skills 1

E

A researcher set up a study in which six people each solved a puzzle in a room alone and a different group of six people each solved the same puzzle in front of an audience.

The following data was collected in this experiment:

Condition A times taken to solve the puzzle without an audience (in seconds): 23, 19, 24, 47, 23, 20

Condition B times taken to solve the puzzle with an audience (in seconds): 45, 44, 43, 44, 46, 48.

What do you notice about the times in the two conditions? Discuss ways of analysing the data from the experiment so that any patterns in the data can be seen.

Mode

The mode is the most frequently occurring value in a set of scores. Sometimes there is no mode and sometimes there is more than one mode.

> Condition A:
> 23, 19, 24, 47, 23, 20: The mode is 23.
> Condition B:
> 45, 44, 43, 44, 46, 48: The mode is 44.

Note that in Condition B above, if the last score had been 45 instead of 48 we would say there were two modes: 44 and 45.

Calculating the range

 Another statistic that can be calculated and used to describe data is the **range**. This is the numerical difference between the highest and lowest value in a set of scores.

> Condition A: the range is 47 – 19 = 28
> Condition B: the range is 48 – 43 = 5

■ Ways of expressing data

There are lots of ways of expressing – or presenting – numerical data. You have probably met these in your GCSE Maths course. You should always choose a way of presenting data so that the information is most appropriate for the study that has been conducted.

Fractions, decimals, percentages, and ratios

 A **fraction** is a way of expressing a part of a whole number. We can see in Table B (page 85) that there are 20 boys, each producing an action. Overall, 15 of those actions are running so the fraction of running is 15/20 or ¾ as a fraction. The same number could be expressed as a **decimal**: 0.75 of their actions would be running.

 Many results in numerical form in psychology are expressed as decimals, for example: the time taken for Sarah to sort the pack of cards was 61.7 seconds, but it took Nicky 73.2 seconds to sort the same pack of cards. It would be appropriate to retain these numbers rather than rounding them up and down, as rounding means that we lose the exact time difference between Sarah and Nicky. You might be instructed to use a particular number of significant figures or decimal places to express an answer that you have calculated. If not, choose a number of significant figures that will balance giving accurate results against giving too much numerical data.

Exam tip

When you are asked to describe the results of a study, you should look for patterns in the data. For example, the participants in Condition A (without an audience) solved the puzzle faster than those in Condition B (with an audience). We can see this because the mean time for Condition A was much lower than that for Condition B.

Sometimes it is useful to round up (or down) figures, especially if we want to **estimate** something. This might be useful if a researcher knows that one interview took 26 minutes and they have 8 more interviews to complete; they could estimate that they would need approximately 4 more hours to finish the study as 8×30 minutes approximately = 4 hours.

A **percentage** is a way of expressing a fraction of a hundred, so 45/100 is 45 per cent. In psychology the frequency of events (the number of times something happens) is sometimes shown as a percentage. So the data in Table B on page 85 could be presented as a table of percentages.

We would calculate those percentages in the following way:

Boys running: $\dfrac{\text{Number of observations in category} \times 100}{\text{Total number of observations}}$

Boys running: $\dfrac{15 \times 100}{20} = 75\%$

When all the other percentages are calculated, the table would be as in Table A below.

Percentages for each category of behaviour			
	Running (%)	Hopping (%)	Skipping (%)	Standing (%)
Boys	75	10	5	10
Girls	15	40	40	5

A *Play behaviour in young children (expressed as percentages)*

A **ratio** is a way to compare amounts of something and is usually expressed in its simplest form. If there were 15 boys and 12 girls in a class, the ratio would be 15:12 and, in its simplest form, 5:4 (divide both sides by 3).

Graphs

The data collected in investigations can often be presented as a graph. Remember, graphs should summarise data, so you should not draw graphs that contain the raw data or individual scores from a study. We have already looked at scatter diagrams, which are a type of graph, in Topic 4.6.

Bar charts

A **bar chart** can be used to display data that is in categories. Each bar represents a separate category and the categories are labelled on the x-axis (horizontal). The frequency or amount for each category is on the y-axis (vertical.) Each bar should be drawn separated from the next bar – they should not touch.

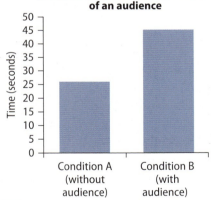

Mean times taken to complete the puzzle in the presence and absence of an audience

B *A bar chart*

Building skills 2

Draw a bar chart to represent the percentage data collected in the observation of children playing (Table A). Remember to label the axes correctly and provide a suitable heading for your chart.

Frequency tables

A **frequency table** is a way of organising raw data into sensible groups of data. If we were to measure the heights of 30 people, it would be sensible to present the data in a summarised form as shown in Table C.

Histograms

Histograms are used to present data that are continuous measurements, such as test scores. The continuous scores are on the x-axis and the frequency of these scores is on the y-axis. There are no spaces between the bars as the data is continuous. We can draw a histogram of the frequency data in Table C: see Figure D below.

Height (cms)	Frequency
140–149	4
150–159	10
160–169	8
170–179	5
180–189	2
190–199	1

C *Frequency table showing heights of 30 people*

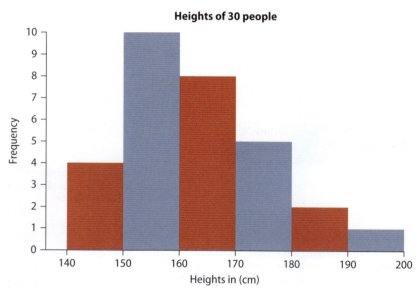

D *Histogram showing heights of 30 people*

Normal distribution

The idea of **normal distribution** is that for any characteristic or quality that can be measured in human behaviour, for example in memory ability or IQ score, most scores of the whole population would be around the mean with decreasing scores away from the mean. In a normal distribution the mean, median, and mode score for the data set are all a very similar value. When the data set is plotted, this produces a distinctive curve shape called a normal distribution curve.

If a researcher has collected data from a sample of participants in a memory experiment and then calculates the mean, median, and mode values for their scores, finding that the mean, median, and mode were all a very similar value might suggest that the sample of people has been drawn from a normally distributed population. The researcher might then conclude that the sample is representative of the larger target population.

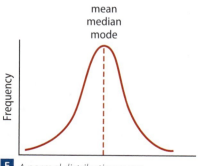

E *A normal distribution curve*

■ Planning and conducting research – some issues to consider

Researchers have to be sure that the way they have planned and conducted their studies means that other psychologists will believe their results are valuable to our understanding of human behaviour. They must always consider the issues of **reliability** and **validity**, and how these might affect their data and conclusions.

If a study is reliable, then when it is replicated or redone in a very similar way, the same results will be found. Some sampling methods are more likely to produce reliable results than others. Random sampling removes possible experimenter biases and this increases the reliability of the data collected. Also, using repeated measures might increase reliability of the data because participant variables of intelligence are eliminated. Similarly, collecting quantitative data that has been accurately measured might be more reliable than asking people what they would do.

Researchers must always try to ensure that their studies are valid too. Any questionnaire that is written by the researcher must measure what is says it is measuring. A questionnaire measuring intelligence should not be focused on general knowledge, because everyone has different general knowledge. A memory study has to be a realistic investigation into memory; for example, learning word lists might be too artificial to tell us about memory ability.

Did you know ?
Sometimes, when psychologists look at the data they have collected, an anomalous result (one that is very different from all other results), can be very interesting. Such a participant might have an unusual ability or behaviour. The researchers might conduct a case study to look for an explanation of the behaviour.

Building skills 3
K **E**

Think about how the issues of reliability and validity might be relevant to the Key research studies you must learn for this course. Remember, the choice of sampling method, experimental design, and whether to collect qualitative or quantitative data, might all affect the reliability and/or validity of the study. Keep a record of your ideas for your final revision.

Exam tip !
Take as many opportunities as you can to get involved in practical activities such as conducting research and designing tasks. This will help you to understand the studies you are presented with on the exam paper.

Synoptic link 🔗
Look at all of the key research studies, and consider how the issues of reliability and validity may have affected the data collected. Draw up a table of your answers and compare them with the answers of others in your class.

Practice exam questions

1. Calculate the mean, mode, and median for the following set of values:

   21, 17, 6, 16, 14, 17, 15, 20. *(3 marks)*

2. Draw a table of results to represent the answers to question 1 above. *(3 marks)*

3. What is the difference between a bar chart and a histogram? *(2 marks)*

4 Revision checklist

You should now be able to:

Formulation of testable hypotheses

☐ formulate testable hypotheses

☐ explain the difference between the null hypothesis and the alternative hypothesis

See pages 66–67

Types of variable

☐ explain the difference between the independent variable, the dependent variable, and extraneous variables

See pages 66 and 70

Designing, planning and conducting research

☐ understand how and when to use the following experimental designs, including the strengths and weaknesses of each:

  ☐ independent groups

  ☐ repeated measures

  ☐ matches pairs

☐ understand how and when to use the following research methods, including the strengths and weaknesses of each, and the types of research for which they are suitable:

  ☐ laboratory experiments

  ☐ field and natural experiments

  ☐ interviews

  ☐ questionnaires

  ☐ case studies

  ☐ observation studies (including categories of behaviour and interobserver reliability)

☐ understand how to plan research so it is reliable and valid

See pages 66–69, 76–87, 99

Sampling methods

☐ explain what the sample and the target population are

☐ understand how and when to select samples using these methods, including the strengths and weaknesses of each:

  ☐ random

  ☐ opportunity

  ☐ systematic

  ☐ stratified

See pages 74–75

Correlation

☐ understand the differences between positive correlation, negative correlation and no correlation

☐ understand how to use scatter diagrams to show correlation

☐ explain the strengths and weaknesses of using correlation

See pages 88–91

Practice exam questions

1. A teacher wanted to know whether her students were more likely to remember information if they were asked to recall it in the same place that they had first learnt it, compared to a different place. She decided to conduct an experiment.

   Each student in her class was a participant in her study. Each participant was shown a list of 20 words in their normal classroom. The class was then divided into two equal groups. One half stayed in the classroom while the other half was taken outside to the playground. Each participant was then given 2 minutes to write down as many of the words on the list that they could remember.

   a) Write a suitable null hypothesis for this experiment. *(2 marks)*

   b) What was the independent variable in this experiment? *(1 mark)*

   c) What is meant by 'extraneous variables'? Identify one extraneous variable in the experiment above. *(3 marks)*

   d) Identify the experimental design that was used in this study. *(1 mark)*

   e) Give one strength of the experimental design used in this study. *(2 marks)*

   f) Outline how the teacher could have allocated the participants to each condition of the experiment. *(2 marks)*

   > This question is worth 2 marks so it is not enough to simply state a strength (such as 'no order effects'); you also need to explain why it is a strength in the context of this study.

2. Look at this table below. It shows the number of words that were recalled by each participant in each condition for the experiment described in question 1.

	Condition 1: classroom	Condition 2: playground
Number of words recalled by each participant	10	7
	12	11
	8	14
	13	6
	12	3
	15	11
	12	13
	16	7
	9	10
	11	6
Range	8	
Mean	11.8	8.8

Research procedures

- [ ] explain how standardised procedures are used in research, including:
  - [ ] giving instructions to participants
  - [ ] using randomisation
  - [ ] allocation of participants to conditions, including counterbalancing
  - [ ] controlling extraneous variables

See pages 70–73

Ethical considerations

- [ ] understand the ethical issues outlined in the British Psychological Society guidelines
- [ ] understand how to deal with these issues in psychological research

See pages 92–93

Quantitative and qualitative data, and primary and secondary data

- [ ] explain the difference between quantitative and qualitative data
- [ ] explain the difference between primary and secondary data

See pages 94–95

Computation

- [ ] be able to recognise and use:
  - [ ] decimals
  - [ ] percentages
  - [ ] ratios
  - [ ] estimates
  - [ ] fractions

See pages 96–97

Interpretation and display of quantitative data

- [ ] be able to construct and interpret:
  - [ ] frequency tables
  - [ ] histograms
  - [ ] bar charts
  - [ ] scatter diagrams

See pages 97–98

Descriptive statistics

- [ ] understand how to calculate the following:
  - [ ] mean
  - [ ] mode
  - [ ] median
  - [ ] range

See pages 95–96

Normal distribution

- [ ] explain the characteristics of normal distribution

See page 98

a) Calculate the range for condition 2. Show your workings.

(2 marks)

b) Using the table above, explain what the teacher might conclude from this experiment. *(3 marks)*

c) Draw a bar chart to represent the mean for each condition. Your answer should include the following:
- an appropriate scale
- an appropriate label on each axis
- a suitable title *(4 marks)*

3. For the experiment described in question 1, the teacher wanted to make sure that each of the students was given the same instructions. Write a short paragraph that the teacher could have read out to the students at the beginning of the experiment. Include reference to the task.

(3 marks)

4. a) For the experiment described in question 1, identify and briefly explain one ethical issue that the teacher should have considered.

(2 marks)

b) Describe how the teacher could have dealt with the ethical issue you have outlined in your answer to 4 a). *(2 marks)*

5. A psychologist wanted to know whether young boys or young girls were more likely to share their toys. He decided to carry out observations of children at a local nursery. He also interviewed four members of staff. While he was there, he put a sign up in the reception asking for parents who were willing to be interviewed.

a) Explain one strength and one weakness of using interviews in this situation. *(4 marks)*

b) Identify which sampling method the psychologist used to obtain the parents he interviewed. *(1 mark)*

c) Give one evaluation of the sampling method used to obtain the parents in this study. *(2 marks)*

6. a) In observation studies, what is meant by a 'behaviour category'? *(2 marks)*

b) Outline one reason why it would be useful to have more than one observer in the study described in question 5. *(2 marks)*

7. Outline the difference between primary and secondary data.

(2 marks)

Providing an accurate working out of your calculations can earn you marks, so make sure you show your workings and that they are clear and easy to follow.

Titles need to be detailed and accurate. They should reference all conditions of the IV and the DV.

Some questions are connected (like 4 a) and 4 b) here). Read them both before answering, because how well you know the answer to the second part could affect what you give as an answer to the first part.

5 Social influence

5.1   What is conformity?

Getting started

Read the scenarios below. With a partner, discuss what you would do and why.

a) You walk past a group of students who have stopped to look at something out of the window. You have no idea what they are looking at. Do you stop and look out of the window too?

b) Your teacher has asked your class a question. You are certain you know the correct answer, but no one else has put their hand up. Do you put your hand up and give your answer?

Objectives

You will be able to:

- understand what is meant by conformity

- identify and explain how social factors affect conformity

- identify and explain how dispositional factors affect conformity

- describe and evaluate Asch's study of conformity.

■ What does conformity mean?

Social influence is a term used to describe how other people can affect our opinions, feelings, and actions. **Conformity** is one type of social influence and is when we think or act like those around us. Sometimes we are aware when we are conforming but this can also be an unconscious process. This means we do not necessarily realise just how much we change what we think, do or say because of others.

Fashion is a good example of conformity. Trends in hairstyles and clothes that were totally normal when the photos opposite were taken may not seem that way to you now. What will people think about current fashions in the future?

Why do we conform?

Deutsch and Gerrard (1955) say there are two reasons why people conform. The first is the need to be right. When we are in an unfamiliar situation such as our first day at a new school or surrounded by people we think have superior knowledge to us, we see what they are doing and assume they are right. In the school canteen for the first time, we may be uncertain about where to queue for food. We watch then follow what other people are doing. In this way, others guide our behaviour. This is known as **informational social influence**.

The second reason we may conform is the need to be liked by others. When we are in social situations, we want to be accepted by other people. This means we are likely to do or say things that make us popular with others to help us fit in. For example, we might watch a film with our friends even if we do not really want to see that film because being with our friends is important to us. Of course, we are motivated to fit in with some social groups more than others. As a result, the extent to which our behaviour is affected by others will depend on who we are

A *Embarrassing fashions*

with and how important it is to us to fit in with that particular group of people. This is known as **normative social influence**.

Social factors affecting conformity

Group size: We are more likely to adopt the behaviour of others when we are in a group with three or more other members who are behaving in a similar way. We are likely to feel increased pressure to fit in when more people are behaving in the same way than when we are in a smaller group (normative social influence).

Task difficulty: We show higher levels of conformity when attempting to complete a difficult rather than an easy task. When we find something challenging, we may look to others to guide our decisions because we lack confidence in our own judgements (informational social influence).

Anonymity: In public situations, we face ridicule from others when they can hear what we say or see what we do. However, when we can express our opinions privately, we are more anonymous. This reduces concern about people disagreeing with our views as they do not know what they are. Anonymity lowers the likelihood of conformity because it reduces normative social influence but does not prevent conformity entirely.

Dispositional factors affecting conformity

Dispositional factors are the individual or personal characteristics everyone has which may affect how that person will behave or conform.

Personality: Some personality characteristics increase the tendency to conform. Low self-esteem, low status in a group, and low IQ have been associated with high levels of conformity. These may lead to insecurity in social situations and assuming others have a better understanding of what to say or do. Therefore, we are more likely to look to others for guidance and follow what they do (informational social influence) so that people will like and accept us (normative social influence).

Expertise: Conformity is less likely in situations where we have a high level of expertise because we are confident in our opinions and know what to do. This may also explain why research has found older people less likely to conform than younger people. With age and experience, we may come to feel more certain about our knowledge base so feel less pressure to conform. Expertise affects conformity due to informational social influence.

Key terms

Conformity: a change in our opinions or behaviour to fit in with social norms or as the result of perceived group pressure

Dispositional factors: internal personal characteristics which may affect how a person will behave

Informational social influence: changing behaviour or opinions because we think other people have superior knowledge to us

Normative social influence: changing behaviour or opinions because we want to fit in and be accepted by others

Social influence: the effect other people have on our opinions and behaviour

Did you know ?

People laugh more at jokes when the jokes are followed by recorded laughter than when they are not. This is an example of normative social influence.

Going further

Use the Internet to find out what percentage of people read product reviews before making a purchase. Use your knowledge of conformity to explain why this might influence what they buy.

Practice exam questions

1. What is meant by the term 'conformity'? Use an example to illustrate your answer. *(2 marks)*

2. Identify one dispositional factor that can influence conformity. Explain why this factor is likely to affect conformity behaviour. *(3 marks)*

3. You and some friends are planning to meet up on Saturday afternoon. You want to go bowling but they all want to go shopping. Outline one social factor that will influence whether or not you go shopping with them. Explain how this factor will affect your behaviour in this situation. *(4 marks)*

Building skills 1

Copy and complete the table below to summarise factors affecting conformity. **K**

Factor	Social or dispositional?	Increases or decreases conformity?	Normative or informational social influence?

Asch's conformity study (1956)

Aim: To investigate if people would conform to the opinions of others to give an answer they knew to be wrong.

Study design: A laboratory experiment in which there was control of possible extraneous variables and all procedures were standardised to ensure the study could be replicated easily. Participants were male American college students.

Method: Groups of 7 to 9 people were shown sets of 4 lines: a standard line and 3 other comparison lines. They were asked to state out loud which comparison line was the same length as the standard line. The correct answer was always clear.

Standard   A   B   C

A *An example of the set of lines Asch showed to his participants*

There was only one real participant in each group. He was told the aim of the study was to investigate visual judgement. Unknown to him, the other members of the group were confederates working for the experimenter who had been instructed to give the same incorrect response for 12 out of the 18 sets of lines. Each real participant was always one of the last to answer so heard the majority of responses before he gave his own judgement. This was to put him under pressure to conform to the incorrect majority.

Asch recorded whether participants gave the correct answer or conformed by giving the same incorrect judgement as the group.

Results: Participants conformed to give the incorrect answer of the group 36.8 per cent of the time. 76 per cent of participants conformed to the incorrect majority at least once. 24 per cent of the participants resisted the pressure to conform and gave the correct judgement in every trial.

Conclusion: The results showed that people conform to fit in with a group, even when they know they are giving an incorrect judgement.

Source: Asch, S.E. (1956) 'Studies of independence and conformity: I. A minority of one against a unanimous majority', Psychological monographs: General and applied, 70(9), 1–70.

■ Evaluation

Why the study is important

■ Asch's study demonstrates the extent to which people will conform in social situations. When people completed the line task alone, with no pressure to conform to the judgements of others, the error rate was less than 1 per cent. It rose to 36.8 per cent when the same task was performed in a group setting. Asch's research suggests that people will conform due to normative social influence to fit in and be accepted by a group of people.

Building skills 1

A

To find out more about the participants' conformity behaviour on the task, Asch carried out an interview with each participant immediately after they had completed his experiment.

Create one open and one closed question he could have used in this interview. (Read more about open and closed questions on pages 76–79.)

This was a laboratory experiment in which Asch had a high level of control over variables. This meant he could alter specific factors to see how they influenced conformity rates. He found conformity rose when he increased the number of people in the majority up to a group size of three. Conformity increased when he made the task more difficult by making the standard and comparison lines closer in length. When participants could respond more anonymously by writing down their judgement instead of saying it out loud, conformity rates fell. This means that Asch's study identified some key social factors that affect conformity.

Limitations of the study

■ Asch's experiment was carried out in a laboratory, which is not a natural situation for participants. This may have caused them to behave in an unnatural way that is different to how they would have behaved in an everyday setting. As a consequence, the results might not reflect everyday conformity behaviour. This low ecological validity means that Asch's findings may not generalise to other settings.

■ Matching line lengths is a fairly trivial task without personal significance to most people. In everyday life conformity behaviour is likely to be about decisions that are more important to us, such as the clothes we wear and whether or not we laugh at a joke. This means that the results may not predict how people respond in real life conformity situations.

■ Asch's research was carried out using American participants. America and the UK are examples of individualistic cultures that place great emphasis on individual needs. Collectivistic countries like China place greater significance on meeting the needs of the group. Cross-cultural research has found higher levels of conformity in collectivistic rather than individualistic cultures. This means Asch's findings cannot be generalised to all countries because the type of culture in which we live is likely to influence conformity levels.

Building skills 2 — A

A repeat of Asch's research used science and engineering students and recorded significantly lower rates of conformity than Asch.

Which dispositional factor best explains these results? Describe why this factor may have led to such low levels of conformity. How can you use this study to evaluate Asch's research findings?

Exam tip !

When you are asked to evaluate research, remember that you are being asked to discuss strengths and weaknesses of the methodology, such as the type of research design used. See Chapter 4 for more on this.

Going further

Use the Internet or library to find out about other studies into social influence. For example, one 1969 study found that when a group of 4 or more people stood on the pavement looking up at the sky, 80 per cent of passers-by would do the same thing. Plan how to carry out a similar study at your school. What ethical issues might you encounter?

Building skills 3 — K

Outline two ethical concerns that arise in Asch's research. If he had conducted his research in a more ethical way, do you think his results may have been different? Make sure you explain your answer fully.

5.1 Key research study: Asch

Getting started

Rank these scenarios, from those where you would be most likely to follow orders to those where you would be least likely to follow orders. Be prepared to justify your answer.

a) A security guard at the airport tells you to open your bag and show them the contents.

b) Your younger brother tells you to take some money from your mum's purse.

c) A doctor in a hospital tells you to roll up your sleeve so they can take your blood pressure.

d) Your boss tells you to wear smarter clothes to work.

e) Your friend tells you to punch someone.

Objectives

You will be able to:

- understand what is meant by obedience

- describe and evaluate Milgram's Agency Theory as a social explanation of obedience

- describe social factors affecting obedience

- describe and evaluate Adorno's theory of the Authoritarian Personality as a dispositional explanation of obedience

■ What does obedience mean?

Obedience is when people follow the orders of an authority figure. Much of the time, this is perfectly acceptable. For example, when we follow an instruction from a lifeguard or a doctor, it probably keeps us safe. However, what happens if you are ordered to do something that you think is wrong? Some of the worst atrocities in history would not have occurred if people had not followed immoral orders. For example, during the Second World War, Nazi soldiers followed orders that led to the deaths of millions of Jews in concentration camps. Psychologists have tried to understand why people follow orders even when they lead us to do things we know are wrong.

Key terms

Agency: the responsibility we feel for our own actions

Agency theory: the idea that a person will obey an authority figure when they believe this authority figure will take responsibility for whatever the person does

Obedience: following the orders of an authority figure

Social factors: external events which may affect how a person will behave

A *German Nazi soldiers followed orders with terrible consequences during World War II*

Milgram's Agency Theory of obedience: a social explanation of obedience

Normally, we feel responsible for our own actions and free to choose how to behave. This is known as an autonomous state. However, Milgram's **Agency Theory** (1963) suggests we are more likely to obey orders when we enter an agentic state. This is when we believe we are acting on behalf of an authority figure so no longer feel accountable for our actions. Instead we see responsibility being with the person who gives us orders. Milgram called the move from an autonomous to an agentic state the agentic shift. He says that we are taught to enter an agentic state as children because we are trained from a young age to respect and follow the orders of authority figures in society. It becomes something we think is normal so that we do it without really thinking about it, but this can lead to blind obedience.

B *James Bond has diplomatic immunity from arrest because the British Government will take responsibility for his actions – he is acting in an agentic state*

Evaluating the Agency Theory of obedience

Many soldiers who have followed orders to commit atrocities appear to have been in an agentic state. For example, Nazi guards at concentration camps during the Second World War claimed that they were simply following orders and that responsibility for their actions lay firmly in the hands of their superiors who gave them the orders.

In Milgram's infamous study of obedience, 65 per cent of his participants were prepared to give what they believed to be a potentially fatal electric shock to another person when an authority figure (an experimenter wearing a lab coat) told them to do so. Milgram argued that they were acting in an agentic state on behalf of the experimenter because participants were being paid to perform a role and were told that the experimenter would take responsibility for their actions. If they had been told that they were responsible for their own actions, it is likely that fewer participants would have followed the orders they were given.

We do not all blindly follow orders, which suggests that some people are less likely to enter the agentic state than others. Milgram's theory focuses on **social factors** that affect obedience, but other psychologists have suggested that dispositional factors such as personality are more important in determining how obedient people are.

> **Exam tip** !
>
> Even though you will not be asked to describe a study of obedience in detail in your exam, you can refer to research evidence to help you explain and evaluate theories of obedience.

■ Social factors affecting obedience

Authority

Some people in society have higher positions of **authority** than the rest of us. As we have seen, we are brought up to obey authority figures, such as parents, teachers, and police officers, from a young age. We learn to obey authority figures without really thinking about it because we think it is what society expects us to do. This means we are likely to follow orders given by people we believe have legitimate authority over us. This is because we trust their expertise (such as a doctor) or because they have the power and social status in society (such as a police officer) to punish us if we do not follow their instructions. Uniforms are often associated with positions of authority and have been shown to increase levels of obedience.

Culture

The **culture** in which we live influences how we are brought up to think about authority figures. Some research has found lower levels of obedience in individualistic cultures compared to collectivistic cultures. It has been suggested that collectivistic cultures place greater importance on group values and respecting authority, while individualistic societies place greater value on independence and individual freedom. This means culture may affect obedience levels because it influences how people respond to authority figures. However, not all research has found higher levels of obedience in collectivistic rather than individualistic cultures.

Proximity

Proximity refers to how far away something is. When we are in close proximity to an authority figure it appears we are more likely to obey them. In Milgram's study, more participants followed orders when the experimenter gave instructions from the same room than over the phone.

Proximity to the consequences of our actions also affects obedience levels. For example, if our boss tells us to fire someone, it is easier to do so by email than in person. This is because when we send an email we do not actually have to see how they react to losing their job. It is easier to follow orders when we are distanced from the consequences of our actions.

C *The police hold legitimate authority in society*

D *Doctors also hold legitimate authority in society, but how does it differ to the police?*

Dispositional factors affecting obedience

As we have seen, dispositional factors are the internal, personal characteristics we each possess, such as high self-esteem or low confidence. These characteristics will affect the likelihood or whether we obey someone or not. For example, Milgram found that people who disobeyed his experimenter often did so because they were confident and articulate, so they could explain their decision not to give people shocks. This means that whether or not a person is obedient is sometimes due to a person's disposition (their characteristics) rather than the situation they are in.

Adorno's theory of the Authoritarian Personality

In 1950, Adorno argued that some people form personalities that make them more obedient than other people, due to their early childhood experiences. He called this type of personality the **Authoritarian Personality**.

Adorno interviewed two thousand American students about their early upbringing. He found that students who had experienced harsh, critical, and strict parenting and physical punishments in the first few years of life were obedient as adults. Although as children they felt angry about the tough punishments they received at the hands of their parents, they could not take out this hostility on their parents because it was not acceptable to do so. As a result, Adorno concluded that these children grew up to be very submissive and obedient towards authority figures.

Evaluating the theory of the Authoritarian Personality

Adorno developed the F scale questionnaire to measure peoples' attitudes and behaviour. People who score highly on this scale are said to have the Authoritarian Personality and some research has found these people to be very obedient.

However, Adorno only found a correlation between personality type and obedience. This means he could not prove that the Authoritarian Personality causes high levels of obedience. Some of the most obedient participants in Milgram's study did not experience the authoritarian upbringing predicted by Adorno.

People with lower educational levels have been found to be more obedient than those who are highly educated. This suggests that other dispositional factors, such as intelligence, may also play an important role in obedience behaviour.

Building skills 3

A

Design an experiment to investigate how one social factor influences obedience in everyday life. Identify your independent and dependent variables (see Topic 4.1, page 66). Explain what participants would be asked to do, how you would measure levels of obedience, and what you would expect to find.

Did you know

In a 2010 French game show called 'Le Jeu de la Mort' (The Game of Death), contestants were told to give electric shocks to other people if they incorrectly answered questions. Over 87 per cent of the contestants followed these orders.

Synoptic link

Deindividuation has also been shown to be a factor affecting obedience. See page 117.

Building skills 4

E

Adorno developed his theory by interviewing adults about their early childhood experiences. Spend a few minutes thinking about your early childhood memories. Use this to identify some problems with Adorno's research method.

Practice exam questions

1. What is meant by the term 'obedience'? Use an example to illustrate your answer. *(2 marks)*

2. Explain the difference between a social and dispositional explanation for obedience. *(3 marks)*

3. Describe and evaluate one theory used to explain obedient behaviour. *(9 marks)*

What is prosocial behaviour?

Getting started

Imagine that someone has dropped a bag of shopping as you are walking past. You may decide to stop and help pick up the spilled contents or you may not.

Make two columns on a piece of paper: in the first write down reasons why you would help and in the second write down reasons why you would not.

■ What does prosocial behaviour mean?

Prosocial behaviour is acting in a way that is beneficial to other people. This can be seen in **bystander behaviour**. Bystanders are people who witness events, such as emergencies where other people need assistance. **Bystander intervention** is when people offer help in such a situation. **Bystander apathy** is when they choose not to help. Psychologists have investigated a range of factors that determine whether or not bystanders will help other people.

■ Social factors affecting bystander behaviour

The presence of others

We are more likely to help others when we are alone than when other people are present. There are two reasons for this. First, it is sometimes hard to determine whether or not a situation is in fact an emergency. When children scream for instance, it might be that they are playing rather than they have hurt themselves. We do not want to overreact and make ourselves look foolish so we look at the responses of those around us. If they do nothing, we are likely to conform to the group behaviour. We assume that the situation is not an emergency and no help is required.

Secondly, if we are alone in an emergency situation, we have to assume full responsibility for helping a person in need because there is no one else who can assist. When other people are present, the responsibility for helping is divided or shared between these people. This is called diffusion of responsibility. The more people present, the more this responsibility becomes diffused. We may not help because we assume that others can and probably will do so.

The cost of helping

It is suggested that we weigh up the cost and rewards of helping a person in need. In some circumstances we may decide it is too costly to intervene: we may get hurt, inconvenienced, or lose money; while in other situations, we may decide the cost to us is low.

Objectives

You will be able to:

- understand what is meant by bystander intervention
- identify and explain social factors that affect bystander intervention
- identify and explain dispositional factors that affect bystander intervention
- describe and evaluate Piliavin's subway study.

Key terms

Bystander apathy: doing nothing when someone is in need of help

Bystander behaviour: the way that someone responds when they witness someone else in need of help

Bystander intervention: when a person who witnesses a person in need offers help

Prosocial behaviour: actions that benefit other people or society

A *Why would someone stop and help, or not stop to help, this man?*

Helping someone who is being beaten up is risky but giving someone directions is not.

There can be rewards for helping others too. Praise, social recognition, financial reward, or simply avoiding the feelings of guilt we may experience if we fail to help someone can all be seen as rewarding. We weigh up the costs and benefits of helping others before we decide whether or not to intervene. If the costs outweigh the rewards, we are less likely to help others.

■ Dispositional factors affecting bystander behaviour

Similarity to the victim

When there are similarities between a bystander and the person in need, bystanders are more likely to offer assistance. If people are the same gender, a similar age, or have other characteristics in common with us, we find it easier to empathise with them because we think they are like us. This means we can put ourselves in their shoes and imagine how they are feeling. When we assist them, it makes us feel better because our distress at their situation is reduced.

Expertise

Bystanders are more likely to help others if they believe they have the skills required to help someone in a specific situation. For example, if a swimmer is in trouble, how can we help if we cannot swim ourselves? If someone is lost, how can we help if do not know our way either?

People without the necessary expertise may not offer assistance because they do not know how to help, and fear causing more harm than good. Bystanders may still be distressed and concerned about victims but, when other people are present, they believe that someone else might be more capable of helping, or can help more easily than themselves.

Building skills 1

K   A

In 1964, a young woman named Kitty Genovese was attacked in New York. She was only metres from her home, and the attack continued for over half an hour before she was eventually killed. Only afterwards did someone call the police, who arrived within four minutes. When the neighbours were questioned, 38 of them were able to say what had happened and to give a description of the murderer. This means that any one of them could have prevented the murder by calling the police straight away. Yet no one did.

In pairs, discuss how social factors could be used to explain why people did not do anything when Kitty Genovese shouted for help.

Going further

The murder of Kitty Genovese inspired Latané and Darley to investigate how the presence of others affects bystander behaviour. Use the Internet to find out about their research.

Practice exam questions

1. Identify one dispositional and one social factor that can influence bystander behaviour. *(2 marks)*

2. Read the following statements about bystander behaviour. Decide whether each statement is true or false.
   A Bystanders are less likely to help people in need when the victim has similar characteristics to them. *(1 mark)*
   B Bystanders are more likely to offer help to someone in need when the rewards of helping are higher than the costs of helping. *(1 mark)*
   C The presence of others may lead to bystander apathy due to the diffusion of responsibility. *(1 mark)*

3. Describe and evaluate one way in which bystander behaviour was investigated in the Piliavin study (see pages 114–115). In your answer include the method used, the results obtained, and the conclusion drawn. *(6 marks)*

Piliavin's subway study (1969)

Aim: To investigate whether the appearance of a victim would influence helping behaviour.

Study design: A field experiment in which there was little control of possible extraneous variables. Participants were male and female passengers who travelled on the 8th Avenue subway train in New York City. They were unaware that they were taking part in a psychological study.

A *A subway train like that used in Piliavin's study*

Method: An actor pretended to collapse in a train carriage. His appearance was altered. In 38 of the trials he appeared to be drunk; he smelt of alcohol and carried a bottle of alcohol wrapped in a paper bag. In 65 of the trials he appeared to be sober and carried a walking stick. Observers recorded how often and how quickly the victim was helped.

Results: When the victim carried a walking stick, he received help within 70 seconds 95 per cent of the time. When he appeared to be drunk he received help within 70 seconds 50 per cent of the time.

Conclusion: A person's appearance will affect whether or not they receive help and how quickly this help is given.

Source: Piliavin, I.M., Rodin, J.A. and Piliavin, J. (1969) 'Good Samaritanism: An underground phenomenon?', Journal of Personality and Social Psychology, 13, 289–99.

■ Evaluation

Why the study is important

- It helps us to understand why some victims are less likely to receive help than others due to the cost of helping. If someone is drunk for example, their behaviour can be unpredictable so helping them may involve putting ourselves in danger. Vulnerable members of society, such as children, pregnant women, and older people, are more likely to receive help from bystanders because they are perceived to be deserving of help and present less risk to us.

Did you know ?

Do you remember the criticism that people do not behave normally in laboratory studies? Well, unlike previous laboratory studies, Piliavin found that bystander behaviour is not affected by the number of people present. This study was conducted in a normal everyday situation, and perhaps that is why this finding is different to that of previous research. (Read more about field experiments on pages 67–68.)

■ This study was carried out in a natural setting. Participants did not know they were taking part in a study so did not show demand characteristics but acted as they usually would. This means that it has high ecological validity and can be applied to explain bystander behaviour in real life situations.

Limitations of the study

■ Piliavin's research was conducted in America. This is an individualistic culture within which people are expected to help themselves and sort out their own problems. In collectivistic cultures, there is a greater emphasis upon reciprocal support and helping others. Research suggests that helping behaviour is not the same in individualistic and collectivistic cultures. This is a weakness of Piliavin's research as it cannot be generalised to explain bystander behaviour in all cultures.

■ There is also evidence to suggest that people living in rural areas are more helpful than those who live in urban environments, such as cities, in both emergency and non-emergency situations. This means that Piliavin's study may not reliably predict bystander behaviour outside cities and towns.

■ Not all people are equally likely to help others. Some people have a stronger belief that it is their duty to help others, or have greater expertise that can be used to help others. Piliavin's research ignores the role of individual characteristics that make bystanders more or less likely to help others.

■ Piliavin's research does not support previous research findings about diffusion of responsibility. He found the characteristics of the person in need were more important than the number of bystanders who were actually present. Piliavin found that help was just as likely to be given on a crowded subway train carriage as a fairly empty subway carriage.

Going further

Piliavin also found that male bystanders were more likely to intervene than females in this study. What might have been the reasons for this?

Building skills 1

K **A**

A 50-year-old American construction worker called Wesley Autrey was waiting for a subway train with his two daughters, when 19-year-old student Cameron Hollopeter suffered a seizure, causing him to fall off the platform onto the train tracks. Wesley jumped off the platform and rolled himself and the young man into the gap between the rails. Two carriages of the train passed within centimetres of their heads before coming to a stop. Both survived the incident and Wesley was hailed as a hero for his actions.

How do you think you would have reacted if you had witnessed this event?

Discuss which dispositional factor you think best explains Wesley's heroic behaviour. Be prepared to justify your answer.

5.3 Key research study: Piliavin

What are crowd and collective behaviours?

Getting started

Try to think of three things that you do which you do not put as much effort into when you are in a group, as when you are on your own. An example could be when singing in a choir compared with singing on your own. Why do you think you do not put in the same amount of effort?

■ What is collective behaviour?

Psychologists have found that people can behave very differently when in groups or crowds than when they are alone. One of the earliest theories of crowd behaviour suggested that crowds had a tendency to act as a violent mob.

A *Violence can errupt in a crowd*

Objectives

You will be able to:

- understand what is meant by collective behaviour

- identify and explain how social factors affect collective behaviour

- identify and explain how dispositional factors affect collective behaviour.

Key terms

Antisocial behaviour: when people do not act in socially acceptable ways or consider the rights of others

Collective behaviour: the way in which people act when they are part of a group

Deindividuation: the state of losing our sense of individuality and becoming less aware of our own responsibility for our actions

Social loafing: putting less effort into doing something when you are with others doing the same thing

Although the majority of research into crowd behaviour has focused on antisocial behaviour, such as violence, most crowd behaviour is peaceful. A growing body of evidence highlights that crowds can act in prosocial ways too. For example, after suicide bombers detonated three bombs in the London Underground in 2005, large numbers of people were trapped underground and united to cooperate and help fellow passengers. People assemble as peaceful crowds showing responsible behaviour on a regular basis; for example at sporting events, train stations, religious gatherings, and tourist attractions. For most people, being part of a

B *Being part of a crowd can be a positive and harmonious experience*

crowd at a music festival or sporting event is a positive and harmonious experience. The rise of social media has led to new forms of **collective behaviour** online, such as crowdfunding where people work together to raise money, often for a charitable organisation. Fundraising is a good example of how collective behaviour unites people in working towards goals to benefit society.

■ How do social factors affect collective behaviour?

Social loafing

Have you ever heard the saying 'two heads are better than one'? We often assume that people work better as part of a team than when they work alone. However, psychologists have discovered that this is not usually the case. In fact, individuals often put less effort into completing a task as part of a group than when they complete the same task alone. This is known as **social loafing**. When a group of people perform a task together, every individual is being helped by other members of the group. This means that diffusion of responsibility occurs as individuals do not need to work as hard as they would if they completed the task alone. As a result, each person contributes less to the task.

C In a tug of war, a person doesn't pull as hard when there are more people pulling

However, there are some key factors that reduce the likelihood of social loafing. People are less likely to show social loafing when:

- in small groups rather than large groups
- completing an activity they think is important
- in competition with another group.

Social loafing can also be reduced by identifying and evaluating each individual's effort in a group task. For example, team leaders can allocate specific roles to each member of their group, and sports coaches can give individual feedback on performance to each member of their team.

Deindividuation

Individuality refers to who we are: our personality, values, and our sense of right and wrong. **Deindividuation** refers to what happens when people lose their sense of individuality. Psychologists have found that people have a tendency to become deindividuated when in a crowd because they feel anonymous. In a crowd, it is hard to identify individuals, especially if they look or behave like other people in the group. This leads people to lose their inhibitions and sense of responsibility for what they do. As a consequence, they are less able to monitor their own behaviour and judge whether their actions are right or wrong because they behave as part of the crowd rather than individuals.

Building skills 1

Read this student's views about group work in school:

A

'I hate doing group work in class. Whenever we have a group project, no one else seems to do very much and I end up having to do all the work myself.'

Use your knowledge of collective behaviour to explain this student's experience of group work. What could teachers do to prevent this from happening when students work together to complete a task?

Going further

Use the Internet to research examples of online collective behaviour that have led to prosocial behaviour, such as social media campaigns supporting charitable causes.

It has been found that when people are in crowds, they look to those around them to guide their own actions, so adopt the mood of that crowd and change their behaviour accordingly. If the crowd is joyful, people joining it will also become happy. If, on the other hand, it is a hostile mob, the people joining it will become angry. If as a result, they behave in antisocial ways, such as shouting abuse, people feel they are less likely to be punished for doing so due to their relative anonymity: if no one knows who they are, they cannot be punished.

Interviews with young people who looted during the riots in London in 2011 found they got involved because they felt swept along by the crowd. They could see other people getting away with antisocial behaviour and felt anonymous, so they joined in too. This is one reason why deindividuation can lead to antisocial behaviour.

Deindividuation can also occur in other collective situations when people behave like the group they are in, rather than as an individual. When people join a group, they are expected to behave like others in that group. There may even be guidelines or 'codes of conduct' for them to follow. Wearing clothing that shows group membership, such as the shirt of a football team or a nurses' uniform, increases the likelihood that deindividuation will occur.

Building skills 2

A

Use the Internet to find out about the riots that took place in London in the summer of 2011. Look at images of the people who were looting from shops. Identify some factors that might have made them anonymous in this situation.

Did you know ?

Research has shown how anonymity affects people's behaviour in real life. When crowds gather to watch someone who is threatening to commit suicide by jumping off a building, the more anonymous the people can be (e.g. the crowd is large, or it is dark), the more likely they are to encourage the person to do it.

D *Is deindividuation always a negative thing?*

E *If people think they can't be identified, they may be more likely to follow the crowd*

Culture

The social norms within a culture can affect collective behaviour. Interestingly, for example, social loafing does not seem to occur in all societies. In some collectivist cultures such as China, people are prepared to work just as hard for the good of the whole group even when they do not need to. This means that it is difficult to assume that collective behaviour will be the same in all cultures.

Synoptic link 🔗

There are other areas of research in which culture has an effect on behaviour. Can you find any other research described in this book that might be affected by cultural differences? Begin by looking at cognitive development in Topic 3.2 and what affects perception in Topic 2.6.

■ How do dispositional factors affect collective behaviour?

Personality

Rotter (1966) said that some people have an internal locus of control, while others have an external locus of control. 'Internals' are people who believe that they can control the things that happen to them, while 'externals' attribute the things that happen to them to factors that are out of their control. For example, if internals did poorly in an assessment, they are likely to say this was because they had not revised well, whereas externals are more likely to blame their result on poor teaching or difficult questions in the test.

Research has found that people with an internal locus of control take greater responsibility for their own behaviour. This means that they are more likely to decide how to behave based on their own idea of what is right or wrong, rather than conforming to the behaviour of those around them. This suggests that people with an internal locus of control are less likely to follow group behaviour and more likely to act as individuals in collective situations, compared to those with an external locus of control.

Morality

Whether people behave in a pro or antisocial way in collective situations also depends on an individual's morality. This is their sense of what is right and what is wrong. For example, if young people do not trust the police and do not believe they are working to protect them and their community, they may feel justified in verbally abusing or even attacking police officers in collective situations. However, this is not the only factor to influence their behaviour. For example, even if people believe their behaviour is right and justified, they may not get involved in antisocial behaviour if doing so presents a personal risk to them, such as getting caught, which might cause them to lose their job.

5 Revision checklist

You should now be able to:

Conformity

☐ identify and explain how the following social factors affect conformity: group size, anonymity and task difficulty

☐ identify and explain how the following dispositional factors affect conformity: personality and expertise

☐ **key research study:** describe and evaluate Asch's study of conformity

See pages 104–107

Obedience

☐ describe and evaluate Milgram's Agency Theory of obedience

☐ identify and explain how the following social factors affect obedience: agency, authority, culture and proximity

☐ describe and evaluate Adorno's theory of the Authoritarian Personality

☐ explain how dispositional factors affect obedience

See pages 108–111

Prosocial behaviour

☐ identify and explain how the following social factors affect bystander behaviour: the presence of others and the cost of helping

☐ identify and explain how the following dispositional factors affect bystander intervention: similarity to the victim and expertise

☐ **key research study:** describe and evaluate Piliavin's subway study

See pages 112–115

Crowd and collective behaviour

☐ explain the difference between prosocial and antisocial behaviour

☐ identify and explain how the following social factors affect collective behaviour: social loafing, deindividuation and culture

☐ identify and explain how the following dispositional factors affect collective behaviour: personality and morality

See pages 116–119

Practice exam questions

1. Explain how group size may affect conformity. *(2 marks)*

2. Describe and evaluate Asch's research into conformity. *(9 marks)*

> In an extended writing question like this one, some of the things that will benefit an answer are: relevant and detailed description, effective evaluation, and being clear and focused throughout.

3. A teacher conducted an experiment into obedience at her school. She told 10 students to each take a note to the school reception. She also asked a student from her class to tell 10 different students to each carry out the same task. She found the following results:

	Teacher giving the instruction	Student giving the instruction
Number of students who obeyed	10	2

   a) Express the number of students obeying when the teacher asked as a percentage. *(1 mark)*

   b) Express the number of students obeying when the student asked as a fraction. *(1 mark)*

   c) Express the results to parts a) and b) above as a ratio. *(1 mark)*

   d) What social factor of obedience was the teacher testing? *(1 mark)*

4. Evaluate Milgram's agency theory of obedience. *(4 marks)*

> When answering a question like this, stay focused on evaluating the theory, rather than evaluating research studies.

5. A psychologist wanted to see how different factors might affect the level of help that a person received at a local football stadium. She used a confederate who was instructed to fall over in front of people. Half the time the confederate was wearing the home team's shirt and the other half he was wearing the away team's shirt. She got the confederate to fall over in crowded areas as well as in front of people on their own.

   Identify one dispositional factor and one social factor that may have affected bystander intervention in this study. Use your knowledge of psychology to explain how each factor might affect bystander behaviour. *(6 marks)*

> There are four things being asked for in this question, so it is important to take the time to read the question carefully and to identify all the different things your answer needs to address.

6 Language, thought, and communication

6.1 What is the relationship between language and thought?

Although research has found that animals use **communication** (see pages 126–127), they do not use **language** like humans do. Animals are also unable to use complex **thought**. This may mean that these two skills are somehow connected.

There are different ideas about the relationship between language and thought. This topic will consider Piaget's theory and the Sapir-Whorf hypothesis.

■ Piaget's theory: language depends on thought

Piaget was very important in helping us to understand how humans develop cognitively. He believed that cognitive development leads to the growth of language. This means that we can only use language at a level that matches our cognitive development.

According to Piaget's theory, children develop language in four stages:

- In the sensorimotor stage, babies are discovering what their bodies can do, and this includes the ability to make sounds. Babies then learn to copy the sounds they hear others making.

- In the preoperational stage, children are egocentric and focused on themselves. They use language to voice their internal thoughts, rather than to communicate with other people.

- In the concrete operational stage, the ability to use language has developed a lot but it is only used to talk about actual, concrete things.

- In the formal operational stage, language can be used to talk about abstract, theoretical ideas.

Piaget believed that while all children move through these stages, some people do not get to the formal operational stage.

Building skills 1

Piaget used his own children for much of his research. Working with a partner, try to think of at least two ways to evaluate his use of this sample.

E

Evaluation

Piaget did many of his observations on his own. When the participants in his research were his own children, they were unlikely to realise that they were being observed. This means that their behaviour was probably natural. However, his research would be more reliable if he had carried out his observations with another researcher, so that they could compare the results afterwards to check if they were similar and had inter-observer reliability (see page 87).

When Piaget's participants were his own children, he may have allowed his personal biases to affect his judgement. This lack of objectivity would affect the validity of his findings.

Because Piaget's sample was very small, and much of his research was based on observing his own children, his findings cannot be generalised because they cannot be said to apply to all children.

There is more research to support other theories about language and thought, including the Sapir-Whorf hypothesis.

■ Sapir-Whorf hypothesis

The Sapir-Whorf hypothesis was developed from the ideas of Edward Sapir and Benjamin Whorf. The hypothesis states that our thoughts and behaviours are affected and formed by the language we speak. This means that **cultures** with different languages and vocabulary will also have different ways of thinking and understanding things.

Language may therefore:

- lead us to focus on certain ways of seeing and understanding things

- make some ways of thinking easier and more likely than others

- lead to memory bias, where the ability to **recall** or retrieve certain information is increased or decreased.

Sapir and Whorf provided evidence for their ideas by studying indigenous (native) languages. Whorf compared Native American languages with English. He used the Hopi's use of different types of words for time and the Eskimo's large number of words for snow to support his claims.

Did you know ?

Piaget's theories of development changed the way that children are taught.

Going further

Vygotsky developed another theory on the relationship between language and thought. Although you do not need to know about Vygotsky for the exam, doing some research on his theory of thought and language will give you more ways to evaluate Piaget.

Exam tip !

Although wider knowledge of both Piaget's stage theory of cognitive development and his theory of language and thought will deepen your overall understanding, remember to focus your exam answers on the specific part of his theories that the question is asking you to address.

A *Does the language that we speak affect the way that we think?*

How does the language we speak affect our view of the world?

Getting started

Draw or write a description of each of the following words:

    phone   orange   camera   computer   cloud   book

Compare your descriptions to others in your class. People might have thought differently about each word. Can you use your knowledge of the Sapir-Whorf hypothesis to explain why?

The Sapir-Whorf hypothesis suggests that the language we speak may lead us to focus on certain ways of seeing and understanding things. Even within the same language, there are cultural and generational differences in the way words are understood. Phones and cameras are very different now compared with those in previous generations, and this will affect how people think about them.

The Sapir-Whorf hypothesis also suggests that some ways of thinking are easier and more common than others. You are probably more familiar with recent meanings for 'orange' and 'cloud' than those from an older generation. This makes it more likely that your descriptions in Getting started, above, will have been affected by the connections that now link the meanings of the words.

B *Does our culture and the language we speak affect our view of the world?*

Evaluation

Some of Sapir and Whorf's claims have been challenged and some of their methods found to be unreliable. For example:

- Eskimos have about the same number of words for snow as English speakers do and Whorf had never even met anyone from the Hopi tribe.

Key terms

Recognition: identification of something or someone, previously known, seen or heard about

Exam tip !

Try to be as precise as possible with the words you use in the exam. An example is the set of terms: 'culture', 'race', and 'ethnicity'. They may seem very similar but actually each means something different, and so it is important to use them correctly.

Building skills 2

What do you think of the Sapir-Whorf hypothesis? Working with a partner, try to think of at least one evaluation point. **E**

Going further

Using the list of words from the Getting started activity above, design and carry out an experiment to test the idea that different generations think differently about language.

 See Chapter 4 for advice on how to design an effective experiment.

 Display your results in an appropriate form, for example a bar chart.

Refer back to Topic 4.8 on data handling to help you with any calculations.

Share your findings with the rest of the class.

Did you know ?

The English language has eleven basic colour terms, but some languages only have two.

- Books and instruction manuals can be translated into a completely different language without developing a whole new meaning for the reader.

- People who grow up without a language, or who lose the ability to speak (such as stroke victims) are still able to think.

However, there is a reasonable amount of evidence supporting the hypothesis.

Variation in recognition of colours

The Sapir-Whorf hypothesis suggests that the language we speak can lead us to focus on certain ways of seeing things and make some ways of thinking more likely than others.

Many languages do not have separate words for blue and green. The Tarahumara, Native Americans from north-western Mexico, have one word for both. Researchers found that English speakers perceived bigger differences between shades of blues and greens than Tarahumara speakers did.

The Russian language has different words for lighter blues and darker blues. Researchers found that Russian speakers were quicker than English speakers to recognise the difference between two shades of blue when one was perceived as lighter and one was perceived as darker.

C *Do Eskimo languages really have lots of words for snow?*

Variation in recall of events

The Sapir-Whorf hypothesis suggests that our ability to recall certain information is affected by the language we speak.

Researchers studied how English speakers and Spanish speakers described intended and accidental actions. Participants were asked about things like seeing someone accidentally bump into and knock a vase to the floor. When the action was intended, all the participants identified the person doing it. But when the action was accidental, the English speakers identified the person more often than the Spanish speakers did. When the participants' recall of the intended actions was tested, the English speakers and Spanish speakers both recalled the people involved. However, the English speakers had much better recall of who was involved in the accidental actions.

> **Synoptic link** 🔗
>
> Applying what you learned about memory as an active process in Topic 1.3 will allow you to discuss how the theory of reconstructive memory might help to explain the variation in the recall of events by speakers of different languages.

> **Exam tip** !
>
> When a question requires the evaluation of a theory, criticism of the research used to support the theory can be a valid part of your answer. However, it is important that your answer clearly shows you understand that the research and the theory are not the same thing.

Practice exam questions

1. What is meant by the term 'language'? *(2 marks)*

2. Outline Piaget's theory of the relationship between language and thought. *(4 marks)*

3. Use your knowledge of psychology to evaluate Piaget's theory of language and thought. *(5 marks)*

How are human and animal communication different?

Getting started

Think of as many ways as you can that animals might communicate with each other. One example would be whistling.

Which of these ways do you think are also used by humans to communicate with each other?

Although animals do not use language to communicate as humans do, they do use vocalisation (communication with sound) in a variety of forms, from the singing of birds and chirping of insects to the growling of lions and other big cats. Many of the messages being conveyed by these vocalisations are similar to those humans might communicate – expressing interest in a mate, showing alarm, or letting others know that they need to back off! Research has also found many similarities between human non-verbal communication and that used by some animals, especially primates. Similarities include the use of facial expressions to show emotion, using body **posture** to show dominance and submission, and the use of **touch** for bonding and reassurance.

■ Limited functions of animal communication

Even though research has found animal communication to be more complex and elaborate than it might first appear, animals use communication for far fewer purposes than humans.

Building skills 1

Think of as many reasons as you can for animals to communicate with each other. Some examples are given above.

Objectives

You will be able to:

- identify differences between human and animal communication

- identify functions of animal communication

- identify properties of human communication that animals do not use.

Key terms

Posture: the positioning of the body, often regarded as a non-verbal communication signal

Territory: an area defended by an animal or group of animals against others

Touch: a form of non-verbal communication in which information is conveyed by physical contact between people

Did you know ?

Cats only meow at humans. They use other ways to communicate with animals, such as hissing, arching their backs, and yowling.

A *Like humans, animals can communicate through touch*

Four of the main reasons animals communicate with one another are: for survival, reproduction, **territory**, and food.

Animal use of communication is linked in a variety of ways to survival. Animals call to their young who have wandered off, they use alarm calls to warn others of the presence of predators, and they use threat signals (such as bared teeth, making fur stand up to look bigger, and growling) to warn others to back off.

Displays involving colour are used by a number of species (such as peacocks) to attract a mate and ensure reproduction, and ultimately survival. Other animals use colour to frighten or warn off predators.

Karl von Frisch discovered that bees tell each other where to find food using dance-like movements (see the Key research study on page 128). Ants communicate with each other using different chemical smells called pheromones. Pheromones can be used for a variety of messages, including the location of food.

Researchers studying rhesus monkeys found that when they made unbroken eye contact with them, the monkeys would start to behave aggressively. They concluded that the monkeys use eye contact to show their dominance and that they became aggressive because they saw the researchers' behaviour as threatening.

A cat defending its territory

Building skills 2

Copy this table and complete it using your answers from Building skills 1 and as many other examples as you can think of. (Some of your answers may go in more than one column.)

K A

Survival	Reproduction	Territory	Food	Other
Calling young			Directions to food source	
Alarm calls				
Threat signals		Threat signals		
Colour displays	Colour displays			

Did you know ?

In 1995, a budgie named Puck appeared in the *Guinness Book of World Records* for his large vocabulary. It was reported that he knew 1728 words.

Researchers have discovered that birds like budgies copy each other in the wild. This may allow them to recognise members of their group among competing groups.

Going further

This topic has focused on animal-to-animal communication. How might animal-to-human communication be different?

Use the examples from the Did you know? boxes to start you off. What other examples can you also think of or find out about? Share your research with the rest of your class.

Exam tip !

The forms (ways) and the functions (reasons) are both important when answering questions about the differences between human and animal communication.

Von Frisch's bee study (1950)

Aim: To investigate how bees communicate the location of a food source to each other.

Study design: A field experiment carried out in the real-life environment of the participants (the bees in this case). The researcher still manipulates the independent variable, but there is limited control of extraneous variables.

Method: Food sources for a hive of bees were created by placing glass containers of sugar-water at different locations.

A hive with glass sides was used so that the bee's behaviour could be easily observed. When the bees visited the containers of sugar-water to feed, they were marked with tiny spots of different coloured paints. This made the bees easy to identify when they returned to the hive.

The researcher observed and recorded the movements that the bees made when they returned to the hive after collecting the food.

Results: The bees were observed making different movements that seemed to depend on how far away the food source was from the hive.

When the food source was no further than 100 metres from the hive, the bees did a round dance by turning rapidly in circles to the right and then the left.

When the sugar-water was moved further away, the bees performed a tail-wagging or waggle dance. The bees moved forward in a straight line, wagging their abdomens from side to side, before turning in a circle towards the left. This was followed by the bees moving straight forward again before turning in a circle towards the right. This pattern was then repeated a number of times.

Von Frisch found that the number of turns a bee makes in fifteen seconds of waggle dancing is actually communicating how far away the food source is. He also found that bees use the straight part of the dance to communicate where the feeding place is in relation to the current position of the sun.

Conclusion: Von Frisch concluded that bees use a variety of different movements to communicate to each other the distance and the direction of food sources.

round dance   waggle dance

A *Bee communication*

Source: Von Frisch, K. (1950) Bees: Their vision, chemical senses and language, *London: Cornell University Press.*

B *A bee gathering food from a natural food source*

■ Evaluation

Why the study is important

- Von Frisch's research was some of the earliest into animal communication and encouraged others to carry out research in this area of study.

- Other researchers have repeated this study and found the same results. This consistency allows us to be more certain that the results are trustworthy and that the original study was reliable.

Limitations of the study

- Gathering sugar-water from glass containers is not a natural, everyday behaviour for bees. Therefore, it can be argued that the study lacks ecological validity. However, when researchers put the sugar solution on flowers instead, the bees acted in the same way.

- Bees do not generally live in glass hives and this may also have affected their natural behaviour. However, research that has used wooden hives and other methods (such as video cameras) to observe the bees, has had the same results.

- Other researchers have suggested that in order for bees to find food, they also use cognitive maps based on their memory of landmarks.

Building skills 1   **A**

Although von Frisch's bee study was carried out in a natural setting, the sugar-water that was used is not a natural food source for bees. The bees' normal behaviour might also have been affected by the hive with glass sides. Working with a partner, think about how the research could be carried out without these extraneous variables. (Read more about extraneous variables on page 70.)

Going further

The *Code of Ethics and Conduct of the British Psychological Society* (2009) says that research using animals should protect them by keeping 'pain, suffering, fear, distress, frustration, boredom, or lasting harm' to a minimum. Working in pairs, discuss whether or not von Frisch's bee study would have met the British Psychological Society guidelines.

Did you know   **?**

Karl von Frisch also found out that bees can see in colour and are able to recognise different flowers by their fragrance. His work studying bees led to him being given the Nobel Prize in 1973.

Exam tip   **!**

The diagrams of the round dance and the waggle dance in the study details are included just to assist your understanding. Drawing them would not gain you extra marks if you were asked to describe von Frisch's bee study in the exam.

6.2 Key research study: von Frisch

What properties are only part of human communication?

A linguist looking at the differences between animal communication and human languages developed the idea of language having certain properties. These properties are known as the design features of language. Productivity and displacement are two design features of language. All communication has some design features, but only human language is believed to have all of them.

Productivity is the ability to create an unlimited number of different messages. It allows language to be used creatively and is not found in animal communication. Although von Frisch found that bees could vary the messages conveyed by their dancing, there are limits to what they can say. For example, they do not appear to have movements that mean up or down.

Displacement is the ability to communicate about things that are not present or events that will happen in the future. It allows language to be used for planning ahead and discussing future events. Although it is rarely seen in animal communication, von Frisch's research provides one example of when it is. Bees demonstrate displacement by communicating about a food source that is some distance from the hive where they are dancing.

Planning behaviours in animals, such as squirrels storing nuts for winter, are likely to be instinctive or innate, rather than communicated ideas.

C *A property of communication rarely used by animals*

Koko is a female gorilla who has been taught sign language. She is believed to understand around one thousand signs and two thousand spoken words.

Koko's trainer has reported that Koko can create new signs when she does not know an existing one. For example, Koko put together the signs for finger and bracelet (i.e. finger-bracelet) to refer to a ring. This would suggest that she has the ability to use language productively.

Building skills 4

E

What do you think of the research into animal communication and the various concepts that have been described in this topic? Working with a partner, try to think of at least two evaluations.

Going further

With a partner, discuss how you feel about teaching animals to behave in ways that are not natural. Does it meet the British Psychological Society's guidelines on the use of animals in research? For more on the guidelines, see pages 92–93.

D *Koko the gorilla communicating through sign language that she is hungry*

Evaluation

It is hard to know for sure which properties or design features are only used by humans because more is being learned about animal communication all the time.

Although research, such as that with Koko, suggests some animals can use properties of communication generally only used by humans, this is not naturally occurring behaviour. These animals may be simply imitating humans.

There are also ethical issues around keeping wild animals in captivity and training them to behave in ways that are not natural.

Exam tip

!

The command word in Practice exam question 2 below is 'discuss'. This type of question needs you to give the key points about the ideas in the question as well as the strengths and weaknesses of these ideas.

1. Decide whether each of the following statements is true or false.
   A Bees do a waggle dance to communicate to other bees that there is a food source close to the hive. *(1 mark)*
   B Bees use the straight part of the waggle dance to communicate the direction of a food source to other bees. *(1 mark)*

2. Using your knowledge of psychology, discuss properties of human communication that are not present in animal communication. *(9 marks)*

Practice exam questions

6.3 What is non-verbal communication?

Building skills 1

Working in a small group, make a list of at least ten different ways that people communicate with each other. Rather than putting 'body language' on your list, be more specific about ways people use their bodies to communicate.

When you have completed your list, rearrange it into three columns with these headings: Communicating with words, Communicating without words, and Communicating using technology.

K

Objectives

You will be able to:

- understand the distinction between non-verbal and verbal communication
- understand the functions of eye contact
- recognise different types of body language
- understand factors that affect personal space.

Key terms

Body language: a general term to describe aspects of non-verbal communication

Eye contact: when two people in conversation are looking at each other's eyes at the same time

Non-verbal communication: conveying messages without the use of words

Verbal communication: conveying messages using words

Exam tip !

When distinguishing between two terms, remember that examples can be helpful and could earn extra marks.

Did you know ?

In trying to work out the total impact of a message, psychologists have suggested that 7 per cent is verbal (the words used), 38 per cent is vocal (for example, tone of voice), and 55 per cent is non-verbal (for example, facial expression).

■ The difference between verbal communication and non-verbal communication

There are many ways in which people communicate; the list is almost endless. In your list you have probably included email, texting, social networking websites, and many others methods that use technology. However, in this section we are focusing on ways in which we communicate without the use of technology.

Communication that requires the use of words is called **verbal communication**, for example talking to someone or reading a letter.

Communication that does not require the use of words is called **non-verbal communication**. This includes aspects of speech (aside from the words themselves) that help to communicate meaning, such as the tone, pitch or volume of someone's voice. It also includes visual cues such as **eye contact** and **body language**.

A *It is not just the words that are important in conversation*

■ Functions of eye contact

Building skills 2

Working with a partner, have a two-minute conversation while you sit facing one another. Then have another two-minute conversation while you are sitting back to back.

Think about whether the conversations felt the same or different. Compare your answers with others in your class.

We are often unaware of what our eyes are doing when we are having a conversation and yet eye movements have very important functions.

In Building skills 2, you might have found that the back-to-back conversation felt less comfortable and did not flow so well. One reason for this is that we use eye movements to signal turn-taking in a conversation. When someone is about to finish speaking, they give the other person a prolonged look. So when we cannot see someone's eyes, we are unsure when their turn to speak is finishing and ours is starting.

Researchers carried out an experiment into the effects of interrupting eye contact. Pairs of participants were observed having conversations. In some conversations, one participant wore dark glasses. The results showed that there were more pauses and interruptions when dark glasses were worn. This shows that one function of eye contact is regulating the smooth flow of conversation.

Research has found that pupil dilation expresses emotion. Dilation is when the pupils expand and look larger. When young men were shown two nearly identical pictures of the same girl and asked which picture they found more attractive, the majority of participants chose the picture of the girl whose pupils had been altered to look dilated. The participants' pupils also dilated when they looked at the altered photo.

Research has also found that people prefer those who look at them more frequently. This may be because we interpret a high level of looking as a signal of attraction.

Going further

Working with a partner, design and conduct an experiment to test the idea that people tend to prefer those who look at them more frequently.

See Chapter 4 for advice on how to design an effective experiment.

Report your findings to the rest of the class.

Synoptic link

In Topic 2.6, you considered how factors such as culture and emotion can influence our perception. You can apply this learning when discussing the functions of eye contact.

B *Wearing dark glasses can affect the flow of conversation*

How do we use body language?

Getting started

Working with a partner, have a two minute conversation while you both have your arms folded across your chests. Then have another two minute conversation while your arms are not crossed.

Think about whether the two types of posture made any difference to the way the conversations went. How did you feel when you were talking to someone who had their arms crossed?

Posture

As shown in Topic 6.2, posture is used by animals to communicate dominance, threat, and submission. Humans also use posture to communicate non-verbally.

Crossing your arms while you are in conversation is known as **closed posture**. Psychologists say that this could indicate rejection, disagreement, or feeling threatened. Having your arms uncrossed and relaxed is known as **open posture**. This may indicate approval or acceptance.

Research has found that the posture that someone adopts will make a difference to how much they are liked. If you have an open posture, you are more likely to be seen as friendly and attractive. Having a closed posture means you are more likely to be seen as unfriendly and less attractive.

People who are getting on well together tend to adopt each other's posture when they are having a conversation. This is known as **postural echo**. Research has found that postural echo gives an unconscious message of friendliness and people are liked more when they use it.

Key terms

Closed posture: positioning the arms so that they are folded across the body and/or crossing the legs

Open posture: positioning the arms so that they are not folded across the body, and not crossing the legs

Postural echo: mirroring another person's body position

Building skills 3

Imagine you are going to carry out a study into the effects of adopting different types of posture when having a conversation. You may want to look back at Topic 4.1 on pages 66–67 to refresh your memory of the experimental method.

The dependent variable is how much a person is liked on a rating scale of 1 to 10. Decide on your independent variable (IV) and then write an appropriate hypothesis.

What do you think the likely results would be if you carried out your experiment?

C People who are getting on well together tend to mirror each other's posture

Touch

Touch is another form of non-verbal communication. It is a very powerful signal that can produce unconscious emotional reactions. There are huge cultural differences in the amount of touch that is permitted between individuals. British society seems to be more restricted than other Western societies in its use of touch when communicating.

Psychologists studied the effect of touch on attitudes by asking a librarian to very briefly touch the hand of some students as they returned their books. Even though the students were not aware that they had been touched, they were found to have a much more positive attitude towards the library and the librarian than those who had not been touched.

Research has found that when you briefly touch other people, they are more likely to agree to your request. Researchers studying this persuasive effect, found that when a man touched women's arms for a second while asking them for a dance, two-thirds agreed to dance with him. When the same man did not use touch, his success rate halved.

D *Touch is a very powerful social signal*

Building skills 4

In order to study concepts such as the effects of posture and touch, psychologists have often used confederates. A confederate carries out a role for the experimenter but the participants do not know that they are part of the experiment. The librarian in the research on touch is an example of a confederate.   **E**

Working with a partner, try to think of at least one criticism and one benefit of using confederates in non-verbal communication studies.

Because the participants do not realise the true nature of the confederate's role and are unaware that they are helping the experimenter, the participants are being deceived. Therefore, the use of confederates in psychological research can be seen as unethical.

However, because the participants are not aware, they are less likely to change their behaviour. This allows researchers to study the natural behaviour of people. This means that the results can be said to be ecologically valid because they give an accurate account of real-life behaviour.

Going further

Working with a partner, design and carry out an investigation into body language. Then report your findings to your class.

Exam tip   **!**

It will be helpful to be able to briefly describe research into each of the areas of non-verbal communication covered in this section.

What factors affect our personal space?

Getting started

Stand as close to your neighbour as feels comfortable for you. Try doing this facing each other. How far apart are you standing?

Now do the same thing, side by side. How far apart are you now?

Now try it back to back and note the distance.

Were there differences in how far apart you stood each time?

The distance that feels comfortable between you and another person is known as your **personal space**. After eye contact, personal space is perhaps the second most important non-verbal communication signal that we use.

Building skills 5

Working with a partner, try to think of things that might cause our personal space to be larger or smaller.

A

Differences in personal space

Research suggests that there are a number of **gender** differences in personal space. Men tend to have a bigger personal space than women, and both genders prefer to have a greater amount of space between themselves and members of the opposite sex. There are also gender differences in how we are positioned when close to other people. Women prefer to sit beside their friends and men prefer to sit opposite them.

Women's personal space is more often invaded by men than the other way around. Men feel more uncomfortable when their personal space is invaded from the front and women feel more uncomfortable when their personal space is invaded from the side.

E *We tend to stand closer to people of the same gender and further away from people of the opposite gender*

Key terms

Cultural norms: the range of behaviours that members of a particular social group or society can be expected to show

Gender: the psychological state of being male or female, often distinguished by social behaviours and cultural roles

Personal space: the physical distance we prefer to keep between ourselves and other people in order to feel comfortable

Status: a person's rank or position within society

Did you know ?

Psychologists have found that our personal space has four zones: an intimate zone (less than 0.5 metres) into which we allow only very close friends; a personal zone (0.5–1.2 metres) for casual acquaintances; a social zone (1.2–3.6 metres) for people we do not know very well; and a public zone (over 3.6 metres) for more formal occasions such as speaking to an audience.

There are a number of other things that have been found to affect personal space. Age and personality type are two of them. People tend to sit or stand nearer to each other if they are a similar age, while introverts have a larger personal space than extroverts.

Status is another factor affecting personal space. Researchers have found that people of lower status stand closer to people of equal status than to people of a higher status. Other research has found that people of higher status feel freer than people of lower status, to choose how close they get to someone.

Researchers have found that **cultural norms** also affect personal space. Groups of white English people and groups of Arab people were observed having conversations. The results showed that the comfortable conversation distance for the white English people was 1–1.5 metres, whereas the comfortable conversation distance for the Arab people was much less than that.

F *Personal space during conversations tends to be less in Arab cultures*

Evaluation

The research looked at in this topic studied the effect of individual factors. However, it is more likely that a combination of factors will affect our personal space in real-life situations.

There are many other factors that may also affect personal space, such as how much we like the other person, or how well we know them. With so many factors having a potential effect, it is very difficult to design research in which it is definitely only the independent variable that is affecting the dependent variable. (Read more about the independent and dependent variables on page 70.)

Cultural and social norms (for example those around gender roles) may change over time and this can result in research findings into social behaviours becoming less valid.

> ### Going further
>
> Working with a partner, design and carry out an investigation into personal space.
>
> See Chapter 4 for advice on how to design an effective investigation.
>
> Display your results in an appropriate form, for example a bar chart.
> Refer back to Topic 4.8 on data handling to help you with any calculations.
>
> Then report your findings to your class.

> ### Exam tip !
> For each mark available, you should try to add an additional piece of information to your answer.

> **Practice exam questions**
>
> 1. State one function of eye contact. *(1 mark)*
> 2. Explain the difference between open posture and closed posture. *(3 marks)*
> 3. Discuss factors that have been found to affect personal space. *(6 marks)*

Getting started

You may have heard of Charles Darwin and the theory of evolution before. Work with a partner to write down the key ideas that you remember.

One key idea is natural selection. For an organism to **evolve** successfully, survival and reproduction are essential. Genetic characteristics that increase an organism's chance of surviving and successfully reproducing are more likely to be passed on to successive generations.

The second key idea is known as 'survival of the fittest'. Successful **adaptive** organisms that have made the best changes in order to fit their situation and environment, are the ones most likely to survive and reproduce.

■ Darwin's evolutionary theory of non-verbal communication

In his book, *The Expression of the Emotions in Man and Animals* (1872), Darwin suggested several principles for the evolution of non-verbal communication that expresses emotions.

One of these principles is serviceable associated habits. A serviceable behaviour is one that has a purpose. For example, humans may have used biting as an early form of self-defence. In the same way that many animals do, they may have exposed their teeth as a threat signal. A serviceable associated habit happens when we have a similar experience, but now the behaviour does not have the same purpose. The behaviour is now a habit associated with feeling a certain way or certain situations. This may be why people expose their teeth when they have an angry facial expression.

Darwin also suggested the principle of actions due to the constitution of the nervous system. This simply means that some forms of non-verbal communication are caused by our nervous system. Dilated pupils and an open mouth are part of a frightened facial expression, but they are also some of the effects of adrenaline being released into our bodies by our nervous system during the fight or flight response.

Did you know ?

The phrase 'survival of the fittest' is strongly associated with Darwin's theory but was actually first used by English philosopher Herbert Spencer.

Objectives

You will be able to:

- describe and evaluate Darwin's evolutionary theory of non-verbal communication
- understand the distinction between innate and learned
- describe evidence that non-verbal behaviour is innate
- describe evidence that non-verbal behaviour is learned.

Key terms

Adaptive: being able to change in order to fit different situations and environments

Evolve: to slowly develop over successive generations into a different state or condition

Innate: inborn or inherited – that is, not learned

Learned: abilities or characteristics gained through experience

Synoptic link

For more information about the fight or flight response, see pages 148–149.

Building skills 1

Can you think of any ways in which facial expressions or eye contact could help humans' chances of survival and reproduction?

Examples of facial expressions that could help with our survival are the pupil dilation and open mouth seen in a frightened facial expression. Pupil dilation increases visual information, potentially allowing us to see the best way to avoid danger. An open mouth increases oxygen supply, allowing us to move away from a threat much faster.

As we learned earlier, pupil dilation also happens when we are attracted to someone. It also makes us more attractive to other people. We also interpret a high level of looking as a signal of attraction. These are examples of non-verbal communication that could help with reproduction.

A *Does this expression help to ensure our survival?*

Building skills 2

What do you think of Darwin's theory of non-verbal communication? Working with a partner, try to think of at least one evaluation. **E**

Going further

Think about some other forms of non-verbal communication (for example, posture and personal space). How might they help with human survival and reproduction?

B *Charles Darwin*

Evaluation

There is research to support Darwin's claims. Medical evidence supports the idea that the function of our nervous system causes certain actions, such as pupil dilation. Other research suggests that at least some non-verbal behaviours are genetic or **innate** (see page 140).

It is possible that some non-verbal behaviours are not genetic but that they are instead **learned** by watching others. Social learning theory believes behaviours are learned through observing and copying others. Research that supports the theory that non-verbal behaviour is learned is explored on pages 134–135.

Some behaviours may be both innate and learned. We are born with the ability to cry and to laugh and these behaviours can happen spontaneously – but we can also learn to control them and to use them in a way that is considered socially and culturally appropriate.

Not all human behaviours obviously help humans to survive or reproduce. This may also be the case with some non-verbal behaviours, such as the use of gestures.

> **Did you know**
> Darwin went to medical school but left because he hated the sight of blood and found the lectures boring.

> **Exam tip**
> You may have learned about Darwin's theory of evolution in other subjects. When answering psychology exam questions about Darwin, it is important to make sure that your answer focuses on your psychological knowledge of his theory.

■ Where does our ability to use non-verbal behaviour come from?

Is non-verbal behaviour innate?

Darwin believed that facial expressions are the same in all cultures and are therefore innate and not learned. Some research also suggests that expressions of anger, disgust, fear, happiness, sadness, and surprise are recognised by most cultures throughout the world.

An experiment filmed people from Papua New Guinea telling a story using non-verbal communication. The film was then shown to American college students, who were able to accurately identify the emotions being shown.

Darwin's theory that emotional expressions are genetic or innate, suggests that they should be found in **neonates**. The younger a baby is when they make these expressions, the less likely it is that they have learned them by observing others.

Research has shown that neonates use a pre-cry expression that suggests sadness, as well as smiles and facial expressions that show disgust, pain, and surprise.

C *Are facial expressions like these recognised by everyone?*

The information we receive through our different senses helps us to learn. If non-verbal behaviours are learned, people who are **sensory deprived** should not be able to use them in the same way.

Research has shown that babies who are born blind have smiling behaviours that are similar to that found in babies with normal vision.

Researchers used 4800 photographs of sighted and blind athletes to compare the facial expressions they made at significant moments. They found that both the sighted and the blind athletes expressed their emotions in similar ways. For example, 85 per cent of silver medallists produced social smiles during the medal ceremony. A true smile causes the eyes to narrow and the cheeks to rise, but a social smile only uses the mouth muscles. This suggests that the silver medallists were not truly happy to come second and they had learned to give a social smile in this situation.

D *Is the ability to use non-verbal behaviour something we are born with or something we learn?*

Building skills 3

The research considered so far in this topic has focused on facial expressions. Do you think that other forms of non-verbal behaviour (such as eye contact, touch, and personal space) are also the same in all cultures? Give reasons for your answer. **K**

Is non-verbal behaviour learned?

While research does seem to suggest that some non-verbal behaviour is innate, there is also evidence that some is at least partly learned.

Topic 6.3 explored the cultural differences in the use of personal space and touch. Cultural differences are learned by observing and copying others around us. Yuki's study of emoticons suggests that the way we understand facial expressions is partly affected by culture.

Non-verbal communication and speech are closely linked. This is seen in the way eye contact is used to help a conversation flow smoothly. This non-verbal behaviour is learned at the same time as we learn to use language, and both are learned through social interactions.

Historical and generational changes in the use of non-verbal communication help to support the argument that it is a learned behaviour.

Did you know ?

The handshake as a gesture is quite a recent addition to British society. Until the seventeenth century, people bowed or curtsied instead. The handshake was only used to seal agreements.

Going further

Do some research into cultural or historical differences in the use of non-verbal communication. Share your findings with the rest of the class.

Practice exam questions

1. What is meant by the term 'innate'? *(2 marks)*

2. Give an example of a non-verbal behaviour that is considered to be innate. *(1 mark)*

3. Evaluate Darwin's evolutionary theory of non-verbal communication. *(5 marks)*

Yuki's emoticons study (2007)

Aim: To investigate if culture affects how facial cues are used when understanding other people's emotions.

Study design: A questionnaire with standard questions for all the participants and a rating scale of 1 to 9. Participants were American and Japanese students.

Method: Yuki showed participants emoticons with six different combinations of eyes and mouths. The eyes and mouths were happy, neutral, or sad. Participants were asked to rate how happy they thought each face was.

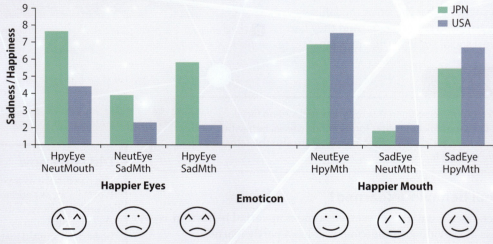

A *Emoticons similar to those used by Yuki*

Results: The Japanese students gave the highest ratings to the faces with happy eyes and the lowest ratings to the faces with sad eyes. The American students gave the highest ratings to the faces with happy mouths and the lowest ratings to the faces with sad mouths. The results suggest that Japanese and American people give more weight to different parts of the face when interpreting another person's emotions. The Japanese focus more on the eyes, while Americans focus more on the mouth. This may lead to a difference in their understanding of facial expressions.

Conclusion: Yuki concluded that people learn their own culture's norms for the expression and interpretation of emotions. Yuki suggested that the results may be related to how openly a culture expresses emotion. Research has shown that the eyes muscles are not as easy to control as those around the mouth. Therefore, the eyes might be seen as the most truthful facial cue in cultures that try to limit their outward emotional expression (such as Japan). But the mouth may be seen as the best guide in a culture where open emotional expression is normal (such as the USA).

Source: Yuki, M., Maddux, W. and Masuda, T. (2007) 'Are the windows of the soul the same in the East and the West?', Journal of Experimental Social Psychology, 43, 303–311.

■ Evaluation

Why this study is important

Yuki's study provides support for the theory that non-verbal behaviour is learned.

Limitations of the study

- Yuki used emoticons instead of real faces. Interpreting the emotion shown by emoticons is not a natural, everyday behaviour. Therefore, it can be argued that the study lacks ecological validity. However, when researchers used photos instead, the results were the same.

- The participants were aware that they were taking part in a piece of research, so they may not have given true responses. One reason for this is demand characteristics. The researchers may have given subtle clues to the participants about the answers they were expected to give. This would make the research less reliable.

- The sample is limited because all the participants were students. This means that the findings are not representative of younger or older people.

- The study only looked at happy and sad expressions and not at any other emotions. Therefore, the findings cannot be generalised to facial expressions of all emotions.

B *Could these two women be interpreting each other's facial expressions differently?*

■ Support for Yuki's findings

Yuki carried out a second study using photographs. He used computer software to create faces with different combinations of happy and sad eyes and mouths. The results were the same as in the previous study with emoticons.

Going further

Working with a partner, use the emoticons shown to conduct your own investigation into people's interpretation of facial expressions. Do your findings suggest that your participants gave more weight to the eyes or the mouth?

Compare your results with Yuki's.

Building skills 1

Yuki used emoticons, not real faces. Therefore, his study does not test people's normal behaviour. Working with a partner, think about how the research could be carried out in a way that is more ecologically valid. **A**

Building skills 2

Imagine you are going to carry out a study using photos just like Yuki did in his second study. Work out what the independent variable (IV) and the dependent variable (DV) are and then write an appropriate hypothesis (see pages 66–67 for help with writing a hypothesis). **K A**

Then ask someone else to check if it is a testable statement. This means that your hypothesis needs to have both conditions of the IV as well as a DV that can be measured.

Synoptic link

In Topic 2.6, you considered how factors such as culture and emotion can influence perception. You can apply this learning when discussing the findings of Yuki's study.

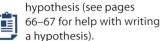

6.4 Key research study: Yuki

6 Revision checklist

The relationship between language and thought, and the effect of language and thought on our view of the world

- [ ] describe and evaluate Piaget's theory (that language depends on thought)
- [ ] describe and evaluate the Sapir-Whorf hypothesis (that thought depends on language)
- [ ] explain how recall of events and recognition of colours may be affected by the language we speak

See pages 122–125

Differences between human and animal communication

- [ ] explain the limited functions of animal communication: survival, reproduction, territory and food
- [ ] key research study: describe and evaluable Von Frisch's bee study
- [ ] explain the properties of human communication that are not present in animal communication

See pages 126–131

Explanations of non-verbal behaviour

- [ ] describe and evaluate Darwin's evolutionary theory of non-verbal communication, including how non-verbal communication is evolved and adaptive
- [ ] explain evidence that non-verbal behaviour is innate
- [ ] explain evidence that non-verbal behaviour is learned
- [ ] key research study: describe and evaluate Yuki's emoticons study

See pages 138–143

Non-verbal communication

- [ ] explain the difference between non-verbal communication and verbal communication
- [ ] explain the functions of eye contact, including: regulating the flow of conversation, signalling attraction and expressing emotion
- [ ] explain how body language is used to communicate, including: open and closed posture, postural echo and touch
- [ ] understand how the following factors affect personal space: culture, status and gender

See pages 132–137

Practice exam questions

1. Read the following descriptions of types of non-verbal communication.

Mirroring another person's body position	
Positioning arms and/or legs so that they are not folded or crossed over the body	
Positioning arms and/or legs across the body	

From the following list of terms, choose the one that matches each description and write either **A**, **B** or **C** in the box next to it. Use each letter only once.

A Open posture   B Postural echo   C Closed posture   *(3 marks)*

> Be sure to take the time to read the instructions for multiple-choice questions. Under the stress of exam conditions, it is easy to make mistakes that cost marks.

2. Describe and evaluate the Sapir-Whorf hypothesis that thinking depends on language. *(9 marks)*

3. Identify one difference between animal and human communication. *(1 mark)*

4. The following conversation took place between two work colleagues.

   Faye: 'Have you noticed that our new boss always looks down at the ground when you have a conversation with him?'

   Julie: 'Yes. I think that's why I find it hard to know if it's my turn to speak when I am talking to him.'

   Explain one function of eye contact. Refer to the conversation in your answer. *(3 marks)*

5. A psychologist conducted a study in which she used computer software to create faces with different combinations of happy and sad eyes and mouths. She asked participants from France and China to rate how happy they thought each face was on a scale from 1–10. A rating of 1 meant very sad and a rating of 10 meant very happy.

   a) Identify the dependent variable in this experiment. *(1 mark)*

   b) Write a suitable hypothesis for this experiment. *(2 marks)*

> A hypothesis needs to include all conditions of the IV and the DV. It also needs to be a statement rather than a longer answer, and it should be written in the future tense.

   The results for the experiment described above are shown in the table below.

Culture of participants	Median rating for happiness for a face with sad eyes and a happy mouth	Median rating for happiness for a face with happy eyes and a sad mouth
Chinese	3.5	9
French	8.5	4

> In a question like this, it is important to refer to the actual results in your answer.

   c) What conclusions can the psychologist draw from the results shown in this table? Explain your answer. *(4 marks)*

7 The brain and neuropsychology

7.1 What is the nervous system?

Getting started

It has been said that the nervous system is a massive information processor. Think about a typical hour in the middle of a usual day, for you. What different types of information would your nervous system have to process during that hour? Try comparing your list with a similar list made by a friend. Did you both identify the same things?

Objectives

You will be able to:

- distinguish between the major sections of the nervous system
- identify the major functions of the nervous system
- describe the central and peripheral nervous systems.

■ The structure of the nervous system

We have looked at lots of different aspects of human psychology, but how does it all happen? We grow, remember, perceive, and interact with other people quite automatically, but underneath all of these processes is the complex set of instructions that allows our bodies and minds to work in the way that they do.

The nervous system is a complex network of nerve fibres and nerve cells which passes information around the body (see Figure A). Since it is very complicated, and has many different functions, it is useful to divide it into sections. The first division is between the central nervous system(**CNS**) and the peripheral nervous system (**PNS**). The central nervous system coordinates incoming information and

Key terms

ANS: the autonomic nervous system, which is a network of unmyelinated nerve fibres running through the body and connecting the senses and internal organs with the central nervous system

CNS: the central nervous system, which consists of the brain and spinal cord

PNS: the peripheral nervous system, which is the network of nerve fibres connecting the various parts of the body with the central nervous system. It is made up of the SNS and the ANS.

Sensory information: information which is picked up by the sense organs of the body and passed on to the central nervous system

SNS: the somatic nervous system, which is the network of myelinated sensory and motor neurons that carry sensory information to, and instructions for movement from, the central nervous system

Stimulus: something that is detected by the sense receptors, which the nervous system will react to

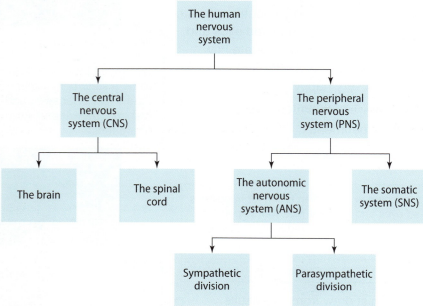

A *The structure of the nervous system*

makes decisions about movement or other activities. It consists of the brain and the spinal cord. The peripheral nervous system collects information from, and sends messages to, different parts of the body.

The peripheral nervous system itself consists of two sections: the somatic nervous system (**SNS**) and the autonomic nervous system (**ANS**). The somatic nervous system is a network of nerve fibres that runs throughout the body, and sense receptors such as those in our skin, muscles, and internal organs. The nerve fibres pass information to and from the CNS using sensory and motor neurons, and they are myelinated, that is, they are covered with the myelin sheath (a fatty wrapping), which helps the messages to travel quickly.

The other part of the peripheral nervous system is the autonomic nervous system. This is a network of special nerves which also takes information to and from the central nervous system, but more slowly because its nerve fibres are not myelinated. The autonomic nervous system uses information from our internal organs to coordinate most of our general physiological functioning, and it also responds directly to some information, like stressful or emotional events.

■ Functions of the nervous system

Each division of the nervous system has different functions. The function of the central nervous system is to coordinate incoming **sensory information** and to respond to it by sending appropriate instructions to the other parts of the nervous system. It also contains our store of knowledge, habits, and other kinds of learning, so we can combine our past experience with what is happening right now and make relevant decisions. Thinking, memory, decision-making, and language are all part of what the central nervous system does.

The two sections of the peripheral nervous system (the SNS and the ANS) have the following functions. The somatic nervous system collects information, both from the outside world and from our internal organs, and passes it on to the central nervous system. It also receives instructions from the central nervous system, for big movements or small reactions to stimuli. In general, it is what allows us to feel and move.

The autonomic nervous system acts more slowly because it is concerned with moods and feelings (see Topic 7.2). It deals with the many different emotions that we feel, responds to threats, and is also involved in major changes to the body like those which happen during puberty or pregnancy.

Building skills 1

Which of these are almost entirely CNS activity, and which involve the SNS as well?

1. Thinking about a puzzle
2. Watching a bird fly past
3. Tasting food
4. Daydreaming
5. Feeling the warmth of a scarf

Going further

Our sense organs each detect certain kinds of **stimulus**: for example, the ear picks up vibrations in the air, while the eye picks up changes in light levels. Their job is to convert that information into electrical information which can pass through the nervous system. The conversion process is called transduction. But how does it happen? Investigate this with a partner and write a short explanation for another student in your class.

Synoptic link

In Chapter 2, we looked at the difference between sensation and perception. Sensation is the information that is carried by the somatic nervous system from our sense organs to the brain or spinal cord. Perception happens after the brain has taken that information and made sense of it in some way, so it happens in the central nervous system.

Practice exam questions

1. Decide whether each of the following statements is true or false.
   a) The function of the central nervous system is to coordinate incoming sensory information. *(1 mark)*
   b) The only function of the somatic nervous system is to pass information about our internal organs to the central nervous system. *(1 mark)*
2. Using an example, explain the function of the peripheral nervous system. *(3 marks)*

Getting started

See if you can get hold of a blood pressure or pulse rate monitor. There are some phone apps that are monitors, so you might not need special equipment. Monitor your heart rate for one minute while you sit quietly. Then deliberately imagine a peaceful scene, putting yourself in that place and feeling as though you were there. Monitor your heart rate again. Did it slow down? Alternatively, think of a recent event or scene in a film that annoyed or frightened you. Did your heart rate speed up?

■ The autonomic nervous system

The autonomic nervous system (ANS) has two divisions:

- The sympathetic division sets off arousal, which can be mild like a feeling of anxiety, or extreme like the fight or flight response. It is activated when we are 'under threat'.

- The parasympathetic division allows the body to store up energy when we are not 'under threat'.

Therefore, the ANS is the part of the nervous system that helps us to react quickly and strongly in an emergency. It has lots of other functions too: for instance, it controls breathing and digestion, and is the main link between the brain and the endocrine system, which is a set of glands in the body that releases hormones into the bloodstream

Objectives

You will be able to:

- describe the key features of the fight or flight reaction

- distinguish between the sympathetic and parasympathetic divisions of the ANS

- outline the James-Lange theory of emotion.

Key term

Fight or flight response: an automatic reaction to threat, stimulated by the ANS and maintained by the endocrine system, which activates the body's reserves of energy to prepare it for action

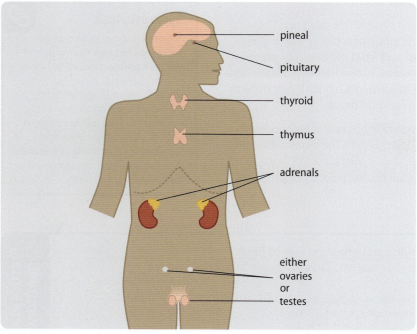

pineal	
pituitary	
thyroid	
thymus	
adrenals	
either ovaries or testes	

A *The endocrine system*

(Figure A). Hormones change the state of the body: adrenaline, for example, activates the heart, making it ready for action.

Imagine that you are trying to survive in a primitive forest. You suddenly see a fierce animal coming, which would quite like to eat you. What can you do?

Effectively, you have a choice. You can run away ('take flight') or you can try to fight. In either case, you will need all the energy and strength you can manage, so that you can survive. There is no point in keeping reserves of energy if it means you end up dead, so this is where the ANS steps in. When it detects a threat, it sends messages all over your body, to make you ready for action. It is called the **fight or flight response**.

The ANS switches from parasympathetic activity to sympathetic activity during the fight or flight response. As a result, we breathe more deeply, our heart rate increases, and the blood carries more oxygen. We sweat more to cool our muscles, the pupils of our eyes dilate, and our digestive system changes so we metabolise sugar quickly, for instant energy. We also prepare for possible injury: the blood thickens so it clots more quickly, and the brain produces natural painkillers called endorphins. These and other changes are also maintained by the endocrine system, which releases adrenaline into the body to keep the aroused state going. It all helps to make us as efficient as possible, so we can fight or escape successfully.

So, under normal circumstances, the parasympathetic division is in control of the body, storing energy. But if a threat is detected, the sympathetic division automatically switches on and the body prepares for action – the fight or flight response. Once the threat has gone away, the ANS switches back to having the parasympathetic division in control.

Figure B shows some of the different ways that the two divisions work.

> **Synoptic link**
>
> In Chapter 6 we looked at Darwin's theory of evolution. The fight or flight response is found in mammals of all kinds. How can we explain this finding?

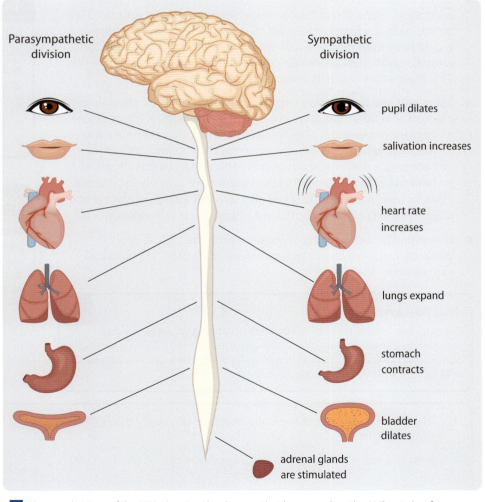

Parasympathetic division

Sympathetic division

pupil dilates

salivation increases

heart rate increases

lungs expand

stomach contracts

bladder dilates

adrenal glands are stimulated

B *The two divisions of the ANS, showing the changes that happen when the ANS switches from parasympathetic activity to sympathetic activity*

■ The James-Lange theory of emotion

One of the founding fathers of psychology, William James, noticed how the fight or flight reaction happens. He gave the example of tripping as you go downstairs, and saving yourself from falling by grabbing the banister. Your reaction happens very quickly. But afterwards, you feel your heart speeding up, you breathe deeply, you start sweating – in short, arousal kicks in. And it is then, James said, that you begin to feel scared. You experience the changes felt by your body and then interpret these as the **emotion**.

James believed that our emotions are really us perceiving physical changes in the body. The brain makes sense of these changes by concluding that we are feeling certain emotions. In James' words: 'We do not weep because we feel sorrow: we feel sorrow because we weep.'

This theory led to a number of studies investigating different aspects of this idea.

Evaluation of the James-Lange theory of emotion

- Other researchers have not been convinced that the theory is an accurate explanation of how we experience emotional arousal. This is especially the case because for the theory to be correct, there would have to be separate and distinctive patterns of physiological arousal – a different pattern for every different emotion we experience. This is not something that researchers have found.

- Schachter and Singer have suggested that it is not only physiological changes that occur when we are in a 'threat' situation. There is also a cognitive component. This means that when we experience the stimulation in the ANS, we also interpret the situation we are in, and come to a decision about how we should feel in this situation. It is these two things that lead to the emotion we actually experience. There is research supporting the idea that physiological change *and* cognitive interpretations both lead to emotional experiences.

- However, the James-Lange theory did promote a great deal of research and recognised the importance of the ANS in emotional experiences.

> ### Key term
>
> **Emotion:** the moods or feelings that a person experiences

> ### Building skills 1
>
>
>
> Which of the following might involve an arousal response?
> - Being excited about a holiday
> - Worrying about exams
> - Eating lunch
> - Watching a scary film
> - Chatting with friends

> ### Going further
>
> Many psychologists have investigated different aspects of our emotional reactions to fear and anger. What can you find out about their research?

> ### Did you know   ?
>
> Lie detectors are machines which can pick up the slight changes caused by anxiety or arousal. When someone is lying, their concern about whether it will be detected results in tiny changes to sweating, heart rate, voice timbre, and so on, and lie detectors pick up on these.

> **Practice exam questions**
>
> 1.   Identify three ways that the body responds physically during the fight or flight response. *(3 marks)*
>
> 2.   Describe and evaluate the James-Lange theory of emotion. *(6 marks)*

■ Are brains electric?

Did you know that your brain works by electricity? Your nervous system is made up of special cells which exchange chemicals to generate small electrical impulses. This is how they pass information around. These special cells are called **neurons**. There are three types of neurons in the human nervous system, each with a different function:

■ **Sensory neurons** carry information from the sense organs to the CNS. They have a cell body, with two 'stems' on either side. One end receives information from the sense organs, and the other passes it on. Each stem ends in small branches called dendrites, which spread out and connect with other cells (Figure A).

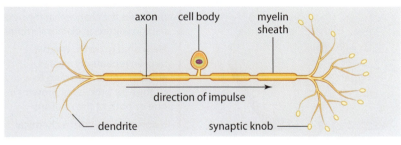

A *A sensory neuron*

■ The second type of neuron is called a **motor neuron** (Figure B) because it stimulates the muscles for movement. Motor neurons send messages from the brain to the muscles. They begin in the spinal cord, and a long axon, or 'stem', leads to the muscle, where it divides into a spread-out set of dendrites called the motor end plate, which connects with the muscles.

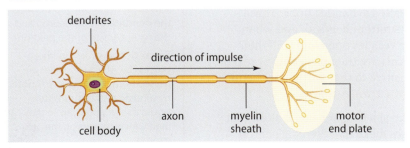

B *A motor neuron*

■ The third type of neuron has a cell body which is entirely surrounded by dendrites. It is called a **relay neuron** (Figure C), and it passes messages to other neurons within the CNS. Relay neurons make millions of connections between each other, the sensory neurons, and the motor neurons.

All three types of neuron were involved in the Getting started activity on page 151. When your knee was tapped, it stimulated sense receptors which generated an electrical impulse. That impulse was picked up by the sensory neurons and carried to the CNS – in this case, to your spinal cord. There, it was passed on to the relay neurons, which in turn stimulated motor neurons, which carried electrical impulses to your leg muscles, causing your leg to kick out. It was an automatic reaction, known as a reflex (Figure D). The fatty myelin sheath covering the axons helps the electrical impulse to travel fast, so you react quickly.

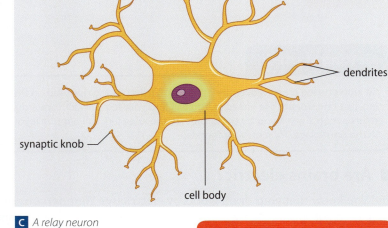

C *A relay neuron*

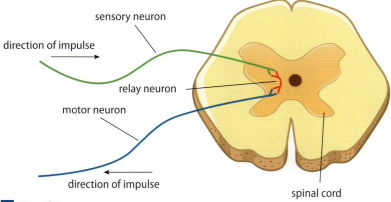

D *The reflex arc*

■ The synapse

Neurons pass messages to other neurons or muscles by releasing special chemicals, called **neurotransmitters**, into tiny gaps between dendrites. Those tiny gaps are called **synapses**. The chemical is released from swellings at the end of each dendrite, called synaptic knobs. These contain vesicles (pockets) of neurotransmitter chemical, and when an electrical impulse reaches them, the vesicles open and spill their chemicals into the synapse. The chemicals are then picked up at receptor sites on the next neuron, which are sensitive to that particular chemical (Figure E). This process is called **synaptic transmission**.

Each time a neurotransmitter is picked up at a receptor site, it alters that neuron's chemistry a little. Some synapses make the receiving neuron more likely to generate an electrical impulse. We call this **excitation**. Other

Key terms

Excitation: when a neurotransmitter binds with a receptor on the next neuron, and increases the chance that the next neuron will fire an electrical impulse

Inhibition: when a neurotransmitter binds with a receptor on the next neuron, and decreases the chance that the next neuron will fire an electrical impulse

Neuronal growth: when a neuron repeatedly excites another neuron, leading to a change (or process of growth) in one or both of the neurons

Neurotransmitter: a chemical which is released into the synapse by one neuron, and picked up by the next neuron

Relay neuron: a nerve cell that passes messages within the CNS

Reuptake: a process by which neurotransmitter is reabsorbed into the synaptic knob after it has been used during synaptic transmission

Synapse: the small gap between the dendrite of one neuron and the receptor site of the next one

Synaptic transmission: the process by which messages are passed from one neuron to another by sending neurotransmitters across the synaptic gap so they can bind with receptors on the next neuron

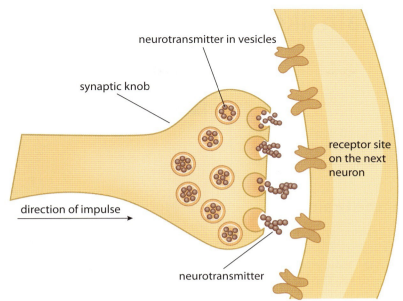

neurotransmitter in vesicles

synaptic knob

receptor site on the next neuron

direction of impulse

neurotransmitter

E *The synapse*

synapses make the neuron less likely to fire. We call this **inhibition**. Once the next neuron has fired or not, the neurotransmitter in the receptor sites will be released back into the synapse. The **reuptake** process then happens so the neurotransmitter can be reused when the next impulse arrives.

■ Hebb's theory of learning and neuronal growth

Donald Hebb suggested that if a neuron repeatedly or persistently excites another neuron, **neuronal growth** takes place, so the synaptic knob becomes larger. This means that when certain neurons act together frequently, they become established as a connection and form neural pathways. Hebb called these combinations of neurons 'cell assemblies', and suggested that each cell assembly formed a single processing unit.

Hebb argued that whenever we learn to do or remember certain things, we are developing stronger cell assemblies, and the more we use them, the better we learn and hold on to the information in that neural pathway.

Although this theory was proposed in the 1950s, it has been the basis for some research into how computers should be developed, and modern neuropsychology supports Hebb's ideas.

Building skills 1   K

Draw a diagram or a flow chart that shows how your nervous system responds when you accidentally touch a hot kettle and then automatically pull your hand away. The diagram should show how the three different types of neuron are involved in your response.

Did you know   ?

People who suffer spinal or brain damage are often paralysed, but can sometimes regain functioning by 'teaching' the brain to form new neural pathways. It takes a lot of practice and time, and is easier for young people, but even older people can sometimes be successful.

Going further

There are several neurotransmitter chemicals, but any one receptor site will only accept a particular chemical, or one which is very similar. Some drugs, such as morphine, affect the brain because they have chemical structures which are almost the same as natural neurotransmitters.

Find out more about this and write a short report that you can present to your classmates.

Practice exam questions

1. Explain what is meant by the term 'neurotransmitter'. *(2 marks)*

2. Draw and label a diagram of a sensory neuron. On your diagram label the following: axon, cell body, myelin sheath, dendrite, synaptic knob, and the direction of the impulse. *(4 marks)*

Synoptic link

As well as affecting neurotransmitters, drug use and misuse can cause many other symptoms. Look at Topic 8.5 to consider these.

Getting started

Imagine that you are trying to design a robot that can read aloud to you from a book. Make a list of the different abilities it would need to be able to do this. Compare your list with a partner's. What differences and similarities are there?

■ The structure and function of the brain

The brain is made up of millions of relay neurons that are tightly packed together. The **cerebrum** is the top layer of the brain. There are two cerebral hemispheres – one on each side of the head – and each hemisphere is divided into four areas known as **lobes**. The four lobes in each hemisphere are:

■ The **frontal lobe**: this controls thought, memory, planning, problem-solving, cognitive and social behaviours, and movement such as facial expressions. This brain region is often affected by traumatic brain injuries, particularly those caused by the forces that occur in motor vehicle accidents.

■ The **parietal lobe**: this is responsible for integrating information from other areas to form the basis of complex behaviours, including all behaviour involving the senses (such as vision, touch, body awareness and spatial orientation), so we are aware of our body position. It also has responsibility for language, helping us to form words and thoughts.

■ The **temporal lobe**: this helps us to understand and process what we hear. It is responsible for the comprehension and production of spoken language. It is also involved in how we learn and organise information, and responsible for emotions and emotional memory.

■ The **occipital lobe**: this is where all visual information is processed such as colour, shape and distance. Injury or damage to the primary visual cortex can cause vision impairments such as blindness or blind spots in visual fields.

A fifth area of the brain is called the **cerebellum**. This is a wrinkled structure and is found at the back of the brain. It is concerned with balance and coordination. These activities are carried out automatically by this area of the brain and are not under conscious control. As we become more practiced in our physical skills like walking and running, the cerebellum controls these actions so they become smoother and more automatic.

Objectives

You will be able to:

● name the major lobes of the cerebrum

● describe some functions of the cerebrum and cerebellum

● identify sensory, motor, and language areas of the cerebral cortex.

Key terms

Cerebellum: a small, wrinkled structure at the back of the brain which coordinates motor movement, dexterity, and balance, among other things

Cerebrum: the largest part of the brain in humans, which consists of two large cerebral hemispheres

Frontal lobe: the area of the brain that controls cognitive processes such as thought and memory

Lobes of the brain: each half of the brain is divided into four areas or lobes: the frontal lobe, the temporal lobe, the parietal lobe and the occipital lobe

Occipital lobe: the area of the brain where visual information is processed

Parietal lobe: the area of the brain that is responsible for integrating information from other areas to form complex behaviours

Temporal lobe: the area of the brain that is responsible for aspects such as the comprehension and production of spoken language

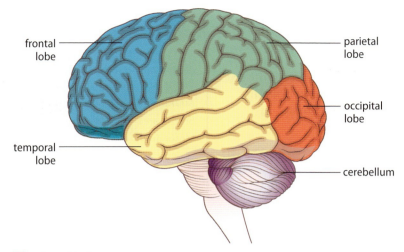

frontal lobe

parietal lobe

occipital lobe

temporal lobe

cerebellum

A *Lobes of the brain*

While it is reasonable to identify major separate functions of the lobes of the brain, it is generally recognised that most actions and abilities result from the cooperative work of multiple regions of the brain (functional networks). Injury to any component of a functional network can impair abilities associated with that network.

■ Localisation of function in the brain

We do not know what every part of the brain does. But we know that some brain functions are associated with particular areas on the cerebral cortex (the folded outer layers of the cerebrum). These **localised functions** include movement, touch, vision, hearing, and language.

The area which controls movement is called the **motor area**. It controls deliberate movement, using motor neurons to send messages to our muscles. Active parts of the body, such as our fingers and thumbs, have a larger share of the motor cortex than less active parts of the body, like the torso. The area behind this is the **somatosensory area**, which deals with touch. The more sensitive an area of the body is, the larger the amount of somatosensory cortex it involves.

The two cerebral hemispheres control the opposite sides of the body. So the sensory and motor strips on the right hemisphere deal with the left side of the body, and those on the left hemisphere deal with the right side.

Did you know

It is often said that humans have five senses: vision, hearing, touch, taste, and smell. But really there are at least seven:

- a sixth sense, called proprioception, which tells us the position of our bodies and limbs
- a seventh sense, called kinaesthesia, which tells us when the body, or any part of it, is moving.

Synoptic link

Look at the diagram of the cortical homunculus on page 159. It is a way of showing the relationship between how sensitive an area of the body is and how much of the somatosensory area it requires.

Going further

When parts of the brain have been damaged by injury or disease, it is likely that people with such damage will lose some abilities. These may be motor related (such as not being able to walk steadily) or cognitive related (such as experiencing memory problems). New research has involved looking at ways of replacing damaged tissue in the brain with new cells. Use the Internet to look up research into embryonic stem cell treatments. Discuss the benefits and ethical issues of such research.

Exam tip !

Make sure you can produce a sketch of the brain on which you can accurately label the four lobes and the cerebellum.

The **visual cortex** is in the occipital lobe, just above the cerebellum. It was first identified from servicemen in the First World War who suffered shrapnel damage to the back of the head, and became partially blind as a result. The visual cortex receives information from both eyes through the optic nerves, and a different area on the temporal lobe, the **auditory cortex**, does the same job for hearing. It receives information from the ears, so damage to this part of the brain produces hearing loss.

Language areas of the brain

One of the things which distinguishes human beings from animals is how we use language. Humans have specialised areas on the left hemisphere, which are devoted to language processing. **Broca's area** is at the base of the left frontal lobe and deals with speech production. People with damage to Broca's area can understand what is said to them, but have problems saying things themselves (a condition known as motor aphasia).

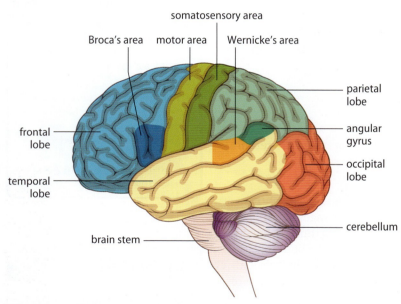

B *Sensory and language areas in the brain*

Wernicke's area, in the temporal lobe, is concerned with understanding speech. People with damage to this area can speak perfectly well, but they have problems understanding what other people are saying to them (a condition known as Wernicke's aphasia). The **angular gyrus**, at the back of the parietal lobe, receives information about written language from the visual cortex, and interprets it as being like speech. People who have suffered injury to this area can experience difficulties in reading (a condition known as acquired dyslexia).

Key terms

Angular gyrus: an area on the parietal lobe which deals with reading

Auditory cortex: the area of the cerebral cortex concerned with hearing

Broca's area: an area on the frontal lobe which deals with speech production

Visual cortex: the area of the cerebral cortex concerned with vision

Wernicke's area: an area on the temporal lobe which deals with understanding speech

Synoptic link

In Topic 2.2 we saw how some depth perception comes from comparing the images from both eyes. When we judge where a noise is coming from we compare messages from both ears. For this reason, our eyes and ears send messages to both cerebral hemispheres for vision and hearing.

C *Speech therapy is a treatment for aphasia*

Did you know **?**

If we become very practised with a particular part of the body – like the gamers who play video games for hours with thumb-driven controllers – the area of the motor cortex devoted to that part of the body becomes larger too.

Building skills 2

Use the information you have learned from this section to work out what parts of the brain would be involved if you (not a robot) were reading aloud from a book.

Exam tip **!**

Draw an outline of the brain. On a set of sticky notes, write down the names of localised functions of the brain, and also the major lobes. When you have done this, put it aside for at least a day. Then take up the set of sticky notes, and attach each one to the outline of the brain in the right place to test your knowledge.

1. Briefly explain where the cerebellum is and what two of its functions are. *(3 marks)*

2. Explain what might happen to a person's ability to use language if there is damage to a language area of the brain. *(2 marks)*

3. Draw and label a diagram of the human brain. On your diagram label the following: frontal lobe, temporal lobe, parietal lobe and the occipital lobe. *(2 marks)*

4. Explain what is meant by localisation of function in the brain. *(6 marks)*

Practice exam questions

Penfield's interpretive cortex study (1959)

Aim: To investigate the workings of the conscious mind.

Study design: Clinical case studies – an investigation of brain function in a number of patients who were undergoing open brain surgery.

Method: Some types of brain surgery require the patient to be conscious, so the surgeon can be confident that any actions occur in the right place. This is painless because the brain has no sense receptors. In this study, the surgeon probed different areas of the cortex using gentle electrical stimulation, and asked the patients to say what they experienced.

Results: The results were qualitative, and these are some examples.

Stimulation of the temporal lobe made one patient report that he could hear a piano playing, and could even identify the song. When a different place was stimulated, the patient reported a clear memory. As a control, the surgeon informed this patient that he was about to stimulate again, but did not activate the electrode. After a pause, the patient reported 'nothing'.

A female patient reported hearing an orchestra playing a particular tune when the temporal lobe was stimulated. The music stopped when the electrode was removed, and came back when the same place was stimulated again. This was repeated several times, always with the same result. The patient herself could hear the tune so clearly that she believed that a gramophone (music player) was being turned on in the operating theatre at these times, and still insisted this was true some days after the operation.

A boy heard his mother telling his brother that he had got his coat on backwards. When the same area on the temporal lobe was stimulated again, he heard the same conversation, even after some lapse of time.

In earlier research, Penfield had stimulated the visual cortex, and found that people 'saw' images, such as balloons floating into the sky. He had also found that stimulation of the motor and sensory areas produced movements or the sensation of being touched. From these and other cases – for example, Wernicke's area is also in the temporal lobe – Penfield was able to conclude that the temporal lobe is active in interpreting meaning.

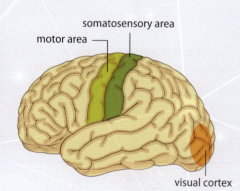

A *Some of the areas of the brain stimulated in Penfield's study*

Conclusion: Penfield concluded that there was evidence for localisation of function (the idea that some psychological functions are controlled from particular places in the brain) in the cerebral cortex.

Source: Penfield, W. (1959) 'The Interpretive Cortex', Science, 129, 1719–1725

Building skills 1

What examples of brain surgery can you find in TV and films? Collect as many examples as you can. Are they realistic, and do they fit with real research into brain functioning?

 E

■ Evaluation

Why the study is important

- The study shows how certain areas of the cerebral cortex may be involved in particular functions of the brain. The study investigated living brains instead of just looking for damage in dead brains during post mortems.

- The study showed that even complex memories, such as conversations, are stored in the brain.

Limitations of the study

- The patients were having brain surgery because they were severely epileptic. Therefore, they may not have been typical of the general population (see Topic 4.2).

- The findings were different for each individual, so it is hard to make generalisations, for example about memory storage.

- People may have found it difficult to put some of their experiences into words.

Synoptic link

 In Chapter 4 we looked at the distinction between quantitative and qualitative data. This is a study which uses qualitative data. In this study, what advantages does this method of data collection give us?

Going further

Wernicke and Broca investigated localised language functions in the nineteenth century. What research methods were they able to use? How is it different for modern researchers?

Exam tip

 Revise the structure of the neuron and the synapse (Topic 7.3) so you are able to explain clearly how electrical stimulation can make a part of the brain more or less active.

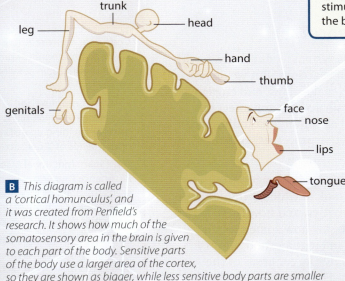

B *This diagram is called a 'cortical homunculus', and it was created from Penfield's research. It shows how much of the somatosensory area in the brain is given to each part of the body. Sensitive parts of the body use a larger area of the cortex, so they are shown as bigger, while less sensitive body parts are smaller because they use a smaller area of the somatosensory cortex.*

Objectives

You will be able to:

- define neuropsychology and cognitive neuroscience
- distinguish between three main methods of scanning the brain
- explain how neural damage can affect behaviour.

A *Do you remember more details about the left side of this image than the right?*

■ What is cognitive neuroscience?

We have seen how the peripheral nervous system feeds the brain with information and how the brain directs our reactions. But we do not just react, we also think, decide, imagine, make plans, and engage in social activities. All of these involve brain activity and affect our behaviour. **Cognitive neuroscience** is all about understanding the relationship between the brain, our cognitive processes, and our behaviour.

Neuropsychologists are psychologists, who study how brain activity relates to psychological processes. They look at which different areas of the brain are involved in cognitive activities, and how these areas link up with one another. In Topic 7.4 we saw how some specific areas of the cerebral cortex are involved in language and sensory functions. Other brain functions may involve larger areas of the cortex, or several areas working together. For example, the parietal lobes of the brain – particularly on the right side – are involved

Key terms

Cognitive neuroscience: the study of how cognitive processes connect with brain activity and structure

CT scan: Computerised Tomography, which scans the brain by building up a 3D image from a series of X-ray 'slices'

fMRI scan: functional Magnetic Resonance Imaging, which scans the brain by identifying the magnetic activity of water molecules in active brain cells

PET scan: Positron Emission Tomography, which locates blood flow in the brain by detecting radioactive tracers

in attention. There is no single part of the brain for memory, but neuropsychologists have found that our memory for places links the temporal lobes of the cortex with a small sub-cortical structure called the hippocampus.

So some areas of the brain have specific functions, some are part of complex systems processing other functions, and some appear to be involved in the general functioning of the brain but are not, as far as we know, involved in any specific psychological process. Brain scans have helped neuropsychologists to find out more about how the brain works, but we are still far from understanding everything.

■ Scanning the brain

Brain scans are ways of looking at the brain in living people. There are many types of brain scan, but we will look at three: **CT scans**, **PET scans**, and **fMRI scans**.

CT scans

CT scans map the brain by taking a number of X-ray 'slices' of the brain, and combining them to build up a full image. Some types of tissue are denser than others, and this shows up in the X-rays. Bone is the most dense, but nerve cell bodies (grey matter), are less dense than myelinated nerve fibres (white matter), so they look different too. Tumours and blood clots also show up with this method, so it is useful for medical purposes.

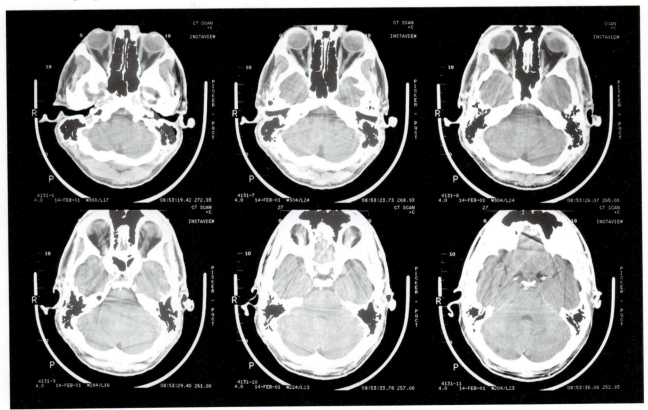

B *A CT brain scan*

PET scans

PET scans work by monitoring a small amount of radioactive chemical which is put into the blood supply. Active brain cells use more blood than passive ones, so the scanner can see which parts of the brain are particularly active. PET scans can highlight brain pathways as well as specific areas of activity, and they can show if there are blockages in the blood flow around the brain. PET scanning is not used by researchers much nowadays, partly because of the slight risk from radioactivity, but it can be useful in medical contexts. (PET scanning was used in Tulving's 'Gold' memory study – see pages 164–165.)

fMRI scans

Perhaps the most popular modern method is functional Magnetic Resonance Imaging (fMRI). It works because the water molecules in brain cells have tiny magnetic fields which can be influenced by the strong magnetic field of the scanner, and which are slightly different if the cell is active than when it is quiet. A whole fMRI brain scan only takes about 2 seconds, so researchers can explore brain activity and cognition. For example, the person may read a word, or think of a special event, and the scan shows which parts of the brain are active as they do it. It is a popular method for researchers, partly because of its accuracy, but also because there are no X-rays or radioactive substances involved.

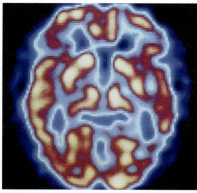

C *A PET brain scan*

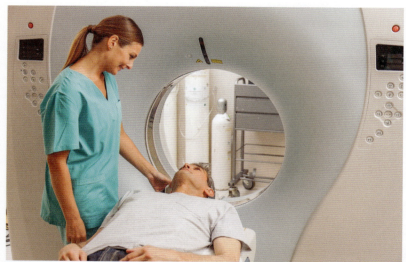

D *A patient undergoing an fMRI scan*

■ When the nervous system gets damaged

Neurological damage, such as injuries to the spinal cord, can produce physical problems like paralysis, or an inability to control particular muscles. If motor nerve fibres are severed, the brain cannot send messages to the muscles, and if sensory nerves are damaged, the person cannot feel anything in those areas. The location of the damage affects which parts of the body are affected. For example, damage to the spinal cord near the neck may paralyse the whole body; damage lower down may paralyse the lower limbs, and so on. Head injuries that damage the motor cortex can also produce paralysis, and if the cerebellum becomes

Key terms

Neurological damage: injury or harm to the nervous system, which affects how the neurons work

Stroke: a sudden interruption to the blood supply in a part of the brain

Symptom: one of a collection of physical changes that tell us that some kind of disorder or problem exists

damaged the patient may lose their balance and become unable to coordinate movements.

The brain can also become damaged by **strokes**. A stroke is an interruption to the blood supply to the brain, either through bleeding or because some blood vessels have become blocked. Nerve cells can die because of a lack of nutrients carried by the blood, so if the blockage or bleeding continues, it can produce permanent damage. If the blood supply is restored quickly, damage can be minimised. This is why strokes need to be treated quickly, usually with drugs that will thin the blood and remove clots. **Symptoms** of strokes include slurred speech, dragging muscles on one side of the face, and lessened function of the muscles on one side of the body.

After a stroke, people often experience emotional and behavioural changes. This is because a stroke affects the brain, and our brain controls all of our behaviour and emotions, not just our movements. Injury from a stroke may make a person forgetful, careless, irritable or confused. Stroke survivors may also feel anxiety, anger or depression.

Stroke survivors may have a problem with memory. Someone who fails to bathe or change clothes may need a checklist on the bathroom mirror as a reminder. There may be other problems. The person may not respond appropriately in social situations – shouting out loud, for example. Inappropriate behaviour should be discussed immediately and in a matter-of-fact way. Many physical disabilities resulting from a stroke improve with time. Behaviour changes and emotional health can also improve over time.

Recovery from neural damage is sometimes possible, but it is always very hard work. The brain has to learn to create new neural pathways, and that needs lots of effort. But recent research has shown that sometimes, those efforts can even result in growing new nerve fibres, although this could take months or years.

> ## Synoptic link
> As we saw in Chapter 1, a mnemonic is a way of helping people to remember things. How does the FAST mnemonic help people to remember what to do?

Going further

Measuring the overall activity of the brain using EEGs (electro-encephalograms) can show us patterns of brain activity, such as sleep, wakefulness, relaxation, and even epileptic seizures.

What can EEGs tell us about how we sleep? Write a short presentation to make to your class.

Did you know   **?**

FAST is a mnemonic to remind people what to do if they think someone has had a stroke. It stands for:

- Face weakness: Is one side of the person's face drooping? Can they smile properly?
- Arm weakness: Can the person raise both of their arms, and keep them raised for ten seconds or more?
- Speech problems: Can they speak clearly, or has their speech become slurred?
- Time: If they have any of these three symptoms, it is important to call medical help immediately, so normal blood supply can be restored as quickly as possible.

Practice exam questions

1. Give two scanning techniques used to identify brain functioning. *(2 marks)*

2. Identify one possible cause of neurological damage. *(1 mark)*

3. Briefly outline two different effects that neurological damage can have on motor abilities or behaviour. *(2 marks)*

Tulving's 'Gold' memory study (1989)

Aim: To explore connections between types of memory and brain activity.

Study design: Case studies

Method: Six people were injected with a mildly radioactive gold isotope, which spread through the bloodstream and into the brain. The gold isotope had a half-life of only 30 seconds, so it presented minimal risk to the participants. The distribution of these particles was measured using a form of PET scanning called regional cerebral blood flow, which measures blood flow in different areas of the brain. The study compared **episodic memory**, in this case the memory of something they had experienced personally, like a holiday or a trip, with **semantic memory**, such as knowledge they had learned through reading a book. The researchers also looked at whether the memory was recent or whether it had been established some time ago. The participants were all volunteers, and chose their own topics.

Each participant lay on a couch with eyes closed and began thinking about the topic. After 60 seconds, the gold isotope was injected, and after 7–8 seconds a reading of rCBF was taken. The reading lasted 2.4 seconds, and consisted of 12 rapid scans of 0.2 second each.

Each participant experienced eight trials in all, with a rest of two minutes in between. The design involved two kinds of memory (episodic and semantic), two time periods for the memories (recent or remote), and each of these conditions was investigated twice.

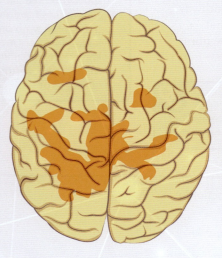
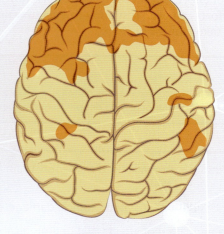

semantic memory   episodic memory

A *The difference between episodic and semantic memory*

Source: Tulving, E. (1989) 'Memory, performance, knowledge and experience,' European Journal of Cognitive Psychology 1(1) 3–26

Results: Three of the participants were dropped from the analysis because their results were inconsistent. However, the remaining three showed clear differences in blood flow patterns depending on whether they were remembering episodic or semantic information. This difference was the same regardless of whether what they were remembering was recent or had taken place a long time ago. Figure A shows the general differences in blood flow patterns between episodic memories and semantic memories found in this study. In general, episodic recollection produced more activation of the frontal and temporal lobes, while semantic recollection produced more activity in the parietal and occipital lobes of the cerebral cortex.

Conclusion: Tulving concluded that semantic and episodic memories produce activity in different parts of the brain.

■ Evaluation

Why the study is important

- The study was one of the first to show how we can investigate cognitive processes in the living brain.

- The study showed different areas of brain activity are related to cognitive processes.

- It used ethical procedures and the participants were fully informed before giving their consent.

Limitations of the study

- Only three participants showed the effects, so they may not apply to everyone.

- There was no way of controlling what people were actually thinking about at the exact moment of the scan.

- The participants were fully informed volunteers who may have tried very hard to get the procedure to work.

Key terms

Episodic memory: unique memories which are concerned with personal experiences or events

Semantic memory: memories which are concerned with general knowledge rather than personal experience

Building skills 1

Using your own memories, make a list of five examples each of episodic and semantic memories. **K**

Synoptic link

In Chapter 1 we looked at the different types of memory. Tulving distinguished between episodic memory and semantic memory. How many other types of memory did you learn about, and how might you convert them into mental activity that could be studied during a brain scan?

Going further

What is meant by the half-life of a radioactive substance? Explain why it was important in this study that the radioactive material used had a very short half-life.

Exam tip

 The design of this study involved two pairs of conditions. Revise counterbalancing as a research method (see page 72), so that you could describe how the conditions should have been arranged to control for order effects.

7.5 Key research study: Tulving

7 Revision checklist

You should now be able to:

Structure and function of the nervous system

- [ ] explain how the human nervous system is divided into the central nervous system and peripheral nervous system (including the somatic and autonomic nervous systems)

- [ ] describe the basic functions of these nervous systems

- [ ] explain the fight or flight response and how it is controlled by the autonomic nervous system

- [ ] describe and evaluate the James-Lange theory of emotion

See pages 146–150

Neuron structure and function

- [ ] describe the differences between sensory, relay and motor neurons, and explain their functions

- [ ] explain how synaptic transmission works, including the release and reuptake of neurotransmitters, and excitation and inhibition

- [ ] describe and evaluate Hebb's theory of learning and neuronal growth

See pages 151–153

Structure and function of the brain

- [ ] describe the basic structure of the following parts of the brain: the frontal lobe, the temporal lobe, the parietal lobe, the occipital lobe and the cerebellum

- [ ] explain the basic functions of the following parts of the brain: the frontal lobe, the temporal lobe, the parietal lobe, the occipital lobe and the cerebellum

- [ ] explain the localised functions of the following parts of the brain: the motor, somatosensory, visual, auditory and language areas

- [ ] **key research study:** describe and evaluate Penfield's interpretive cortex study

See pages 154–159

An introduction to neuropsychology

- [ ] understand what cognitive neuroscience is

- [ ] explain how the following scanning techniques are used to identify brain functioning: CT, PET and fMRI scans

- [ ] explain how neurological damage can affect motor abilities and behaviour

- [ ] **key research study:** describe and evaluate Tulving's 'gold' memory study

See pages 160–165

Practice exam questions

1. Read the following statements and decide whether they are true or false.

   a) Functions of the cerebellum include coordination of motor movement, dexterity, and balance. *(1 mark)*

   b) Neurons are special cells which exchange chemicals to generate small electrical impulses. *(1 mark)*

   c) A synapse is a series of connections between neurons which act in sequence to make a familiar 'route' from one area of the brain to another. *(1 mark)*

2. Describe and evaluate Hebb's theory of learning and neuronal growth. *(6 marks)*

   > These type of questions require an answer that has a balance of description and evaluation. Writing an extremely detailed description cannot make up for not giving any evaluation at all. Both are important.

3. Scientists used an fMRI scan to examine the motor cortex of 20 participants. Half of the participants regularly played video games for more than 3 hours a day and the other half rarely played any video games. The scientists measured the area of the motor cortex devoted to the use of the arms and hands.

   a) Identify the independent variable in this experiment. *(1 mark)*

   b) The results for the experiment described above are shown in the table below.

Participants	Percentage of the motor cortex devoted to the use of the arms and hands
Regular gamers	32.5%
Non-gamers	26.8%

   How much larger is the area of the motor cortex devoted to the use of arms and hands in the regular gamers compared to the non-gamers? Show your workings. *(2 marks)*

4. a) Other than an fMRI scan, identify one other scanning technique used to identify brain functioning. *(1 mark)*

   b) Describe the scanning technique you have identified in 4 a). *(3 marks)*

   > It is important in questions that are connected, like these two, that both parts of your answers match. If your described scanning technique does not match with the one you identified, you will lose valuable marks.

5. Evaluate Tulving's 'gold' memory study. *(6 marks)*

   > Generic statements about research, such as 'it's not ecologically valid', will earn few if any marks. It is important to elaborate these types of statements to show clear understanding of the idea being used.

8 Psychological problems

8.1 What is mental health?

Getting started

Take two minutes to write down what you think would be a good definition for the term 'mental health'.

■ Characteristics of mental health

Mental health is more than not having a **mental health problem**. It is also how you feel about yourself and how you deal with life. Mental health has a number of different characteristics. A mentally healthy person will display some, but not necessarily all of them. They include:

- not being overcome by difficult feelings
- having good relationships with others
- being able to deal with disappointments and problems
- being able to cope with stresses and demands of everyday life
- effectively coping with difficulties and challenges
- being able to make decisions
- functioning as part of society
- positive engagement with society.

Although a mentally healthy person will generally have many of these characteristics, not having some of them, does not mean someone has a mental health problem.

■ Mental health problems

Mental health problems affect the way you think, feel, and behave. Some mental health problems are more common, such as depression and anxiety. Other mental health problems occur less often, such as schizophrenia and bipolar disorder.

There are two recognised ways of identifying and diagnosing mental health problem. These are version ten of the World Health Organisation's **International Classification of Diseases** (ICD-10) and edition five of the American Psychiatric Association's *Diagnostic and Statistical Manual of Mental Disorders* (DSM-5).

Objectives

You will be able to:

- describe the characteristics of mental health
- describe cultural variations in beliefs about mental health problems
- understand how and why the incidence of significant mental health problems has changed over time.

Building skills 1

Working with a partner, try to think of at least three ways in which people can show positive engagement with society. Then think of at least three effective ways for coping with difficulties and challenges. Use the bullet list to the left to help you.   K   A

A *Ways to stay mentally healthy*

Cultural variations in beliefs about mental health problems

Throughout history, mental health problems have often been believed to have a supernatural or spiritual origin. Suggested causes for people's symptoms included possession by evil spirits, being cursed, and being a witch. In Europe and North American during the fourteenth to the seventeenth centuries, many people, especially women, were accused and tried for being witches. It is now believed that mental health problems may have resulted in some of the behaviours that led to people being accused.

In many cultural groups, having mental health problems is seen as shameful. In Asian cultures, for example, mental health problems are strongly stigmatised and seen as a form of personal weakness. The **stigma** of mental health problems can result in people experiencing economic, social, and legal discrimination. In cultures where a person's behaviour reflects on their whole family, it is common for people with mental health problems to be kept away from other people and cared for by the family.

Cultural beliefs also influence the type of treatment people receive. Treatments are closely linked to beliefs about the cause of mental health problems. In cultures where these are viewed as having a biological cause, medication is commonly used. In cultures that view mental health problems as having a spiritual cause, treatments may range from prayer to exorcisms. Self-help groups and therapy are most popular in cultures where sharing openly about yourself and your emotions is valued. In cultures where shame over having mental health problems is very common, people may be kept completely isolated, and unable to talk to anyone at all about what they are experiencing.

Key terms

International Classification of Diseases (ICD): lists of symptoms and other features of different physical and mental health problems, which also provide the criteria for diagnosing them

Mental health: a person's emotional and psychological wellbeing; this allows them to cope with the normal stresses of everyday life and to function in society

Mental health problems: diagnosable conditions in which a person's thoughts, feelings, and behaviours change and they are less able to cope and function

Stigma: situations, people, or characteristics that are disapproved of and seen as shameful by much of society

Did you know ?

One in four people in the UK have a mental health problem in any given year.

Building skills 2

Working with a partner, design a questionnaire to find out about attitudes and beliefs about mental health problems within different cultures. Look back at Topic 4.3 on questionnaires to help you.

A

Going further

Significantly more money is spent on mental health care in Western countries than elsewhere in the world. However, this does not necessarily mean that people with mental health problems are better cared for.

Do some research on the provision of care for young people with mental health problems in the UK. Share your findings with the rest of your class.

B *The diagnosis of mental health problems can be affected by culture*

Are mental health problems becoming more common?

Getting started

Working with a partner, look at the characteristics of mental health and think about our modern way of life. How might modern life negatively affect our mental health?

Key term

Isolation: being or feeling alone and separate from other people

Data suggests that, worldwide, more people than ever before are being diagnosed with a mental health problem. Although some conditions (such as schizophrenia) seem to occur at a consistent rate, others (like depression) have growing rates of diagnosis.

But rising diagnosis levels may not actually mean that more people have a mental health problem. Some medical professions believe that changes in the classifications of some conditions mean that more people now meet the criteria for diagnosis. More people are also seeking medical and psychiatric treatment as many cultures come to rely less on traditional methods of dealing with mental health problems.

Changes in diagnosis levels may explain some of the upward trend in mental health problems, but there may also be other factors involved.

Challenges of modern living and its effects on mental health

Living in more populated areas can increase stress. Brain scans show that people living in cities have more active amygdala than people living in less populated areas. One role of the amygdala is responding to threats.

Loneliness and **isolation** can be factors in mental health problems such as depression and anxiety. A recent survey for the Mental Health Foundation found that one in ten people in the UK report feeling lonely and that this is increasing amongst young people. Changes in the way we live may be behind increasing levels of loneliness.

Synoptic link

See pages 160–163 for more information about the use of brain scans in psychology.

More people are living on their own, often some distance away from family members. This may be down to needing to move for work, family breakdown, and people living longer.

Technology and social networking sites have changed the way that people interact. People can connect with others all over the world, but there are also concerns that technology may be making isolation worse as it increasingly replaces face-to-face communication. 18 per cent of the participants in the Mental Health Foundation survey said they thought they spent too much time communicating with family and friends online rather than in person.

C *Are social network sites reducing the amount of time we physically spend with friends?*

Increased recognition of the nature of mental health problems

Although there has been recognition of mental health problems throughout history, they have been viewed as having many different causes.

Current Western understanding of biological and psychological causes began to develop during the nineteenth century. At this time, classification systems were first developed and psychiatry became a specific area of medicine. The early twentieth century saw the development of psychoanalysis and the mid-twentieth century saw drugs increasingly become the most common way of treating mental health problems.

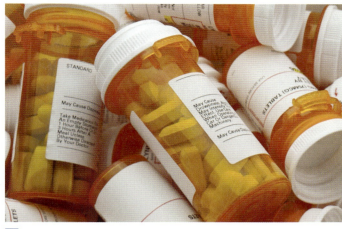

D *Prescription medication is increasingly used to treat mental health problems*

Traditional understanding has generally focused on supernatural and spiritual factors. Although biological and psychological causes are now becoming more accepted, myths and misconceptions are still widespread, especially in rural areas in developing countries.

As more people recognise the biological and psychological nature of mental health problems, they are also more likely to seek medical and psychiatric treatment. This increases worldwide diagnosis rates.

Reducing social stigma

The term 'mental health' was first used in the early twentieth century to try to reduce stigma by focusing on health rather than illness. But a hundred years later, being diagnosed with a mental health problem can still be hugely stigmatising.

However, recent findings in the National Attitudes to Mental Illness survey show that opinions in the UK are changing. This may be the result of a variety of things, including campaigns such as 'Time to Change' and well-known personalities speaking openly about their own experiences.

The World Health Organisation (WHO) views stigma and discrimination towards people with mental health problems as one of the world's most important health issues. Although one reason for diagnosis levels increasing may be the lessening of social stigma, in order for everyone to feel able to seek the treatment they need, more needs to be done.

> ### Building skills 3
>
> Create a poster aimed at helping people to have more positive and accepting views of mental health problems. The 'Time to Change' website (www.time-to-change.org.uk/) may be a helpful resource for this activity. **A**

> ### Did you know **?**
>
> 'Stigma' is a Greek word for a mark used to show that people were traitors, criminals, or slaves.

> ### Exam tip **!**
>
> When you are asked to explain 'what is meant by' a term, you need to give a precise definition like the key terms in this book.

> 1. Decide whether each of the following statements is true or false.
>
>   a) Positive engagement with society and effectively coping with challenges are both characteristics of mental health. *(1 mark)*
>   b) Very few cultures view having a mental health problem as shameful or something to be disapproved of. *(1 mark)*
>
> 2. What is meant by the term 'mental health'? *(2 marks)*
>
> 3. Discuss possible reasons for changes in the number of diagnosed mental health problems. *(6 marks)*

Practice exam questions

What are the effects of mental health problems?

■ Effects on individuals

People with mental health problems can have many difficulties coping with everyday life. Trouble sleeping, low energy levels, and poor concentration levels all make being in education or work more difficult. Developing a condition earlier in life can stop individuals from finishing their education or training. People in the UK who have a mental health problem are four times more likely to be out of work. Unemployment and low income can increase stress and anxiety and may well make mental health problems worse.

Mental health problems can also have a negative impact on physical wellbeing. People can find it hard to follow treatment programmes for their mental health condition or for other health conditions they may have. Possible reasons for this include anxiety about side effects of medication, being too depressed to attend appointments, and forgetting to take medication due to concentration difficulties. Changes in appetite and side effects of medication can result in weight loss or gain, and low energy and mood can reduce physical exercise levels. People with mental health problems also have higher rates of drug and alcohol abuse.

Relationships can be damaged in a number of ways. Research suggests that 50 per cent of family members of someone with a mental health problem may also develop some form of mental health problem. Family members may end up becoming caregivers, which can increase stress and cause conflict. The effect on the household income can also increase stress levels. Children may not understand why their parents are different or unable to care for them and they may blame themselves. Some children end up becoming the parents' caregiver and others may end up in the care system. People can also become very isolated. The stigma of mental health problems may mean that people choose not to talk about their situation and low mood can lead people to simply withdraw into themselves.

A *Parent-child relationships can be affected by mental health problems*

■ Effects on society

The implications for the economy are one of the main societal effects of mental health problems. A study by the WHO found that in developed countries such as the UK, 15 per cent of the economic cost of all health issues is due to mental health problems. The Sainsbury Centre for Mental Health has calculated that decreased work productivity due to mental health problems costs the UK economy over 15 billion pounds every year.

Most individuals with mental health problems do not commit violent crimes, and people with mental health problems are actually more of a danger to themselves. However, a Ministry of Justice study found that 49 per cent of female and 23 per cent of male prisoners were suffering from anxiety and depression. This compares to 19 per cent of females and 12 per cent of males in the general population. These figures may suggest a link between mental health problems and crime or they may indicate a link between imprisonment and mental health problems.

Mental health problems may mean that social care costs increase. A person with a mental health condition may have a variety of needs to be met. In a welfare state such as the UK, this can result in increased spending in areas such as the health system, social housing, and benefit payments.

B *Mental health problems can affect the economic situation of individuals and society*

1. Identify two effects of mental health problems on society. *(2 marks)*

2. Discuss at least one way in which relationships may be affected by mental health problems. *(4 marks)*

Practice exam questions

■ The differences between unipolar depression, bipolar depression, and sadness

Because depression is often linked with its main symptom of **sadness** or low mood, many people are unsure of the difference between them. Sadness is a normal emotional reaction to certain situations or events, while depression often occurs without any obvious trigger. Sadness may seem like it goes on for a long period of time, but is not a continuous feeling that lasts for weeks or months. Sadness hurts and is unpleasant, but it is normal and it does not last. Depression affects every part of our daily lives and often does not get better without medical or therapeutic treatment.

Unipolar depression is also known as clinical depression or depression. Generally, people with depression have a continuous low mood, and loss of enjoyment and energy. 'Uni' comes from Latin and means 'one'. Someone with unipolar depression only experiences a change of mood in one direction.

The medical term for **bipolar depression** is bipolar affective disorder. It is also known as manic depression. 'Bi' comes from Latin and means 'two'. Someone with bipolar depression experiences two types of mood change. As well as having depressive type symptoms such as low mood, people with bipolar disorder also have high moods known as mania. During a manic episode, people may have increased energy and feelings of extreme excitement. They may be unable to sleep, be more talkative, and may do risky or extreme things.

A *Sadness is a normal emotional response*

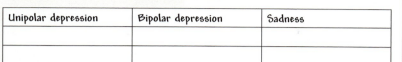
■ Diagnosing unipolar depression

Only a doctor can give a formal diagnosis of depression. In order to diagnose depression, doctors ask a number of standard questions based around the diagnostic criteria set out in the ICD-10 and DSM-5 (see Topic 8.3). Because some medical conditions have similar symptoms to depression, a doctor may also do a physical examination as well as blood and urine tests.

The ICD-10 gives a number of possible symptoms for depression. The number and severity of the symptoms an individual is experiencing, determines whether a depressive episode is considered to be mild, moderate, or severe. Symptoms would generally need to be continuously present for at least two weeks for a diagnosis of depression.

The symptoms given in the ICD-10 for a depressive episode include:

- low mood
- reduced energy and activity levels
- changes to sleep pattern
- changes to appetite levels
- decreased self-confidence
- lack of interest and enjoyment
- reduced concentration and focus
- feelings of guilt and worthlessness
- negative thoughts about the future
- suicidal thoughts.

B *Depression includes continuous low mood*

Getting started

Without looking back, outline the use of the ICD in diagnosing unipolar depression. When you have finished, ask a partner to check your answer.

Theories of depression suggest that the causes are biological, psychological, and social. Each of these areas and the relationship between them is complex and this makes it difficult to determine a definite cause of depression. We will consider two of these areas in more detail.

■ The influence of nature – a biological explanation for depression

One explanation for depression is that it is influenced by **nature**. It is suggested that whether an individual will suffer from depression is predetermined by their genes and biology. Therefore, one biological explanation is that depression can be caused by an imbalance of neurotransmitters (chemicals). The brain uses these chemicals to communicate with itself and with the nervous system and the body. These chemical messages are received and sent by the brain's neurons (nerve cells). Neurons are constantly communicating with each other using neurotransmitters, and this communication is very important for the brain to function properly. Serotonin and norepinephrine are two of the main neurotransmitters to be linked with depression.

Serotonin helps to control biological functions like sleep patterns, aggression levels, appetite, and mood. There are a number of theories about the effect of serotonin levels on depression. Researchers used PET scans to study the brains of depressed people and compared them to the brains of people who were not depressed. They measured levels of a serotonin receptor and found less in the brains of the depressed people, especially in the hippocampus. The hippocampus is part of the temporal lobe and it is involved in storing our memories and connecting them to our emotions. MRI scans have also found that people who are depressed have a smaller hippocampus.

Norepinephrine gets the brain and body ready for action and high levels are released during the fight or flight response. Autopsy studies of people who have had many depressive episodes have found that they have fewer neurons that release norepinephrine. Other research has found that in some people, low levels of serotonin may cause a decrease in norepinephrine levels.

Although research does suggest that neurotransmitters are somehow involved in depression, it is very difficult to actually measure the levels of chemicals in the brain. The brain is also very complex and there are many chemical reactions that affect your mood in some way. Therefore it is unlikely that an imbalance of one neurotransmitter completely explains why depression occurs.

Objectives

You will be able to:

- understand how an imbalance of neurotransmitters may cause depression
- understand how negative schemas and attributions may cause depression
- understand how the use of antidepressant medications may improve mental health
- understand how the use of cognitive behaviour therapy (CBT) may improve mental health.

Key terms

Attributions: the ways people explain situations and behaviour

Nature: the idea that our characteristics and behaviour are inherited

Negative schemas: a biased cognitive model of people, objects or situations based on previous information and experience that directs us to perceive, organise or understand new information by focusing on what is bad

Nurture: the idea that our characteristics and behaviour are influenced by our environment

Synoptic link

Applying what you learned about the brain and neuropsychology in Topics 7.1–3 will help you to discuss the effect of neurons, the nervous system, and brain function on mental health problems such as depression.

■ The influence of nurture – a psychological explanation for depression

A second explanation for depression suggests that it is influenced by nurture: the life experiences and environment which affect how an individual grows up and lives. Cognitive theory is a psychological approach that believes our thought processes affect our behaviour. According to cognitive theory, behaviours and emotions are influenced by the way people explain the things that happen to them and the views that they have about themselves and the world.

The schema we have of ourselves, and the world around us, affects the way we think about things. The term 'schema' was first introduced by Piaget (see Topics 3.2 and 6.1). Schemas are based on our previous experiences and are developed and changed to fit with new experiences and information. Negative schemas have been linked to depression. Traumatic events in childhood may cause negative schemas to be created. These schemas mean that people view themselves and the world in a negative way.

People with negative schemas can also make errors in their thinking. The example in Building skills 1 above can help us to understand thinking errors. One error would be believing we are going to get into trouble even though we know we have not done anything wrong. We might exaggerate how bad things will get, such as believing that we will be permanently excluded from school. We might even ignore the fact that our psychology teacher had told us we might get a headteacher's award for our class project.

A *What is your schema for this situation?*

How attributions influence depression

Attributions have also been linked to depression. Attributions are the ways in which people explain the causes of situations and behaviour. Two dimensions of attributions are internal–external and stable–unstable. With an internal attribution, people explain situations or behaviours as being caused by dispositional factors, such as personality or ability. With an external attribution, people explain them as being caused by situational factors, such as the economy or the weather. When people make a stable attribution, they explain situations or behaviours as being caused by factors that do not change, such as gender, but when they make an unstable attribution, they explain them as being caused by factors that are only temporary, such as tiredness.

Someone who fails a psychology test, and believes it is because they are not clever enough and that cannot do anything about this, explains the failed test as internal and stable. But someone who fails the test and believes it is because they did not do enough revision because their dog was ill, explains the failed test as external and unstable.

Research has found that people are more likely to be depressed if their attributions are internal and stable. People whose attributions are external and unstable, will see bad things as being caused by factors beyond their control and only temporary. They are less likely to be depressed.

Building skills 1   K

Imagine you are told to go and sit outside the headteacher's office. What would you be thinking while you waited to go in?

Synoptic link   🔗

In Topic 3.2, you learned about Piaget's stage theory and the development of schemas. You can apply this learning when discussing the ways that negative schemas affect mental health.

Did you know   ?

The American psychiatrist Aaron Beck, who developed the theory about negative schemas and depression, is also considered to be the originator of cognitive therapy.

What are the treatments for depression?

Getting started

Without looking back, spend a few minutes writing about attributions and how they may be linked with depression.

Antidepressants

Antidepressants are a form of medication used to treat depression. They work by increasing the levels of neurotransmitters such as serotonin and noradrenaline. There are almost 30 different kinds of antidepressants. The most commonly prescribed antidepressants in the UK are Selective Serotonin Reuptake Inhibitors (SSRIs). SSRIs stop the reuptake of serotonin. After a neurotransmitter has communicated its message to the neurons, the message needs to be prevented from being constantly communicated. To do this, the neuron reabsorbs the neurotransmitter it released. This is called reuptake, and stopping it increases the levels of the neurotransmitter, which may reduce the effects of depression.

Antidepressants first became available in the 1950s and have been increasingly prescribed since then. Statistics show that the use of antidepressants in Europe increased by 20 per cent each year between 2000 and 2010. The UK has the fourth highest level of antidepressant use in Europe with more than 50 million prescriptions being written every year.

Despite the large numbers of people using antidepressants, there is some uncertainty as to how effective they actually are. Although many people experience some improvement as a result of taking antidepressants, especially in cases of severe depression, the research suggests that they may not be as effective for mild depression. The Royal College of Psychiatrists says that 50 to 65 per cent of people with depression will improve as a result of taking antidepressants. However, 25 to 30 per cent of people will also improve when they take a fake pill, or placebo. Research into the effectiveness of treating depressed children and adolescents with antidepressants concluded that almost all antidepressants have a very similar effect to that seen when a placebo is taken.

Antidepressants also have a number of possible side effects, which include weight gain, insomnia, and having a dry mouth. Some people may experience more serious side effects such as becoming aggressive or having suicidal thoughts.

Cognitive behaviour therapy

Cognitive behaviour therapy (CBT) is based on cognitive theory and the idea that our thought processes affect our behaviour and that behaviours and emotions are influenced by our thinking. CBT is a talking therapy that helps people to change their thinking patterns (like negative schemas). Unlike some talking therapies, CBT focuses on 'here and now'

Key terms

Antidepressants: a type of medication used to treat depression

Cognitive behaviour therapy (CBT): a talking therapy that can help you manage your problems and emotions by changing the way you think and behave

Holistic: the view that the parts of something are all connected and understandable only by studying things as a whole

Reductionist: understanding complex things like human behaviour by simplifying it to its most fundamental and basic parts

Synoptic link

See pages 152–153 for more information on synaptic transmission and the reuptake of neurotransmitters.

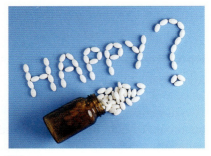

B *Do antidepressants (sometimes referred to as 'happy pills') really work?*

Thought
What we *think* affects how we act and feel.

CBT

Emotion
What we *feel* affects what we think and do.

Behaviour
What we *do* affects how we think and feel.

C *The CBT triangle*

problems instead of looking at ones from the past. CBT sessions can be delivered by a therapist one-to-one or in group sessions. Research has shown positive results for the use of CBT to treat depression. One such study was Wiles' study (see page 180).

Reductionist and holistic perspectives

A **reductionist** approach says that the best way to understand complex things like human behaviour is to study the most fundamental and basic parts of it.

The biological explanation of mental health problems like depression can be considered to be reductionist. The biological explanation views depression as having a biological cause and as being treatable with drugs such as antidepressants.

A **holistic** perspective is that all the parts of something are connected and understandable only by studying the whole. Mental health problems like depression are often explained as a complex mix of biological, psychological, and social factors. A holistic approach to depression treatment is likely to involve a blend of medication, therapy, and positive lifestyle changes, such as increasing exercise levels.

> ### Going further
>
> There are many self-help CBT resources available online. Find some that you can bring in and share with the rest of your class.

> ### Building skills 2
>
> Working with a partner, discuss whether CBT is a reductionist or holistic approach to treating depression.   **A**

> ### Exam tip !
>
> Although wider knowledge of Piaget's stage theory and the development of schemas will deepen your overall understanding of schemas, remember that it is important to keep exam answers focused on the specific question that is asked.

CBT is a reductionist approach. There are two reasons for this. Firstly, it only looks at 'here and now' problems instead of looking at those from the past; this may mean that not all relevant psychological factors are being dealt with. Secondly, CBT only considers an individual's thinking and does not look at biological or social factors.

At present, the National Institute for Health and Care Excellence (NICE) guidelines for the treatment of depression in the UK, for both young people and adults, require a stepped pathway of treatments. CBT and other non-drug therapies are offered and assessed for effectiveness before any antidepressant medication is given.

> **Practice exam questions**
>
> 1. What are 'negative schemas'? *(2 marks)*
>
> 2. Decide whether each of the following statements is true or false:
>   a) Research has found that CBT is much less effective than antidepressants in treating depression. *(1 mark)*
>   b) Research has found that CBT is more effective than antidepressants in treating depression. *(1 mark)*
>
> 3. Outline how negative schemas might be linked to depression. *(4 marks)*
>
> 4. Use your knowledge of psychology to evaluate the use of antidepressants to treat depression. *(5 marks)*
>
> 5. Evaluate Wiles' study of the effectiveness of CBT. *(5 marks)*

Wiles' effectiveness of CBT study (2013)

Aim: To investigate the effectiveness of CBT in treating depressed people who have not improved after taking medication.

Study type: Longitudinal field experiment carried out in the real-life environment of the participants. The researcher still manipulates the independent variable, but there is limited control of extraneous variables. Participants were living in the UK, aged between 18 and 75 years and had been taking antidepressants for at least 6 weeks with little or no improvement.

Method: Participants were randomly allocated into two groups. A total of 234 participants were allocated to have CBT as well as antidepressants and other normal medical care for depressed patients. A control group of 235 participants were allocated and continued to take antidepressants and have normal medical care for depression. Participants in the CBT group had 12, individual, one-hour sessions of CBT with a trained therapist. Participants were followed up regularly.

Results: After six months, 90 per cent of participants were able to be followed up. At this point in the study, 46 per cent of the group having CBT showed a notable improvement in symptoms compared with 22 per cent of the control group. At 12 months, the perceived improvements to quality of life were found to be greater for the participants who had taken part in CBT sessions.

Conclusion: When used in addition to antidepressants and other normal medical care, CBT is an effective way of reducing the symptoms of depression in people who do not respond to antidepressants on their own.

A *46 per cent of the CBT group responded to treatment*

Wiles, N., et al. (2013) 'Cognitive behavioural therapy as an adjunct to pharmacotherapy for primary care based patients with treatment resistant depression,' The Lancet, Volume 381, 375–384

■ Evaluation

Why the study is important

■ It showed that CBT could be an effective way of reducing the symptoms of depression in people who are not responding to antidepressants

Limitations of the study

■ Although nearly half of those in the group having CBT showed a notable improvement in symptoms, 54 per cent of participants did not.

■ This was a longitudinal study that took place over the period of a year. This makes it less likely that participants will complete the entire study. In this study, 32 percent of participants did not attend all 12 sessions of CBT. However, longitudinal studies are positive because they show changes and effects over time.

■ A field experiment happens in a real-life environment in which it is not possible for researchers to control extraneous variables. However, in this study there were controls put in place to ensure that participant variables were limited. People who had bipolar disorder or substance addiction were not able to participate. People who were currently having CBT or counselling for their depression or who had previously had CBT were also not able to participate.

■ Requiring depressed participants to not receive appropriate care in order to be in a research study would go against the ethical consideration of responsibility and is a limitation of research in this area. However, researchers in this study treated participants ethically by ensuring that all participants were able to continue with their usual medical care.

■ Support for Wiles' findings

In another recent study, participants either took antidepressants, a placebo, or had CBT. After four months, people whose symptoms had improved after taking antidepressants either kept taking the medication or began taking a placebo. Participants who improved after having CBT were stopped from having regular sessions and were only allowed three follow-up sessions.

Of the participants given a placebo 76 per cent had their symptoms return. This compared with only 31 per cent of the participants who had CBT. The results of this study fit with those seen in other studies and suggest that CBT has a lasting effect that is not found with antidepressants.

> **Building skills 1** **E**
>
> Research into the effects of antidepressants often uses a control group who take a fake pill known as a placebo. With a partner, discuss the ethics of giving a depressed person medication that is not real.

> **Exam tip** **!**
>
> When evaluating the ethics of research, it is important to fully explain any statements you make. You will not get any marks by simply stating that a study was not ethical – you must explain why.

Wiles' study, and other research such as the study described above, suggest that CBT can have a positive and lasting effect in treating people with depression. However, research also shows that antidepressants do help many people, especially those with more severe depression.

In order to treat participants ethically, it is important that they are fully informed and this would mean explaining any risks involved with taking a placebo rather than an antidepressant. Giving participants a fake pill could be considered to be deception. However, if participants are informed that they may be given a placebo and they consent to this, it would become acceptable. In order to be responsible and to protect participants from harm, they would need to be monitored in case their symptoms became worse and they were at risk of harming themselves. Wiles' study allowed all participants to continue normal medical care and this avoided any ethical issues around the use of placebos.

8.4 Key research study: Wiles

Getting started

Discuss the terms 'substance misuse' and 'substance abuse' with a partner. What do you think might be the difference between them?

■ The differences between substance misuse and substance abuse

Many different substances with an addictive quality are used by individuals. These range from caffeinated drinks (such as coffee and some energy drinks), to legal drugs (such as alcohol, tobacco, and pain killers), and to illegal drugs (such as cannabis, heroin, and cocaine). Some substances are more addictive than others and some are more harmful than others, but they can all be misused and abused.

Substance misuse is using a substance for purposes, or in amounts, that may be harmful and that are different to the recommended pattern of use. A misuse of medication would include not following the doctor's instructions, such as taking more painkillers than the prescribed dose to stop a toothache. Misuse of alcohol is drinking more than the recommended limits, such as drinking more than 14 units in a week. Substance misuse may also lead to **substance abuse** and **addiction**, because it may be something that happens on more than one occasion.

Substance abuse is using a substance in a way that will be harmful or dangerous for the person doing this. Substance abuse often affects other people as well, such as family members. Individuals who abuse substances often do so in order to experience an altered state or to help them deal with difficult emotions. The abuse of substances usually leads to side effects, including dependency and addiction.

A *Enjoying a warm drink or a necessity to get through the day?*

Objectives

You will be able to:

- understand the distinction between addiction and dependence
- understand the distinction between substance misuse and substance abuse
- understand the use of the International Classification of Diseases (ICD) in diagnosing dependence syndrome
- identify symptoms of dependence syndrome.

Key terms

Addiction: repeated use of a substance resulting in an individual becoming entirely focused on the substance, which they need to have regularly in order to avoid withdrawal symptoms

Dependence: repeated use of a substance results in an individual's brain and body only functioning normally when the substance is present; when the substance is not present, withdrawal symptoms occur

Substance abuse: using a substance in a way that is harmful or dangerous, often because of a consistent pattern of use

Substance misuse: using a substance for purposes, or in amounts, that may be harmful and that is different to the recommended pattern of use

Building skills 1

Discuss with a partner what behaviours, choices, emotions, or thoughts might suggest someone is abusing a substance. Share your ideas with the rest of your class.

K

Did you know ?

The 2014 Global Drug Survey found that the four most commonly used drugs are alcohol, tobacco, cannabis, and caffeinated energy drinks.

■ The differences between addiction and dependence

Dependence is a biological effect caused by repeated use of a substance. The body only functions normally when the substance is present and is dependent on regular use. If the substance is not present, the person will experience withdrawal symptoms. Withdrawal symptoms include headaches, irritability, nausea, anxiety, tiredness, and trouble sleeping.

Addiction has biological and behavioural effects. Continued substance abuse causes biochemical changes in the brain as well as noticeable changes to behaviour. Substance use becomes the main focus of the addict, regardless of the harm they may cause to themselves or others. Addicts need to 'use' regularly in order to avoid withdrawal symptoms. It is possible to be dependent without being addicted, but the two are very closely linked.

■ Diagnosing dependence syndrome

The medical term for addiction is dependence syndrome. The ICD-10 describes it as when using a substance becomes more important than other behaviours and there is a strong and overwhelming need to take a substance.

The ICD-10 sets out criteria for diagnosis as being the occurrence of three or more symptoms present together within the past year.

The symptoms given in the ICD-10 for dependence syndrome are:

- a strong desire to use a substance despite harmful consequences

- difficulty in controlling use

- a higher priority given to the substance than to other activities or obligations

- experiencing withdrawal symptoms when substance use is reduced or stopped

- increased tolerance to a substance which means that increasingly larger amounts are needed in order for the same effects to be experienced.

Dependence syndrome may be for one substance, for a group of substances (such as opioid drugs like codeine and morphine), or for a variety of substances (such as alcohol and cannabis).

Exam tip !

There are three symptoms of dependence syndrome that you need to remember for the exam. These are the first three bullet points in the ICD-10 list below.

Going further

Create a poster aimed at helping people to recognise the symptoms of addiction/ dependence syndrome. Your poster should also include information about where to get help for those who are concerned about themselves or others. You can research this on the web, for example at www.talktofrank.com or the NHS website www.nhs.uk/ Livewell.

Synoptic link

As well as causing the symptoms discussed here, drugs affect neurotransmitters. Look back at Topic 7.3 to consider this.

B *Addiction can be a very lonely place*

Practice exam questions

1. What is meant by the term 'addiction'? *(2 marks)*

2. State three symptoms of dependence syndrome. *(3 marks)*

What causes addiction?

Theories of addiction suggest that the causes are biological, psychological, cultural, social, and environmental. Each of these areas and the relationship between them is complex and this makes it difficult to determine a definite cause. We will consider two of these areas in more detail.

■ The influence of nature – a biological explanation for addiction

Some people may inherit a **genetic vulnerability** towards addiction. This does not mean that someone with certain genes will definitely develop an addiction. It means that some people are more likely than others to become addicted to the substances they try because of the influence of nature. However other factors, such as environment, are also involved.

Evidence for there being a genetic vulnerability towards addiction initially came from the study of twins. Kaij's twin study of alcohol abuse was one of the first in this area and we will learn more about it on page 186. Twin and adoption studies strongly suggest that addiction to tobacco, alcohol, and illegal drugs all have a **hereditary** element. Research suggests that environmental factors have a greater effect on someone starting to use a substance, and hereditary factors have a greater effect on an individual's likelihood of moving from regular user to addict.

Modern research methods and greater knowledge of DNA have allowed exact genes to be identified for many disorders and conditions, but although some progress has been made towards identifying the genes involved with addiction, there are thought to be hundreds, possibly thousands, of genetic variations involved.

Objectives

You will be able to:

- understand how hereditary factors may cause a genetic vulnerability towards addiction
- understand how peer influence may affect the development of an addiction
- understand how the use of aversion therapy may help with addiction
- understand how the use of self-management programmes may help with addiction.

Key terms

Genetic vulnerability: a biological susceptibility towards developing certain conditions or disorders when other influencing elements are also present

Hereditary: being transferred from parent to child through their genes

Peer: someone who is from the same social group, or who is the same age or social status, or has the same background, abilities or qualifications, as someone else

A *We may be born with an increased likelihood of developing an addiction to certain substances*

■ The influence of nurture – a psychological explanation for addiction

Environmental conditions, part of the influence of nurture, are also thought to be a key explanation for addiction. Psychologists studying social influence and conformity have found that we change our behaviour as a result of social pressure. We do this in order to avoid rejection and to feel that we are part of a group. Research shows that age is a factor affecting conformity and that young people are more likely to conform.

A report by the National Institute on Drug Abuse found that that 90 per cent of cigarette users in the United States started smoking when they were teenagers. Most of them believe that they were strongly influenced by seeing others, such as their friends, smoking.

Peer influence has also been found to be a strong factor in the use of drugs during teenage years. A study into peer influence found that individuals whose friends used drugs were more likely to start to use drugs. However, they also found that the family members' attitudes towards drug use was an important factor.

Another study found that teenagers are also influenced by peers to *not* use substances. Researchers found that teenagers were influenced by the anti-alcohol views of others, especially when the individual expressing these views was seen as popular amongst their peer group.

Synoptic link

In Topic 5.1 you learned how social influence can lead people to conform to the behaviour of those around them. You can apply this learning when discussing peer influence on drug use.

Did you know

In the UK, 8 out of 10 cigarette users in the UK started smoking before they were 19 years old.

Going further

Working with a partner, design and carrying out a questionnaire aimed at finding out how strong an effect peer influence has on the decisions made about using substances such as tobacco, alcohol, and illegal drugs. Look back at Topic 4.3 on questionnaires to help you.

Report your findings to the rest of the group.

Building skills 1

With a partner, discuss the theory that peer influence may affect the development of an addiction. Do you agree or disagree? Why?

The theory that peer influence may affect the development of an addiction does not take into consideration that people generally choose the groups they want to be a part of. Our thoughts and views on substance use are also likely to have an effect on the peer groups we join.

While peer influence may affect how likely someone is to start using substances, substance abuse and addiction may also be affected by genetics, mental health problems, personality, social and cultural norms, environment, and experiences of trauma.

B *We can change our behaviour because of group pressure*

Kaij's alcohol abuse in twins study (1960)

Aim: To see if hereditary factors influence the development of alcohol addiction.

Study type: Case study using a variety of methods, including questionnaires and interviews of the twins and other family members, and some psychological testing. Information from birth records and a public register of alcohol abusers was used to identify participants. There were 174 pairs of participants. 48 pairs were monozygotic (identical) twins and 126 pairs were dizygotic (non-identical) twins. All of the participants were male and they were all born in Southern Sweden after 1880.

Method: Using the information from the public register of alcohol abusers, and the information from the questionnaires and interviews, Kaij categorised each twin depending on their level of alcohol use. There were five categories ranging from not drinking at all to being a chronic alcoholic.

Results: Kaij found that 54 per cent of identical twins were in the same category of alcohol use but that only 28 per cent of non-identical twins were in the same category of alcohol use. He also found that as the level of alcohol use increased, there was a higher concordance rate for identical twins, with 72 per cent of chronic alcoholic twins being in the same category as their co-twin.

Conclusion: Kaij concluded that there are hereditary factors involved in the levels of alcohol usage and in alcohol addiction.

Source: Kaij L. (1960), Alcoholism in Twins: Studies on the Etiology and Sequels of Abuse of Alcohol, *Vol. I. Stockholm: Almqvist and Wiksell International.*

■ Evaluation

Why the study is important

- It provides evidence that suggests some hereditary factors are involved in the levels of alcohol usage and in alcohol addiction.

Limitations of the study

- The information on alcohol use was provided by the participant and other family members. This type of self-report method is subjective and there are many

A *Twins studies have been used to study the genetic nature of alcoholism*

reasons why the information provided may not be accurate. These include lying about the level of alcohol consumed in order to give a sociably desirable answer.

- The study only looked at rates of alcohol abuse. Therefore, the findings cannot be generalised to include addiction to other substances.

- The sample is limited because all of the participants were twins, male, and Swedish. This means that the findings are not representative of people who are female or who are not twins or Swedish. The participants were also twins where at least one of them was publically known to abuse alcohol. Therefore, the results are not representative of those who abused alcohol but did so in private.

- Identical twins are often treated the same so it may be environment (nurture) and not genetics (nature) that was the cause of the similar levels of alcohol use.

- 46 per cent of the identical twins were not in the same category as their co-twin for alcohol use, which suggests factors other than genetic must also be involved.

- The numbers of identical twin pairs is a lot lower than for non-identical twins. There was also a very small number of identical twins who were categorised as chronic alcoholics. This decreases the validity of the conclusions drawn from these results.

■ Other research

Research since Kaij's study has consistently shown that there are hereditary factors involved in the development of alcoholism in males. While there is some evidence that alcoholism in women may also have a genetic element, the findings are not as strong. Studies suggest that around 20 to 25 per cent of male siblings and male children of alcoholics also become alcoholics. This is compared to only 5 per cent of female siblings and female children.

In one study, pairs of twins were identified from hospital admissions information. While 30 per cent of participants were identical twins, the rest were non-identical twins, evenly split between same-sex and opposite-sex pairs. Investigations showed that levels of drug use were fairly similar for identical twins of both genders and same-sex non-identical male twins, but far less similar for female non-identical twins.

It is likely that the reasons for the gender differences seen in substance use and addiction are complex and suggest that genetic vulnerability and peer influence are just two of the factors involved. Other factors include cultural and social norms, and personality type.

Women are twice as likely to be prescribed antidepressants as men and are far more likely to seek therapy or counselling. It may be that cultural and social norms influence gender choices when dealing with emotional and psychological distress.

A certain personality type has been shown to be more likely to abuse substances. For example, anti-social personality disorder (ASD) is more commonly found in males, and people with ASD are at risk of substance abuse and addiction.

> **Did you know** ?
> In the UK, males are almost twice as likely as females to be treated for an alcohol related injury or condition and almost twice as likely as females to use illegal drugs.

> **Building skills 1**
>
>
>
> Research does suggest a genetic vulnerability towards addiction, particularly in males. However, the differences in the findings for males and females suggest that there are also other factors involved.
>
> Discuss with a partner why the levels of substance use in men and women may be different and what this might suggest about the factors involved in developing an addiction.

> **Exam tip** !
> When you are asked to evaluate research, you can consider a range of different areas to look at including the methodology the researcher has used.

What are the treatments for addiction?

Getting started

Without looking back, spend a few minutes writing about peer influence and how it may be linked to addiction.

Aversion therapy

Aversion therapy tries to help people stop addictive behaviours by regularly experiencing some form of unpleasantness when carrying out the unwanted behaviour. This results in them learning to connect the behaviour with unpleasant feelings rather than with the previously enjoyable feelings such as 'being high'.

The form of aversion therapy used to treat addicts generally involves the individual taking medication or a substance that causes an unpleasant reaction when drugs, tobacco, or alcohol are used. This is usually an emetic, which is a medicine that causes vomiting. The emetic usually given to alcoholics is disulfiram (also known as Antabuse). Drinking even small amounts of alcohol while using this medication will result in instant and severe hangover-type symptoms. Electrical aversion therapy is also used to treat addiction. A safe but painful electrical shock is given to the individual while they carry out the behaviour they wish to stop.

Research shows that aversion therapy is successful in treating addictions, however the research also suggests that the effects tend to be short-term. Aversion therapy tends to be most effective and long lasting when individuals also receive other support, such as attending counselling or **self-management programmes**. Other issues with aversion therapy include the fact that it is a very unpleasant treatment to experience and this means that there is quite a high dropout rate. The unpleasant nature of the treatment also raises ethical concerns and it is important that the process is fully explained and consented to.

Building skills 2

Working with a partner, discuss whether aversion therapy is a reductionist or holistic approach to treating addiction.

A

Aversion therapy is a reductionist approach because it only deals with an individual's learned desire to use a substance and does not look at other factors involved in addiction, such as biological, environmental, or social factors. Aversion therapy also focuses on the 'here and now' problem and does not look at problems from the past, which may have originally influenced the individual to start using substances.

Key terms

Aversion therapy: a treatment to help individuals stop unwanted behaviours such as substance addiction; the individual experiences some form of unpleasantness when carrying out the unwanted behaviour

Self-management programmes: an intervention designed to support and empower individuals so that they can take responsibility for their own choices and behaviour

C *Taking an emetic makes people sick when they drink alcohol*

Self-management programmes

Self-management programmes are interventions that give addicts the help they need to manage their substance abuse. They provide peer support, accountability, and opportunities to develop self-awareness. Groups may have a psychologist, therapist, or experienced group member as a facilitator.

D *Peer support can help people manage their addiction*

Self-help groups are groups of people with a common problem. By sharing their experiences with others, they learn that they are not alone. The more experienced members of the group can also provide an example to newer members. Both of these elements can be very important for someone who has felt hopeless and alone in their struggle with addiction.

Alcoholics Anonymous (AA) and Narcotics Anonymous are two of the best-known 12-step recovery programmes for addiction. These 12-step programmes provide addicts with guidelines for moving towards, and remaining in, recovery. The 12 steps have a strong spiritual element, but they allow for a personal understanding of God rather than any set religious belief. Research shows that many non-religious people have found the 12-step programmes helpful but that people who have no belief at all in God are less likely to continue attending meetings. There are also non-religious 12-step programmes available.

Studies into the effectiveness of self-management programmes are difficult because of the need to allow group members complete anonymity, and the fact that control groups cannot be used for ethical and methodological reasons. Research that has been carried out suggests that these programmes have a similar success rate to other available treatments, and that they are most successful in helping those who attend regularly and for a longer period of time.

Self-management programmes are a holistic approach. They help people deal with their desire to use a substance as well as looking at other factors involved in addiction, such as environmental or social factors. They also provide opportunities for individuals to look at and deal with issues from their past, present, and future.

Going further

Find an example of the 12 steps and share them with the rest of your class.

Building skills 3

Working with a partner, discuss whether self-management programmes are a reductionist or holistic approach to treating addiction.

A

Exam tip   !

When a question states 'use your knowledge of psychology', it is a reminder not to just use your own opinion but to use psychological theories, facts, and research.

Practice exam questions

1. Outline how genetic vulnerability might be linked to addiction. *(4 marks)*

2. Describe Kaij's target population. *(3 marks)*

3. Use your knowledge of psychology to evaluate the use of aversion therapy to treat an addiction. *(5 marks)*

4. Evaluate Kaij's twin study of alcohol abuse. *(5 marks)*

8 Revision checklist

Characteristics of mental health

- [ ] describe the characteristics of mental health
- [ ] describe cultural variations in beliefs about mental health problems
- [ ] understand how and why the incidence of mental health problems has changed over time

See pages 168–171

Effects of mental health problems

- [ ] explain how mental health problems affect individuals
- [ ] explain how mental health problems affect society

See pages 172–173

Characteristics of clinical depression

- [ ] explain the differences between unipolar depression, bipolar depression and sadness
- [ ] understand how the International Classification of Diseases (ICD) is used to diagnose unipolar depression
- [ ] know the symptoms of unipolar depression

See pages 174–175

Causes and treatments of depression

- [ ] explain how an imbalance of neurotransmitters may cause depression
- [ ] explain how negative schemas and attributions may cause depression
- [ ] explain how the use of antidepressant medications may improve mental health
- [ ] explain how the use of cognitive behaviour theory (CBT) may improve mental health
- [ ] **key research study:** describe and evaluate Wiles' study of the effectiveness of CBT

See pages 176–181

Characteristics of addiction

- [ ] explain the difference between addiction and dependence
- [ ] explain the difference between substance misuse and substance abuse
- [ ] understand how the International Classification of Diseases (ICD) is used to diagnose addiction
- [ ] know the symptoms of addiction

See pages 182–183

Causes and treatment of addiction

- [ ] explain how hereditary factors may cause a genetic vulnerability towards addiction (influence of nature)
- [ ] explain how peer influence may affect the development of an addiction (influence of nurture)
- [ ] explain how aversion theory may be used to treat addiction
- [ ] explain how self-management programmes may help with addiction
- [ ] understand the differences between reductionist and holistic approaches to mental health
- [ ] **key research study:** describe and evaluate Kaij's twin study of alcohol abuse

See pages 184–189

Practice exam questions

1. Read the following information and answer the question that follows.

'Researchers have released a new report into how today's teenagers are coping with exam stress. Their research shows that some teenagers are able to deal with the difficulties and challenges of exams more effectively than others. Those teenagers who cope best with exam stress were found to have good relationships with their peers and family members. They were also able to deal with disappointments and problems, and were more able to make decisions. The researchers believe that these characteristics help to reduce the effects of exam stress.'

From the passage above, identify three characteristics of mental health. *(3 marks)*

> This is a good example of why it is important to read all of the question. Here, just identifying any characteristics of mental health is not what the question requires. It would also be advisable to use the actual wording from the passage in your answer.

2. Explain how the International Classification of Diseases (ICD) is used to diagnose unipolar depression. *(3 marks)*

3. Evaluate the use of cognitive behaviour therapy (CBT) in the treatment of depression. *(4 marks)*

> The findings from Wiles' study may help in answering this question, but be careful not to write an evaluation of a research study instead of answering the actual question.

4. Complete the table below, by writing the terms 'addiction', 'dependence' and 'substance abuse' in the correct boxes. Use each term only once.

Terms used in relation to the use of addictive substances	Descriptions of terms
	Using a substance in a way that is harmful or dangerous.
	When an individual becomes entirely focused on a substance which they need to have regularly in order to avoid withdrawal symptoms.
	When a substance is not present, withdrawal symptoms occur.

(3 marks)

5. Outline how peer influence might be linked to addiction. *(4 marks)*

6. a) Describe Kaij's twin study of alcohol abuse. Include in your answer the aim of the study, the method used, the results obtained and the conclusion drawn. *(4 marks)*

   b) Kaij's twin study of alcohol abuse was a case study. Outline one strength and one weakness of case studies. *(4 marks)*

> Avoid using the same wording for the aim and the conclusion of a study. The conclusion should indicate what it is that the research has discovered.

Improve your exam skills

What do we mean when we say 'improve your exam skills'? At its simplest, this means learning how to get more marks on the exam paper. This chapter will give some suggestions about how this can be done.

There is a wide variety of questions in Psychology exam papers. You might find it useful to look through one and find out the ways in which questions differ. They vary in style from multiple-choice questions to those with a large space to write an answer in continuous prose. They vary in the number of marks available, from 1 to 9. They vary in the kind of challenge they present: giving definitions, doing calculations, evaluating studies, and so on. They vary in the 'command' words that they use, such as 'identify', 'describe', 'explain', 'evaluate', 'discuss' or 'calculate'.

This chapter includes a selection of practice exam questions to give you an idea of some of the different types of question you will encounter in your exam. For each question, there are two 'student' answers. One earns more marks, the other fewer. The commentary beside each answer explains what was expected in the answer and why each answer scored more or less. You will notice that the better answers share a few general features. They tend to:

- respond well to the command words in the question
- use appropriate psychological vocabulary
- make detailed, specific points
- use good English
- be well organised
- have been checked to see that the question has been fully answered.

■ Questions based on the key research studies

> Describe Kaij's twin study of alcohol abuse. Include in your answer the aim of the study, the method used, the results obtained and the conclusion drawn. *(4 marks)*

This question is from the Psychological Problems topic. Several key research studies are mentioned in the specification and are dealt with in detail in this book. There will probably be questions about the key research studies in one or both exam papers. In the question above, the first sentence makes it clear which study you need to describe. The second sentence shows that your answer should deal with four features of the study: its aim, its method, its results, and the conclusion drawn from these results.

Lawson's answer

The aim of the study was to find out if levels of alcohol abuse are influenced by inherited factors. The method used involved the case study of groups of identical and non-identical twins in Sweden. Each person's level of alcohol abuse was rated using interviews, questionnaires and public records. Each person got a rating from 'no abuse' to 'chronic alcoholic'. The results showed that more pairs of identical twins got the same rating compared to the non-identical twins. The conclusion was that inherited factors do influence levels of alcohol abuse.

Lawson's answer deals with the four features of the study which are required in the question. Each part contains important details, for example naming the two types of twin, identifying features of the method used, and giving examples of the rating scale. This answer would probably get all 4 marks. It demonstrates the value of learning the details of the key research studies.

Callum's answer

Kaij did a study on two types of twins. He found out what level of alcohol abuse each person had. The results showed that being an identical twin made alcohol abuse more likely. The conclusion was that you can inherit alcohol abuse.

There are enough specific features of Callum's answer to show that he is describing the correct study. However, the answer is missing several key details. This answer would probably get 1 or 2 of the 4 marks. It does not state the aim of the study (what Kaij was trying to find out). The two types of twin are not identified. The method that Kaij used is not identified. In addition, the results are not correct. Improving or dealing with these points, as Lawson did, would lead to a higher mark.

■ Questions asking you to plan a study

Imagine that you have been asked to conduct a study to investigate how motivation affects perception. Use your knowledge of psychology to describe:

- what task you would do to carry out your study
- what you would measure
- the results you would expect to find in your study.   *(5 marks)*

This question is from the Perception topic. It is asking you to devise your own study. The words 'how motivation affects perception' show what the study must be about. The three bullet points tell you what your answer should include. Questions like this may be related to the key research studies in the specification, as this one is. A good answer may use a similar method to one seen in this book, or may make up something that does the same job.

Catherine's answer

I would cut out 10 large pictures of items of food, like burgers, and mount them on pieces of card. I would get 10 other students to take part in the study. Just before lunchtime, when they are

Catherine's answer involves motivation and perception, and has dealt with each of the bullet points in the question. It sounds plausible and it is possible to imagine a student carrying out a study like this. There are two 'conditions' for the independent variable, 'before lunch' and 'after lunch'. Studies that have already been carried out suggest that the results would be as she predicts.

Other good features of this answer are that Catherine suggested a 'measurement' for perception (the score for brightness), and intended to work out mean scores for each participant. This answer would probably get all 5 marks.

hungry, I would ask them, one at a time, to give the pictures a score for how bright they are from 1 (= dull) to 10 (= very bright). I would ask them to repeat the task immediately after they had eaten their lunch. I will be recording the brightness scores and working out a mean score for each person both before and after eating. I would expect to find that most of the participants will make higher mean ratings before they have eaten than afterwards because their hunger will motivate them to perceive the pictures of food as brighter.

Premika's answer

My aim would be to see if motivation affects perception. I would get 10 of my class to miss their lunch one day. I would show them some pictures of food and ask them how bright they seem to be. I would also ask them how hungry they felt. I would expect the participants who were the most hungry to say that the pictures of food were brighter.

Premika's answer deals with motivation and perception, but will not score many of the available marks, perhaps 1 or 2. She has stated the aim of the study, which does not lose any marks, but is not required as part of the answer. The ideas of 'hunger' and 'brightness' are there, but Premika has not stated how they would be measured, recorded or used. The two 'conditions' are not as clearly differentiated as in Catherine's answer. Dealing with any of these weaknesses would earn the answer more marks. The conclusion appears to fit in with studies that have already been carried out.

■ Questions asking you to describe something

> Describe Gibson's direct theory of perception. *(5 marks)*

This question is from the Perception topic. The key command word here is 'describe'. So, a good answer will include several important details and use relevant key terms. There will not be any credit for evaluating the theory.

Jai's answer

The basic idea in Gibson's theory is that we can make sense of what we see using only the various kinds of visual information that enter our eyes. This is called a bottom-up approach. He gives examples of different kinds of visual information we use. There are depth cues which allow us to perceive how far things are from us. These include relative size, height in the field and texture gradient, the fact that things which are further away from us look smoother than those which are closer. There is also motion parallax, which concerns moving objects. We can tell which way we are moving and how quickly by how quickly our surroundings seem to be moving towards us or away from us. Finally, there are affordances, that is the way in which we know what we can do with objects around us, for example a chair looks like something we can safely sit on. Gibson's theory is sometimes called 'ecological' because it shows how the real-world environment gives clues to aid accurate perception.

Jai's answer gives a good general idea of what is meant by direct perception, and then gives details of three features of Gibson's theory. Jai uses several key terms, such as 'affordances', and explains what some of them mean. This answer would probably get all 5 marks.

Max's answer

Gibson suggested that we can make sense of what we see through a variety of clues. We can tell how far objects are from us. If they seem further up, they are further away. We can tell if we are moving or not by what seems to be happening to our surroundings. We can also tell what objects might be used for by just looking at them. For example, we see a berry on a tree and think that we may be able to eat it. Gibson believed that animals perceive in the same way.

> Max's answer offers three appropriate suggestions about how perception is based on clues in the environment, as Gibson's theory suggests. So, his answer might score 2 or 3 marks. To get more marks he should use key terms for the 'clues' he describes, such as 'affordances' when he refers to the berry, and give more detailed examples to show how the 'clues' work.

■ Questions referring to a real-life scenario

> The following conversation took place between two work colleagues.
>
> Faye: 'Have you noticed that our new boss always looks down at the ground when you have a conversation with him?'
>
> Julie: 'Yes. I think that's why I find it hard to know if it's my turn to speak when I am talking to him.'
>
> Explain one function of eye contact. Refer to the conversation in your answer. *(3 marks)*

This question is from the Language, Thought and Communication topic. The exam paper may have several questions where there is a 'story' to read, which will require you to apply some psychological knowledge to a real-life scenario. There are two command words in this question. 'Explain' implies that the answer should state the function of eye contact and give reasons why it is important. 'Refer to' implies that the function of eye contact should be illustrated by use of the conversation. Just copying out parts of it will not be sufficient.

Eleri's answer

One function of eye contact is to help people take turns in a conversation. When one person comes to the end of their 'turn' they may take a long look at the other person to show that it's their turn now. In the story it seems that the new boss does not make eye contact during conversations, as Faye says. Julie explains how lack of eye contact from the boss makes it difficult to know when it is her turn to speak.

> Eleri's answer deals with both command words. She has explained the reason behind using eye contact, and referred to the conversation to illustrate this. Her answer may get all 3 marks.

Romillie's answer

Eye contact helps us know when it is our turn to speak. As Faye says, 'the new boss always looks down when you have a conversation with him'.

> Romillie's answer states a function of eye contact. She has then copied out much of Faye's statement. Her answer might get 1 mark. A better answer, like Eleri's, will give a reason why eye contact is important in conversations, and try to use the conversation to show this.

■ Questions asking you to evaluate a study

> Evaluate Tulving's 'gold' memory study. **(6 marks)**

This question is from the Brain and Neuropsychology topic. The command word here is 'evaluate'. The answer can include the strengths and limitations of this key research study. This question doesn't state the number of points to be made; some questions do. So, here you could write two points with more detail, or three or four points with less. It is likely that a full-mark answer will need at least one point that is elaborated with more detail. While it may help to recall the method and results of Tulving's study in your answer, remember that this will not earn you marks. The focus must be on evaluation.

Jincheng's answer

Tulving's study was one of the first to show that recalling different kinds of memory involved blood flow to different parts of the brain. So it showed that different brain areas were used. So it is possible to link different kinds of thinking to different parts of the brain. Other studies were able to use this idea, too. This is a good point about the study. A problem with the study is that only three participants showed the different blood flow patterns. This is a very small sample so we can't be sure that the same results would be found if lots of participants were used. Another problem is that Tulving had no control over the kind of memory that the participants were recalling.

Jincheng has made three points of evaluation. The first one has extra detail and is linked to what Tulving did. The second point is also elaborated and a third added in less detail. This answer would get 5 or 6 marks.

Tahmid's answer

A good point is that this study was one of the first to show how cognitive processes in the brain can be investigated. A bad point is that the results can't be generalised. Also the process is unethical.

Tahmid's 'good point' about the study will get credit. To get extra marks, Tahmid could expand this point to explain why this is a good feature of the study, as Jincheng's answer did.

The second and third points that Tahmid made appear quite often when students evaluate studies. Tahmid could explain what is meant by 'can't be generalised', and why this may be true of Tulving's study. There are several points to be made about the ethics of Tulving's study. Tahmid's answer could explain why the process may be unethical (for example be referring to the danger of using a radioactive injection). His short answer might score 1 or 2 marks. It would score several more if the points were elaborated as suggested.

■ Questions worth 9 marks

> Two students were talking about a psychology test they had to revise for:
>
> Mike: 'I have been trying to revise for the psychology test this week by saying the information over and over again. I still don't remember it though.'
>
> Caroline: 'You need to do something with the information, turn it into a story or understand what it really means.'
>
> Describe and evaluate the multi-store model of memory. Refer to the conversation above in your answer. **(9 marks)**

This question is from the Memory topic. There will be two questions on each exam paper which require a longer piece of writing and can earn up to 9 marks. These answers in particular will be looked at carefully to check your use of 'continuous prose'. There is advice about this on the front of the exam paper, which reminds you to use good English, organise information clearly, and use specialist vocabulary where appropriate. Before starting to answer a 9-mark question, it is a good idea to write a brief plan to make sure that the command words have been dealt with. There are three here, 'describe', 'evaluate' and 'refer to'. It is worthwhile reading your answer at the end to check that it is complete.

Sheena's answer

There are three memory stores in the multi-store model. The sensory store is where information enters the model through the senses. It can hold a limited number of items for about 1 second. Information moves to the short-term store (STS) if it is attended to. This store can hold about 7 bits of information for about 30 seconds. It is stored as a mainly acoustic code. If information is rehearsed it moves to the long-term store (LTS). This has an unlimited capacity and can store items for a lifetime. It mainly uses a semantic code. The model has been very useful although there are some problems with it. It is supported by many research studies. One of these is the serial position study where participants seem to recall the beginning and end of a list of words better than those in the middle. The first words are stored in the LTS and the last words in the STS, so the study shows that these two stores exist separately. A problem with the model is that the idea of repeating items to get them into the LTS, which is rehearsal, does not fit our experience. We seem to recall vivid memories without ever repeating them and we don't recall everything which we repeat over and over for tests. In the conversation, Mike has been trying just rehearsal as he mentions 'saying information over and over'. Like in the previous paragraph he does not remember much of what he rehearses. Caroline suggests that elaboration of the material 'by turning it into a story or understanding it' will improve retrieval. Their comments actually fit in with evidence from studies.

Saskia's answer

There are three memory stores as follows:
• Sensory store: sensory input; very limited capacity; duration of about 1 second
• STS: coding by sound; capacity of 7 items, duration of 30 seconds
• LTS: coding by meaning; unlimited capacity and duration.
The three stores help to make sense of many studies of memory but there are other ways of looking at memory which sometimes do a better job. Mike and Caroline seem to be talking about rehearsal. Caroline's kind of rehearsal seems to be better for learning things.

Sheena's answer deals with each command word in detail. Many features of the model are described, there are at least two well-developed evaluation points, and the conversation is used to illustrate the value of different kinds of rehearsal. Her answer is in paragraphs and there are no spelling errors. A mark scheme for this answer might divide answers into three categories, 'detailed', 'good' and 'basic'. This is a 'detailed' answer and might score 8 or 9 marks.

The three command words are dealt with in part. There are a number of details about the multi-store model, but they are presented in bullet points rather than full sentences, so the highest marks are not possible. Saskia could improve the first part of her answer by writing in sentences and including the way in which information moves between the stores.

The evaluation points are brief. To get more marks, Saskia should give more detail, for example, of a study which supports the model and of another model which explains some features of memory better.

In the final section, Saskia identifies 'rehearsal'. Using some brief quotes from Mike and Caroline, and explaining the different kinds of rehearsal they mention, would get more marks. Overall, the answer is in the range from 'basic' to 'good' and might score 4 or 5 marks.

■ Research methods questions

A teacher wanted to know whether her students were more likely to remember information if they were asked to recall it in the same place that they had first learnt it, compared to a different place. She decided to conduct an experiment.

Each student in her class was a participant in her study. Each participant was shown a list of 20 words in their normal classroom. The class was then divided into two equal groups. One half stayed in the classroom while the other half were taken outside to the playground. Each participant was then given 2 minutes to write down as many of the words on the list that they could remember.

Number of words recalled by each participant										Range	Mean
Condition 1: classroom	10	12	8	13	12	15	12	16	9	11	8	11.8
Condition 2: playground	7	11	14	6	3	11	13	7	10	6		8.8

(a) What was the independent variable in this experiment?   (1 mark)

(b) Write a suitable null hypothesis for this experiment.   (2 marks)

(c) Calculate the range for condition 2. Show your workings.   (2 marks)

(d) Draw a bar chart to represent the mean for each condition.
    Your answer should include the following:
    • an appropriate scale
    • an appropriate label on each axis
    • a suitable title   (4 marks)

(e) Identify and briefly explain one ethical issue that the teacher
    should have considered.   (2 marks)

(f) Describe how the teacher could have dealt with the ethical issue you
    have outlined in your answer to (e).   (2 marks)

(g) Using the table above, explain what the teacher might conclude
    from this experiment.   (3 marks)

This question is from the Research Methods topic. There will be a full exam question on this topic. The question above shows some of the challenges you will face when answering a question on this topic.

Tom's answer

(a) Where the words were recalled, the classroom or the playground.

(b) Where the words are recalled has no effect on the number of words recalled.

(c) The highest score is 14; the lowest score is 3. The range = 14 − 3 = 11.

(a) would score 1 mark. Tom chose the variable which the researcher changed and wrote it in a form that gives details of the two possibilities. (b) would score 2 marks. The answer makes clear the two variables and the fact that the IV has no effect on the DV. (c) would score 2 marks. The range is correct and the workings are shown.

(d)

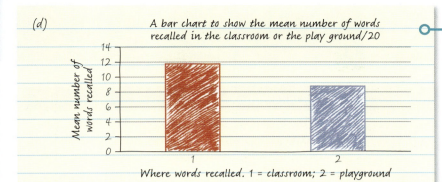

A bar chart to show the mean number of words recalled in the classroom or the play ground/20

Mean number of words recalled

Where words recalled. 1 = classroom; 2 = playground

(e) Informed consent. It is part of the BPS code of ethics that those who take part in a study should be as fully aware as possible what the study is about and what they have to do. Then they can agree to take part.

(f) To deal with this the teacher could write out some standardised instructions about what the students will be asked to do and then get them to sign something to say that they are happy to take part.

(g) The mean number of words recalled for condition 1 is bigger than for condition 2, 11.8 compared to 8.8. This shows that more words are recalled in the same surroundings in which they are learned than in a different environment. The original surroundings may provide clues to help recall.

(d) would score 4 marks as all the demands of the question are properly dealt with. (e) would score 2 marks as Tom chose a relevant ethical issue and explained its importance. (f) would score 2 marks. The suggestion allows the students to make an informed agreement to take part in the study. (g) would score 3 marks. Tom quotes the mean values, compares them and uses them to draw a conclusion. He also suggests an explanation.

Will's answer

(a) The class room or the playground.

(b) Your memory isn't affected by where you are.

(c) The highest score is 14; the lowest score is 3.
The range = 14 − 3 = 12.

(d)

A bar chart to show the number of words recalled

Number of words recalled

Where words were recalled

(e) Respect.

(f) Get the students to sign a piece of paper to say that they agree to take part.

(g) You recall more words if you stay in the same place where you learned them.

(a) might score 0 marks. Will should not only give the two conditions, but also what they represent. (b) might score 0 marks. To gain more marks Will should be precise about the two variables in the study. Tom's answer shows this. (c) would score 1 mark for showing the workings, but the range is incorrect. (d) might score 2 marks. The bars are correctly drawn on a suitable scale. To gain more marks, the title should include detail of the two conditions and the word 'mean'. The 'x' axis label should explain what '1' and '2' represent. The 'y' axis should contain the word 'mean'. (e) might score 1 mark. Will should explain a practical way of treating the participants with respect, such as getting some form of consent from them so they agree to take part. (f) might score 1 mark. To get more marks Will should explain how the teacher would give details of the study to the students. (g) might score 1 mark. Extra marks can be gained by quoting and comparing the mean values in the table.

Maths appendix

6.1 Arithmetic and numerical computation	Link in textbook
6.1.1: Recognise and use expressions in decimal and standard form.	For decimal form, see page 96. Standard form is a way of expressing a very large or very small number in the form $A \times 10^n$. Such expressions are rarely used in psychology.
6.1.2: Use ratios, fractions, and percentages.	pages 96–97
6.1.3: Estimate results.	page 97

6.2 Handling data	Link in textbook
6.2.1: Use an appropriate number of significant figures.	page 96
6.2.2: Find arithmetic means.	page 95
6.2.3: Construct and interpret frequency tables and diagrams, bar charts, and histograms.	Building skills 1, page 43; Building skills 1, page 45; page 98; Going further, page 124; Going further, page 137; Going further, page 173
6.2.4: Understand the principles of sampling as applied to scientific data.	pages 74–75
6.2.5: Understand the terms mean, median, and mode.	page 95
6.2.6: Use a scatter diagram to identify a correlation between two variables.	Building skills 2, page 90
6.2.7: Know the characteristics of normal distributions.	page 98
6.2.8: Understand range as a measure of dispersion.	page 96
6.2.9: Understand the differences between qualitative and quantitative data.	page 94
6.2.10: Understand the difference between primary and secondary data.	page 95
6.2.11: Translate information between graphical and numerical forms.	Building skills 2, page 97
6.2.12: Plot two variables from experimental or other data and interpret graphs.	Building skills 4, page 15; Building skills 1, page 89

Glossary

This glossary lists all of the important terms in the specification. Terms that are not in the specification, but which are still useful for you to know, are given in italics.

A

Accommodation: changing a schema, or developing a new schema to cope with a new situation

Adaptive: being able to change in order to fit different situations and environments

Addiction: repeated use of a substance resulting in an individual becoming entirely focused on the substance, which they need to have regularly in order to avoid withdrawal symptoms

Agency: the responsibility we feel for our own actions

Agency theory: the idea that a person will obey an authority figure when they believe this authority figure will take responsibility for whatever the person does

Allocation to conditions: putting participants into the conditions of an experiment

Alternative hypothesis: the hypothesis the researcher tests by conducting a study and collecting data, which attempts to show the null hypothesis is not supported

Ambiguity: having more than one possible meaning or interpretation

Angular gyrus: an area on the parietal lobe which deals with reading

ANS: the autonomic nervous system, which is a network of unmyelinated nerve fibres running through the body and connecting the senses and internal organs with the central nervous system

Antidepressants: a type of medication used to treat depression

Antisocial behaviour: when people do not act in socially acceptable ways or consider the rights of others

Assimilation: adding new information to an existing schema

Attributions: the ways people explain situations and behaviour

Auditory cortex: the area of the cerebral cortex concerned with hearing

Authoritarian Personality: an obedient personality type, characterised by a belief that authority figures should be obeyed

Authority: when a person is perceived to have the right to give orders

Autonomic functions: involuntary bodily functions such as breathing and heart rate

Aversion therapy: a treatment to help individuals stop unwanted behaviours such as substance addiction; the individual experiences some form of unpleasantness when carrying out the unwanted behaviour

B

Bar chart: a type of graph that is used to display data from different categories

Binocular depth cue: a way of detecting depth or distance, which requires two eyes in order to work

Bipolar depression: a mood disorder that causes an individual's mood, energy, and activity levels to change from one extreme to another

Body language: a general term to describe aspects of non-verbal communication

Brain stem: the part of the brain that controls basic functions such as breathing and heart rate

British Psychological Society (BPS) guidelines: the ethical guidelines produced by the British Psychological Society in its Code of Ethics and Conduct (2006) and Code of Human Research Ethics (2014), which govern the work of all practising and research psychologists

Broca's area: an area on the frontal lobe which deals with speech production

Bystander apathy: doing nothing when someone is in need of help

Bystander behaviour: the way that someone responds when they witness someone else in need of help

Bystander intervention: when a person who witnesses a person in need offers help

C

Capacity: how much information can be stored

Case study: an in-depth investigation of an individual, a small group, or an organisation

Categories of behaviour: the separate actions that are recorded as examples of the target behaviour

Cerebellum: a small, wrinkled structure at the back of the brain which coordinates motor movement, dexterity, and balance, among other things

Cerebrum: the largest part of the brain in humans, which consists of two large cerebral hemispheres

Closed posture: positioning the arms so that they are folded across the body and/or crossing the legs

Closed question: a question where the possible responses are fixed, often as 'yes' or 'no' options

CNS: the central nervous system, which consists of the brain and spinal cord

Coding: the way that information is represented to be stored

Cognition: the mental processes involved in gaining knowledge; these include thinking, planning and problem solving

Cognitive behaviour therapy (CBT): a talking therapy that can help you manage your problems and emotions by changing the way you think and behave

Cognitive development: the changes that take place over time in a person's thinking and intellect

Cognitive neuroscience: the study of how cognitive processes connect with brain activity and structure

Collective behaviour: the way in which people act when they are part of a group

Communication: passing information from one person (or animal) to another

Concrete operational: the ability to apply logic to physical (concrete) objects to solve problems

Condition: an experiment is usually organised so there are two trials, after which the performances of the participants are compared; these are the conditions of the experiment

Conformity: a change in our opinions or behaviour to fit in with social norms or as the result of perceived group pressure

Conservation: knowing that the amount of something stays the same, even though its appearance may change

Constructivist theory: the idea that our perception is built from our prior knowledge and experience

Context: the general setting or environment in which activities happen

Convergence: a form of depth perception which uses how eye muscles focus on images

Correlation: a technique used by researchers to establish the strength of a relationship between two variables

Cortex: the outer layer of the brain where higher cognitive functions take place, e.g. speech

Counterbalancing: an arrangement in which half of the participants in an experiment are given the conditions in one order (A followed by B) while the other half are given them in the opposite order (B followed by A)

CT scan: Computerised Tomography, which scans the brain by building up a 3D image from a series of X-ray 'slices'

Cultural norms: the range of behaviours that members of a particular social group or society can be expected to show

Culture: a group of people who share similar customs, beliefs, and behaviour

D

Decimal: numbers where a point is used to separate whole numbers from parts

Deindividuation: the state of losing our sense of individuality and becoming less aware of our own responsibility for our actions

Dependence: repeated use of a substance results in an individual's brain and body only functioning normally when the substance is present; when the substance is not present, withdrawal symptoms occur

Dependent variable (DV): the factor which will be measured in an experiment to see if changing the IV has had an effect

Depth cue: a feature of an image which indicates distance

Dispositional factors: internal personal characteristics which may affect how a person will behave

Duration: how long information can be stored for

E

Ecological validity: the results of the investigation can be said to apply to real-life behaviour; they are an accurate account of behaviour in the real world

Effort after meaning: making sense of something unfamiliar after it has happened

Egocentric: not being able to see things from another person's point of view

Emotion: the moods or feelings that a person experiences

Encoding: taking information into memory and changing it into a form that can be stored

Episodic memory: unique memories which are concerned with personal experiences or events

Estimate: figures are rounded to make the calculation simpler, which makes the answer roughly, but not exactly, right

Ethical issues: points of concern about what is morally right

Evolve: to slowly develop over successive generations into a different state or condition

Excitation: when a neurotransmitter binds with a receptor on the next neuron, and increases the chance that the next neuron will fire an electrical impulse

Expectation: the beliefs we have about what we are going to experience

Experiment: a research method in which the researcher tries to control all variables other than the independent variable (IV) and dependent variable (DV); this allows the researcher to identify a cause-and-effect relationship between the IV and DV

Experimental design: how the participants are used in the conditions of an experiment

Extraneous variable (EV): a variable that is not the IV but might affect the DV if it is not controlled

Eye contact: when two people in conversation are looking at each other's eyes at the same time

F

False memories: remembering something that has never happened

Fiction: the perception of an object or movement that is not present in the stimulus

Fight or flight response: an automatic reaction to threat, stimulated by the ANS and maintained by the endocrine system, which activates the body's reserves of energy to prepare it for action

Fixed mindset: the belief that ability is genetic and unchanging

fMRI scan: functional Magnetic Resonance Imaging, which scans the brain by identifying the magnetic activity of water molecules in active brain cells

Formal operational: the ability to apply logic in an abstract (non-physical) way to solve problems, for example mental calculation

Fraction: a part of a whole number

Frequency table: a way of displaying data that shows how often something occurs

Frontal lobe: the area of the brain that controls cognitive processes such as thought and memory

G

Gender: the psychological state of being male or female, often distinguished by social behaviours and cultural roles

Genetic vulnerability: a biological susceptibility towards developing certain conditions or disorders when other influencing elements are also present

Growth mindset: the belief that ability comes from hard work and can be increased

H

Height in plane: how high the object appears in the image

Hereditary: being transferred from parent to child through their genes

Histogram: a type of graph that is used to display continuous data

Holistic: the view that the parts of something are all connected and understandable only by studying things as a whole

Hypothesis: a testable statement about the relationship between two variables: the independent variable (IV) and the dependent variable (DV)

I

Independent groups: where two or more separate groups of participants are used in an experiment; each group takes part in one of the conditions

Independent variable (IV): the factor which will be varied or changed in an experiment to look for an effect on the other variable

Inference: a conclusion reached on the basis of past experience or knowledge

Informational social influence: changing behaviour or opinions because we think other people have superior knowledge to us

Inhibition: when a neurotransmitter binds with a receptor on the next neuron, and decreases the chance that the next neuron will fire an electrical impulse

Innate: inborn or inherited – that is, not learned

Instructions: the written (or verbal) information given to participants during an experiment

Inter-observer reliability: how closely the record sheets of two or more people match (when the records do match, they are considered to be accurate; if they do not match they are inaccurate)

Interference: the difficulty in recalling information when other memories get in the way

International Classification of Diseases (ICD): lists of symptoms and other features of different physical and mental health problems, which also provide the criteria for diagnosing them

Interview: a method in which a researcher collects data by asking questions directly

Isolation: being or feeling alone and separate from other people

L

Language: a system of communication used by a specific group of people

Learned: abilities or characteristics gained through experience

Learning styles: the different ways that a person can process information

Linear perspective: when straight lines are angled so that they would come together at a point on the horizon

Lobes of the brain: each half of the brain is divided into four areas or lobes: the frontal lobe, the temporal lobe, the parietal lobe and the occipital lobe

Localised function: a function such as language or vision, which is found in a particular area on the cerebral cortex

Long-term store: memory store that holds a vast amount of information for a very long period of time

M

Matched pairs: where people with similar qualities are grouped into pairs; each member of the pair takes part in a different condition

Mean: a statistic calculated by adding all the scores in a set of values and dividing the total by the number of values in the set; this is sometimes called the arithmetic mean

Median: the middle value in a set of values when the values have been arranged in ascending order

Mental health: a person's emotional and psychological wellbeing; this allows them to cope with the normal stresses of everyday life and to function in society

Mental health problems: diagnosable conditions in which a person's thoughts, feelings, and behaviours change and they are less able to cope and function

Mindset Theory of Learning: a theory that describes how students can achieve success in their learning

Misinterpreted depth cues: when a depth cue is used inappropriately

Mode: the most frequently occurring value in a set of values

Monocular depth cue: a way of detecting depth or distance, which will work with just one eye

Motion parallax: the way that the visual field changes with movement, with close objects seeming to move more than objects that are further away

Motivation: the drives and needs that cause a person to act in a particular way

Motor area: the area of the cerebral cortex concerned with movement

Motor neuron: a nerve cell that takes messages from the CNS to muscles to cause them to move

Multi-store model of memory: the theory of memory that suggests information passes through a series of memory stores

N

Nature: the idea that our characteristics and behaviour are inherited

Negative correlation: a relationship between two variables in which, as the value of one variable increases, the value of the other variable decreases

Negative schemas: a biased cognitive model of people, objects or situations based on previous information and experience that directs us to perceive, organise or understand new information by focusing on what is bad

Neonates: a newborn infant of less than 4 weeks of age

Neurological damage: injury or harm to the nervous system, which affects how the neurons work

Neuron: a specialised nerve cell which generates and transmits an electrical impulse

Neuronal growth: when a neuron repeatedly excites another neuron, leading to a change (or process of growth) in one or both of the neurons

Neurotransmitter: a chemical which is released into the synapse by one neuron, and picked up by the next neuron

No correlation: there is no relationship between two variables

Non-verbal communication: conveying messages without the use of words

Normal distribution: an arrangement of data in which most values group in the middle of the range and the rest taper off symmetrically towards each end

Normative social influence: changing behaviour or opinions because we want to fit in and be accepted by other

Null hypothesis: a hypothesis that exists and states that no variables affect any other variables

Nurture: the idea that our characteristics and behaviour are influenced by our environment

O

Obedience: following the orders of an authority figure

Observation study: a method of collecting information about behaviour by watching and recording people's actions

Occipital lobe: the area of the brain where visual information is processed

Occlusion: when one object seems to cover part of another object

Open posture: positioning the arms so that they are not folded across the body, and not crossing the legs

Open question: a question where the person answering can give any response they like

Opportunity sample: people who are members of the target population and are available and willing to take part in research

Order effect: when a participant's performance in the second condition of an experiment is affected because they have already done the first condition. They may do better because of practice or worse because of tiredness. This may happen in a repeated measures design.

P

Parietal lobe: the area of the brain that is responsible for integrating information from other areas to form complex behaviours

Participant variables: the differences between the people who take part in the study. These may affect the results of an experiment that uses an independent groups design

Participant: someone who takes part in a study and, by taking part, provides data for the researcher to analyse

Peer: someone who is from the same social group, or who is the same age or social status, or has the same background, abilities or qualifications, as someone else

Percentage: a proportion expressed as a fraction of 100

Perception: how we interpret or make sense of the sensory information that we receive

Perceptual set: a state of readiness to perceive certain kinds of stimuli rather than others

Personal space: the physical distance we prefer to keep between ourselves and other people in order to feel comfortable

PET scan: Positron Emission Tomography, which locates blood flow in the brain by detecting radioactive tracers

PNS: the peripheral nervous system, which is the network of nerve fibres connecting the various parts of the body with the central nervous system. It is made up of the SNS and the ANS.

Positive correlation: a relationship between two variables in which, as the value of one variable increases, the value of the other variable also increases

Postural echo: mirroring another person's body position

Posture: the positioning of the body, often regarded as a non-verbal communication signal

Praise: an expression of approval

Pre-operational: before logic – being unable to apply reason to solve problems

Prediction: a statement about what will happen, made before the event occurs

Primacy effect: more of the first information received is recalled than subsequent later information

Primary data: data collected firsthand from the source (participants), by the researcher

Procedural memory: our memory for carrying out complex skills

Prosocial behaviour: actions that benefit other people or society

Proximity: how near or close something is to us

Q

Qualitative data: data in descriptive (non-numerical) form, such as verbal or written answers to questions, or observed behaviour

Qualitative method: any method which provides descriptive (non-numerical) data

Quantitative data: data in numerical form, such as scores or times taken to do a task

Quantitative method: any method which provides numerical data

Questionnaire: a set of standard questions about a topic that is given to all the participants in the survey

R

Random allocation: sorting participants into groups in a way that depends on pure chance

Random sample: every member of the target population has an equal chance of being selected for the sample

Randomisation: using chance to provide an order for a procedure

Range: the difference between the lowest and highest value in a set of values

Ratio: the relationship between two amounts showing the number of times one value contains, or is contained within, the other

Recall: to bring a memory back into one's mind (similar to 'retrieval')

Recency effect: more of the information received later is recalled than earlier information

Recognition: identification of something or someone, previously known, seen or heard about

Reconstructive memory: altering our recollection of things so that they make more sense to us

Reductionist: understanding complex things like human behaviour by simplifying it to its most fundamental and basic parts

Relationship: a connection or association between two or more variables

Relative size: how large an object appears in an image

Relay neuron: a nerve cell that passes messages within the CNS

Reliability: describes the consistency of a study or some measuring device such as a test or scale used in a study

Repeated measures: where only one group of participants is used in an experiment; this group takes part in both conditions

Representative: when the sample of participants is made up of people who have the same characteristics and abilities as the target population

Retinal disparity: a form of depth perception which compares the images from two eyes, side by side

Retrieval: recovering information from storage

Reuptake: a process by which neurotransmitter is reabsorbed into the synaptic knob after it has been used during synaptic transmission

S

Sadness: a normal emotional response to an unpleasant, painful, or unhappy situation or experience

Sample: the small group of people who represent the target population and who are studied

Sampling methods: strategies used by researchers to obtain people from the target population to take part in their studies

Scatter diagram: a type of graph for representing correlations

Schema: a cognitive model of people, objects, or situations; based on previous information and experiences which helps us to perceive, organise, and understand new information

Secondary data: data that is already published and just used, rather than gathered, by the researcher

Self-efficacy: the belief in your own ability to succeed at a task

Self-management programmes: an intervention designed to support and empower individuals so that they can take responsibility for their own choices and behaviour

Semantic memory: memories which are concerned with general knowledge rather than personal experience

Sensation: the information that we receive through our senses

Sensorimotor: learning through the senses and by physical (motor) activities

Sensory deprived: receiving little or no sensory stimuli, such as light or sound

Sensory information: information which is picked up by the sense organs of the body and passed on to the central nervous system

Sensory neuron: a nerve cell that picks up information from sense receptors and carries it to the CNS

Sensory processing: the brain receives messages from the senses and turns them into appropriate motor and behavioural responses

Sensory store: memory store that holds information received from the senses for a very short period of time

Serial position curve: the name given to the graph that displays the results of a serial position experiment

Serial position effect: the chances of recalling any item depends on its position in the list

Short-term store: memory store that holds approximately seven bits of information for a limited amount of time

Size constancy: the way we keep our original perception of the size of an object, even when the information received by the eyes changes

SNS: the somatic nervous system, which is the network of myelinated sensory and motor neurons that carry sensory information to, and instructions for movement from, the central nervous system

Social factors: external events which may affect how a person will behave

Social influence: the effect other people have on our opinions and behaviour

Social loafing: putting less effort into doing something when you are with others doing the same thing

Society: a group of people living together in an area or country with common values, laws, and customs

Somatosensory area: the area of the cerebral cortex concerned with sensory feeling

Standardised procedures: a set order of carrying out a study that is applied to all participants when necessary

Status: a person's rank or position within society

Stigma: situations, people, or characteristics that are disapproved of and seen as shameful by much of society

Stimulus: something that is detected by the sense receptors, which the nervous system will react to

Storage: holding information in the memory system

Stratified sample: the different subgroups in the target population are identified; then people are selected randomly from these subgroups in proportion to their numbers in the target population

Stroke: a sudden interruption to the blood supply in a part of the brain

Structured interview: an interview in which all the questions are pre-set, given in a fixed order, and every interviewee is asked the same questions

Substance abuse: using a substance in a way that is harmful or dangerous

Substance misuse: using a substance for purposes, or in amounts, that may be harmful and that is different to the recommended pattern of use

Survey: a method used for collecting information from a large number of people by asking them questions, either by using a questionnaire or in an interview

Symptom: one of a collection of physical changes that tell us that some kind of disorder or problem exists

Synapse: the small gap between the dendrite of one neuron and the receptor site of the next one, which allows signals to pass between them

Synaptic transmission: the process by which messages are passed from one neuron to another by sending neurotransmitters across the synaptic gap so they can bind with receptors on the next neuron

Systematic sample: every 'nth' member of the target population is selected for the sample

T

Target population: the large group of people the researcher wishes to study

Temporal lobe: the area of the brain that is responsible for aspects such as the comprehension and production of spoken language

Territory: an area defended by an animal or group of animals against others

Thalamus: the part of the brain that passes information from the sense organs to the cortex

Thought: the mental activity of thinking, which involves reasoning and considering, and that produces ideas and opinions

Touch: a form of non-verbal communication in which information is conveyed by physical contact between people

U

Unipolar depression: a mood disorder that causes an individual to feel constantly sad, to lose interest and enjoyment, and to have reduced energy and activity levels

Unstructured interview: an interview in which only the first question is set and all other questions are determined by the answers of the interviewee

V

Validity: the extent to which a study or measuring device actually does what it claims to be doing

Variable: a factor or thing that varies: it can change

Verbal communication: conveying messages using words

Verbaliser: someone who processes information by speaking and listening (auditory processing)

Visual cortex: the area of the cerebral cortex concerned with vision

Visual illusion: a visual perception which is wrong or misinterprets what is actually there in reality

Visualiser: someone who processes information by looking at it (visual processing)

W

Wernicke's area: an area on the temporal lobe which deals with understanding speech

Index